Lovecraft

From a screenplay written by
Hans Rodionoff

Adapted by
Keith Giffen

Illustrated by
Enrique Breccia

Lettered by
Todd Klein

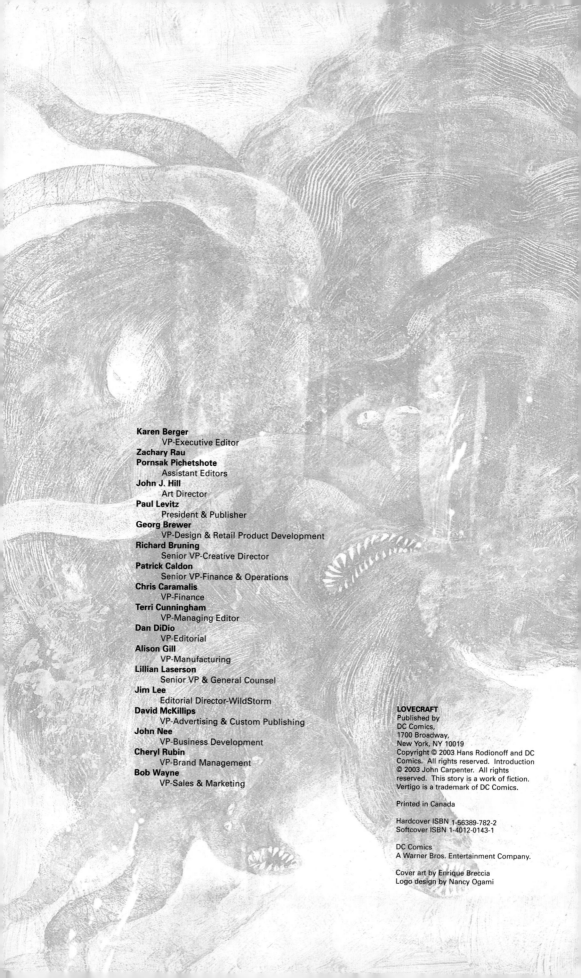

Karen Berger
   VP-Executive Editor
Zachary Rau
Pornsak Pichetshote
   Assistant Editors
John J. Hill
   Art Director
Paul Levitz
   President & Publisher
Georg Brewer
   VP-Design & Retail Product Development
Richard Bruning
   Senior VP-Creative Director
Patrick Caldon
   Senior VP-Finance & Operations
Chris Caramalis
   VP-Finance
Terri Cunningham
   VP-Managing Editor
Dan DiDio
   VP-Editorial
Alison Gill
   VP-Manufacturing
Lillian Laserson
   Senior VP & General Counsel
Jim Lee
   Editorial Director-WildStorm
David McKillips
   VP-Advertising & Custom Publishing
John Nee
   VP-Business Development
Cheryl Rubin
   VP-Brand Management
Bob Wayne
   VP-Sales & Marketing

LOVECRAFT
Published by
DC Comics,
1700 Broadway,
New York, NY 10019

Printed in Canada

Hardcover ISBN 1-56389-782-2
Softcover ISBN 1-4012-0143-1

DC Comics
A Warner Bros. Entertainment Company.

Cover art by Enrique Breccia
Logo design by Nancy Ogami

Introduction

The question I get asked the most is, "What scares you?" My answer is simple. "The same things that scare you. We're all afraid of the same things. And one of them is evil."

Evil can come from many places. Oftentimes, the evil comes from beyond, from outside, from the darkness out there farther on than our flickering firelight can reach. The evil is the dreaded Other, the Outsider, the Alien.

This kind of evil is something that I find myself continually exploring. During many of these explorations I've looked down and seen footprints -- the footprints of someone who had passed the same way before me -- the footprints of Howard Phillips Lovecraft.

Most people who have watched my movies will notice my recognition of those footprints. From Innsmouth references in THE FOG, to the general premise of IN THE MOUTH OF MADNESS, I have used the tools of the cinema to put my own unique spin on the Lovecraftian mythos.

Few authors can claim the distinction of becoming an adjective. Lovecraftian. As much as Frankenstein and Dracula are considered classics, people don't often claim a story to be "Shellian" or "Stokeresque".

Lovecraft, a reclusive writer of weird fantasy stories, who during his lifetime couldn't even pay the rent with his odd stories, now has the ability to inspire readers and filmmakers around the globe.

Which brings me to the book that you hold in your hands, the love sonnet of another Lovecraft aficionado. It's something of a rite of passage among those of us who work in the horror trade. Almost everyone who writes in the genre, from Stephen King to Clive Barker, has written at least one Lovecraftian tale.

But this one is a little different, because it deals with the man behind the mythos. This is a frightening, ultimately tragic story about a man's slow descent into madness.

Is it possible that all of the horrible, slithering things that Lovecraft wrote about were real and that good old Howard was the only thing standing between us and those unspeakable, unnamable things from beyond?

The story is strengthened because the details of Lovecraft's life are all dutifully followed in this tale. The insanity, the peculiar upbringing, the failed relationships, are all based on fact. The only liberties taken were with the reasons for the insanity and the failed relationships.

In the end, the only person who could tell us for certain that this story is a work of fiction or not is Howard himself. But I imagine that if he were here...

He'd say every word of it was true.

John Carpenter
Los Angeles
July 7, 2003

"Those who dream by day are cognizant of many things which escape those who only dream by night."

—Edgar Allan Poe

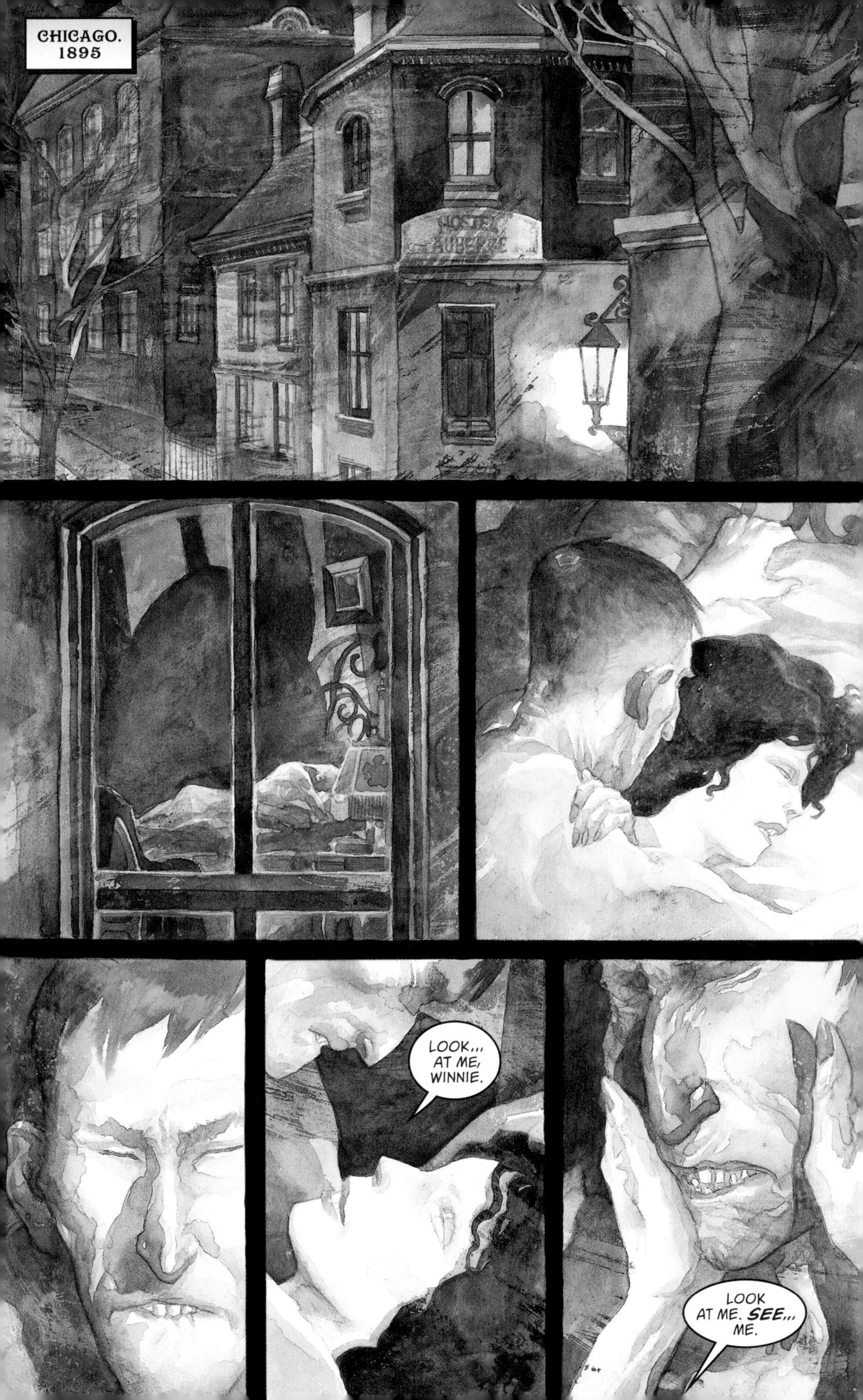
CHICAGO. 1895
LOOK... AT ME, WINNIE.
LOOK AT ME. **SEE**... ME.

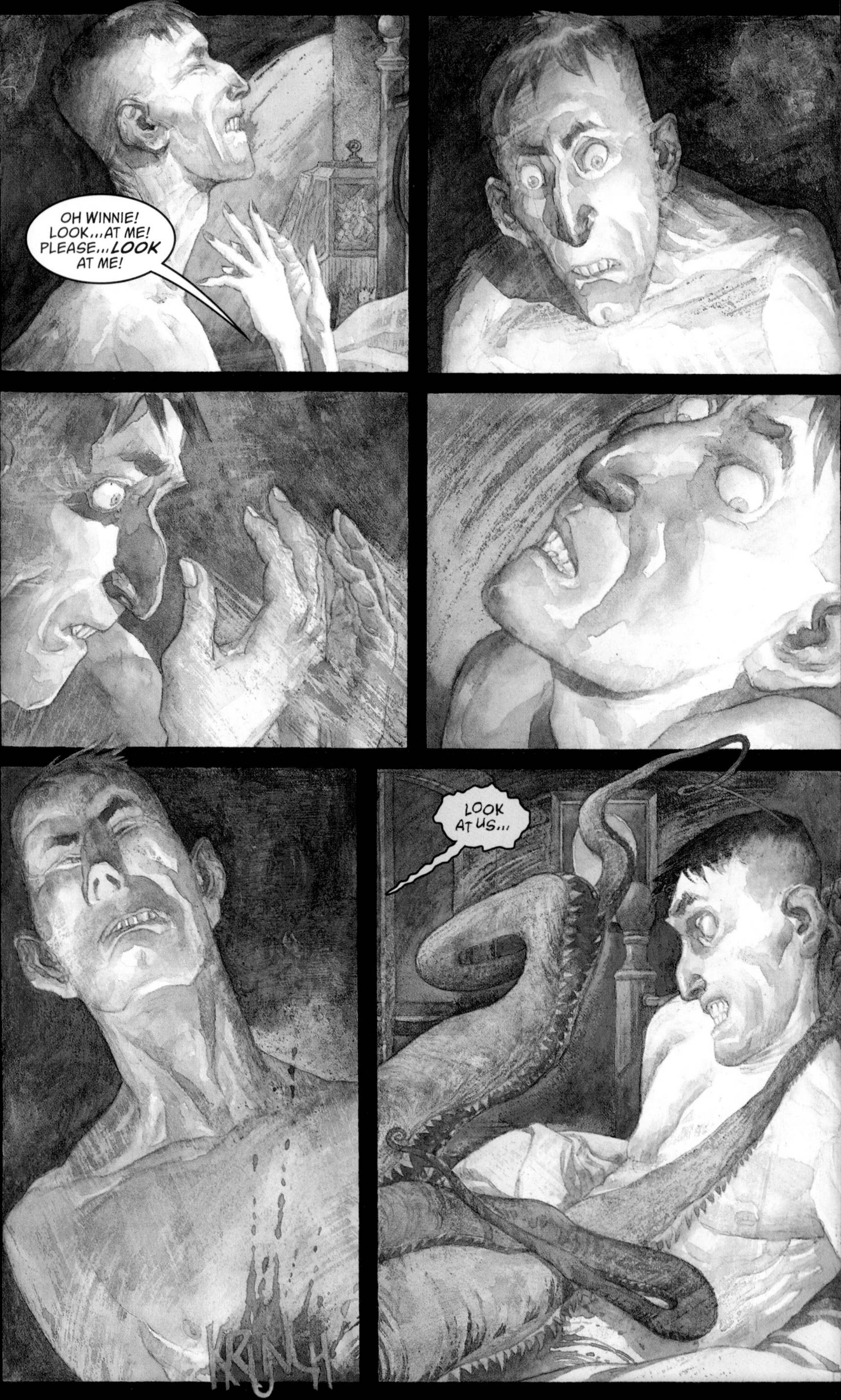

OH WINNIE! LOOK...AT ME! PLEASE...LOOK AT ME!
KRUNCH
LOOK AT US...

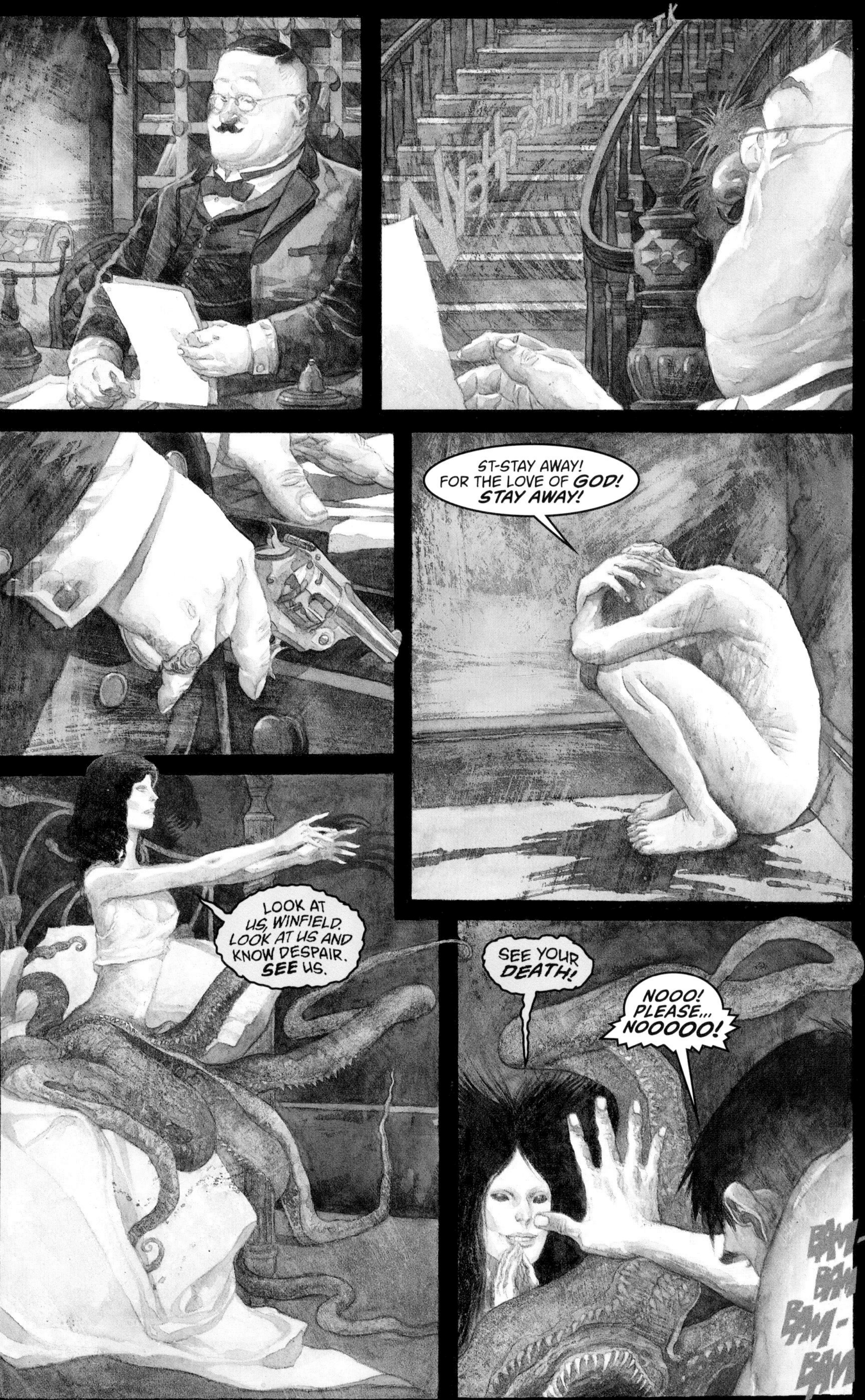
ST-STAY AWAY! FOR THE LOVE OF GOD! STAY AWAY!
LOOK AT US, WINFIELD. LOOK AT US AND KNOW DESPAIR. SEE US.
SEE YOUR DEATH!
NOOO! PLEASE... NOOOOO!

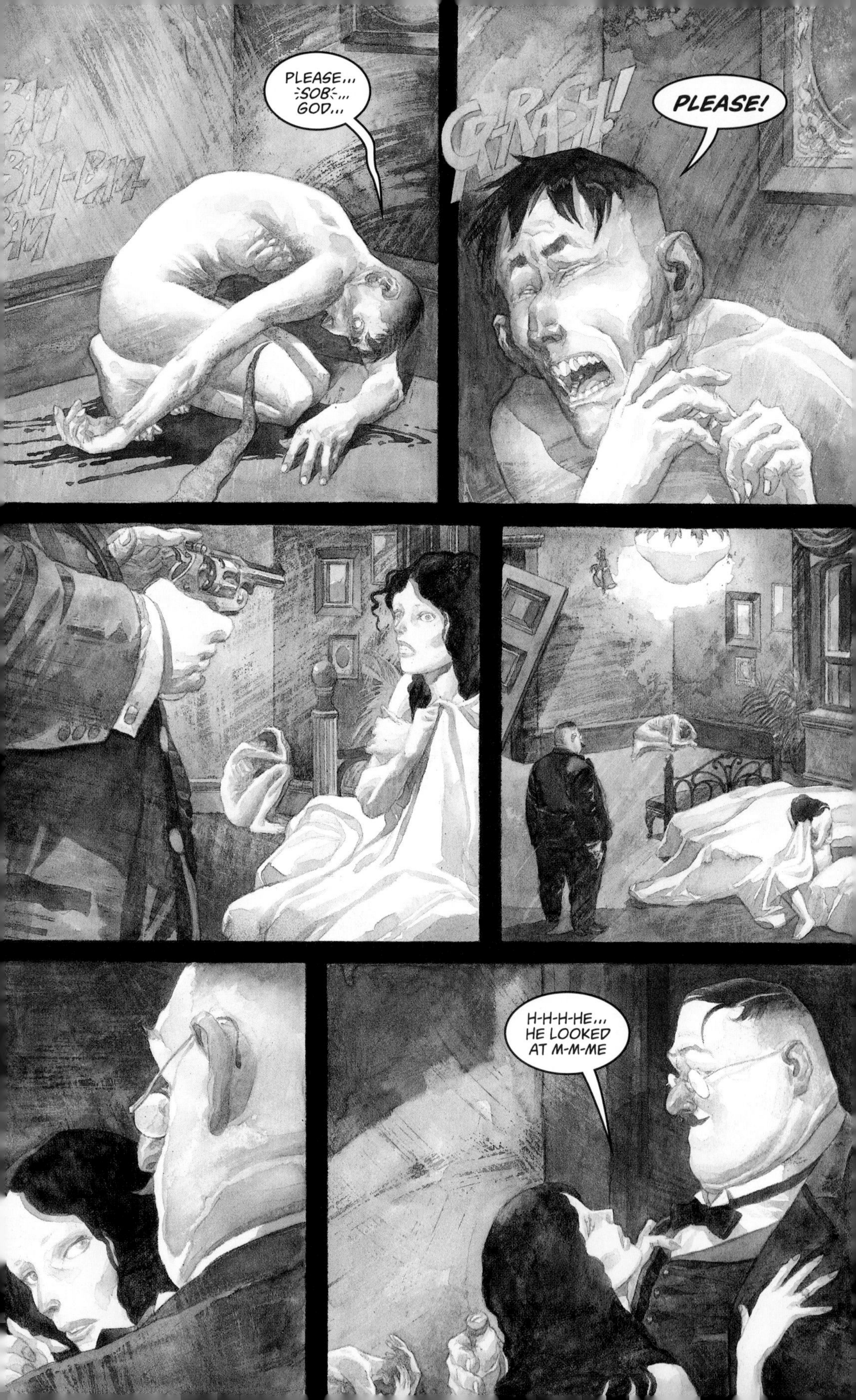
BAM BAM-BAM BAM
PLEASE... -SOB-... GOD...
CR-RASH!
PLEASE!
H-H-H-HE... HE LOOKED AT M-M-ME

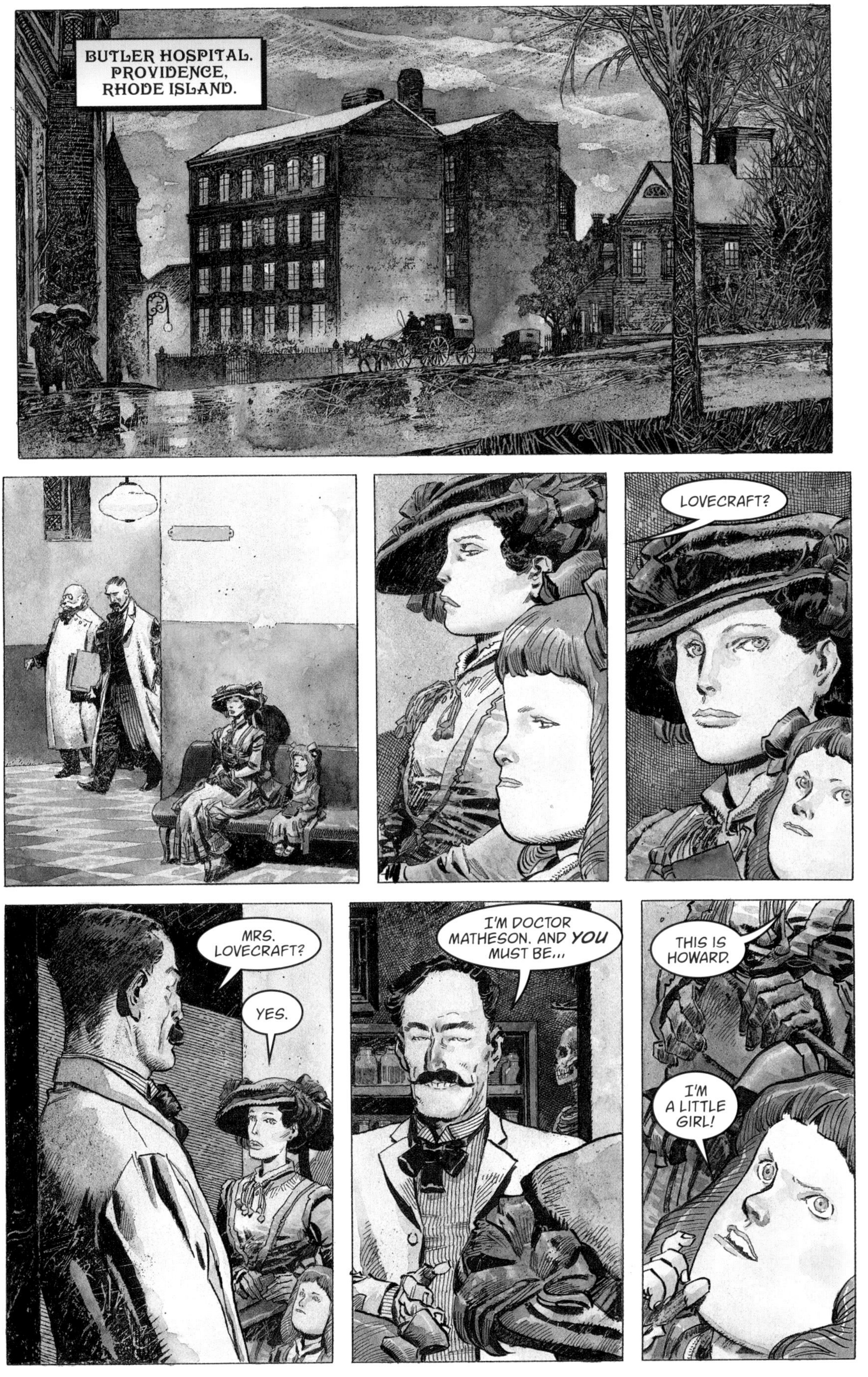
BUTLER HOSPITAL. PROVIDENCE, RHODE ISLAND.
LOVECRAFT?
MRS. LOVECRAFT?
YES.
I'M DOCTOR MATHESON. AND *YOU* MUST BE...
THIS IS HOWARD.
I'M A LITTLE GIRL!

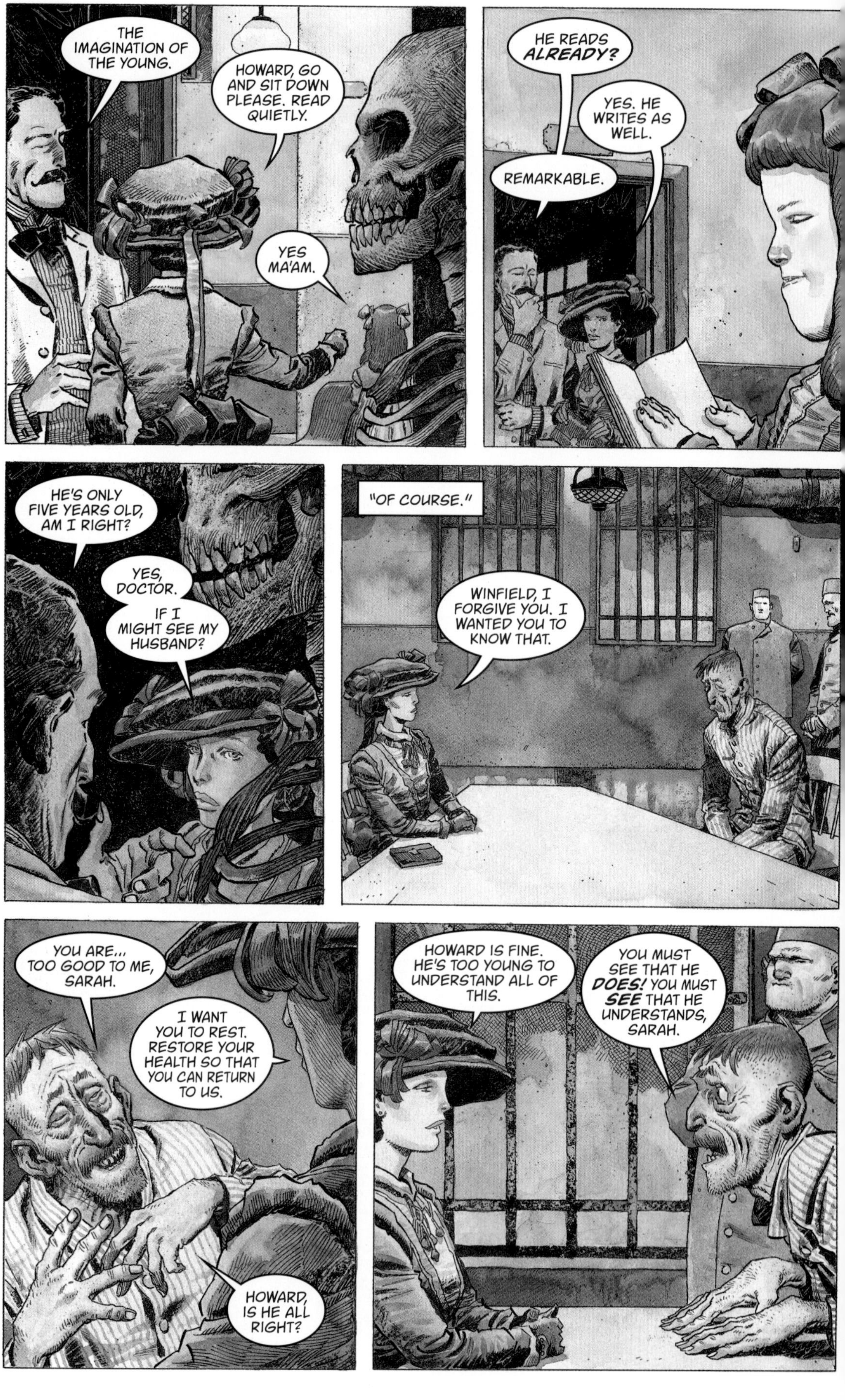
THE IMAGINATION OF THE YOUNG.
HOWARD, GO AND SIT DOWN PLEASE. READ QUIETLY.
YES MA'AM.
HE READS ALREADY?
YES. HE WRITES AS WELL.
REMARKABLE.
HE'S ONLY FIVE YEARS OLD, AM I RIGHT?
YES, DOCTOR.
IF I MIGHT SEE MY HUSBAND?
"OF COURSE."
WINFIELD, I FORGIVE YOU. I WANTED YOU TO KNOW THAT.
YOU ARE... TOO GOOD TO ME, SARAH.
I WANT YOU TO REST. RESTORE YOUR HEALTH SO THAT YOU CAN RETURN TO US.
HOWARD, IS HE ALL RIGHT?
HOWARD IS FINE. HE'S TOO YOUNG TO UNDERSTAND ALL OF THIS.
YOU MUST SEE THAT HE DOES! YOU MUST SEE THAT HE UNDERSTANDS, SARAH.

YOU *MUST* TELL HIM. THE TIME IS NEAR. THE WALLS... THE BARRIERS ARE THINNING. THEY'RE CLOSER THAN EVER, AND HE *WILL* SEE THEM.

HE HAS THE GIFT, AS I DO. YOU *MUST* LET ME SPEAK WITH HIM.

PLEASE, DEAREST, THIS IS NOT THE TIME. YOU'RE DISTRAUGHT AND TIRED. YOU MUST REST, AND THEN...

REST! I *CANNOT* REST! THEY'RE COMING, SARAH! THEY'RE RIGHT OUTSIDE, PUSHING IN! I'VE *SEEN* THEM! THE BOOK IS THE GATE! YOU *MUST BURN* IT!

WINFIELD, *PLEASE*...

BURN IT, SARAH! BURN IT IMMEDIATELY!

THAT'S ENOUGH, MR. LOVECRAFT. LET'S JUST STAY CALM.

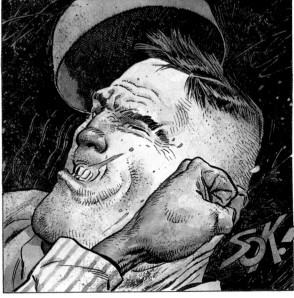

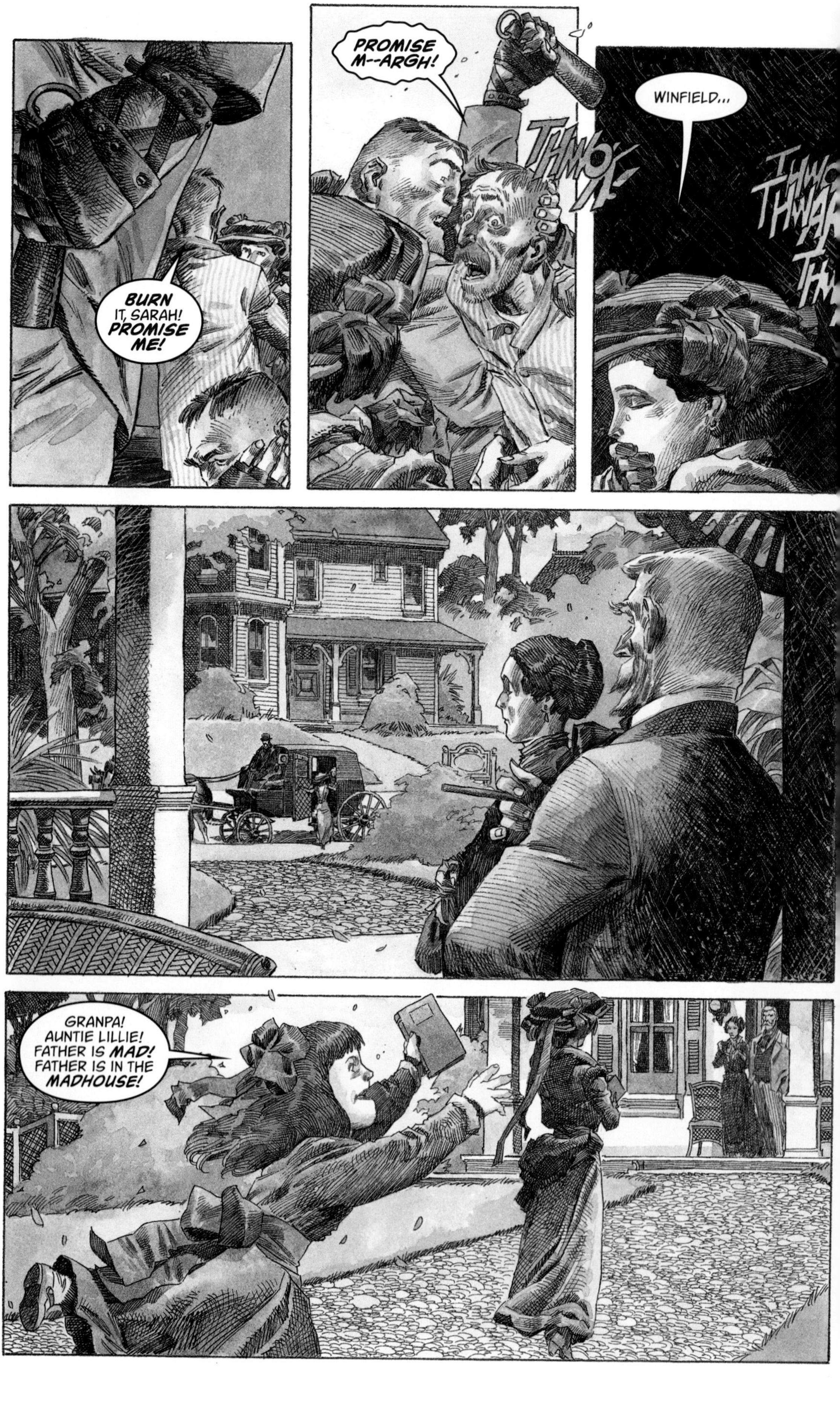
BURN IT, SARAH! PROMISE ME!
PROMISE M--ARGH!
THWOK!
WINFIELD...
GRANPA! AUNTIE LILLIE! FATHER IS MAD! FATHER IS IN THE MADHOUSE!

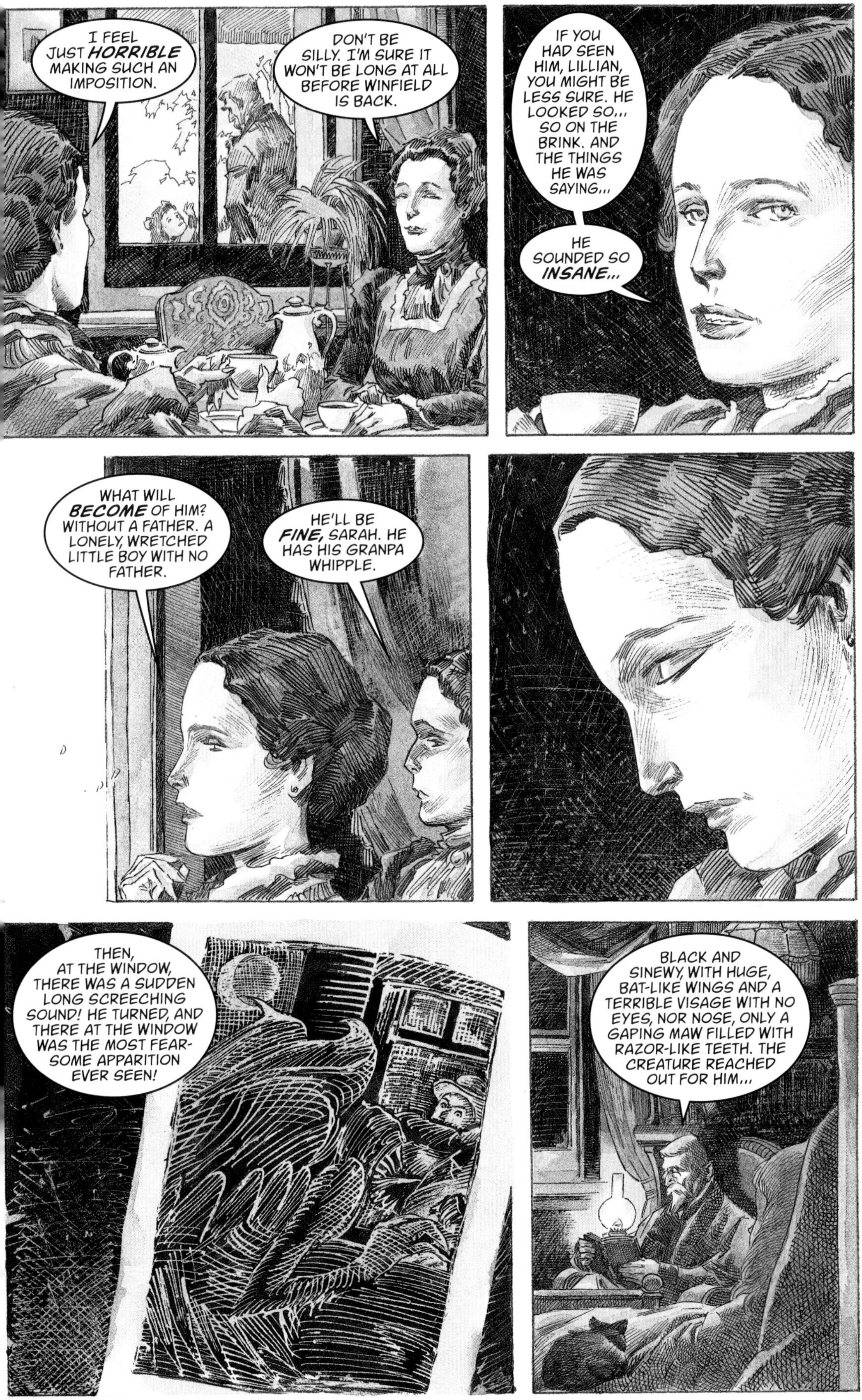
I FEEL JUST HORRIBLE MAKING SUCH AN IMPOSITION.
DON'T BE SILLY. I'M SURE IT WON'T BE LONG AT ALL BEFORE WINFIELD IS BACK.
IF YOU HAD SEEN HIM, LILLIAN, YOU MIGHT BE LESS SURE. HE LOOKED SO... SO ON THE BRINK. AND THE THINGS HE WAS SAYING...
HE SOUNDED SO INSANE...
WHAT WILL BECOME OF HIM? WITHOUT A FATHER. A LONELY, WRETCHED LITTLE BOY WITH NO FATHER.
HE'LL BE FINE, SARAH. HE HAS HIS GRANPA WHIPPLE.
THEN, AT THE WINDOW, THERE WAS A SUDDEN LONG SCREECHING SOUND! HE TURNED, AND THERE AT THE WINDOW WAS THE MOST FEAR-SOME APPARITION EVER SEEN!
BLACK AND SINEWY, WITH HUGE, BAT-LIKE WINGS AND A TERRIBLE VISAGE WITH NO EYES, NOR NOSE, ONLY A GAPING MAW FILLED WITH RAZOR-LIKE TEETH. THE CREATURE REACHED OUT FOR HIM...

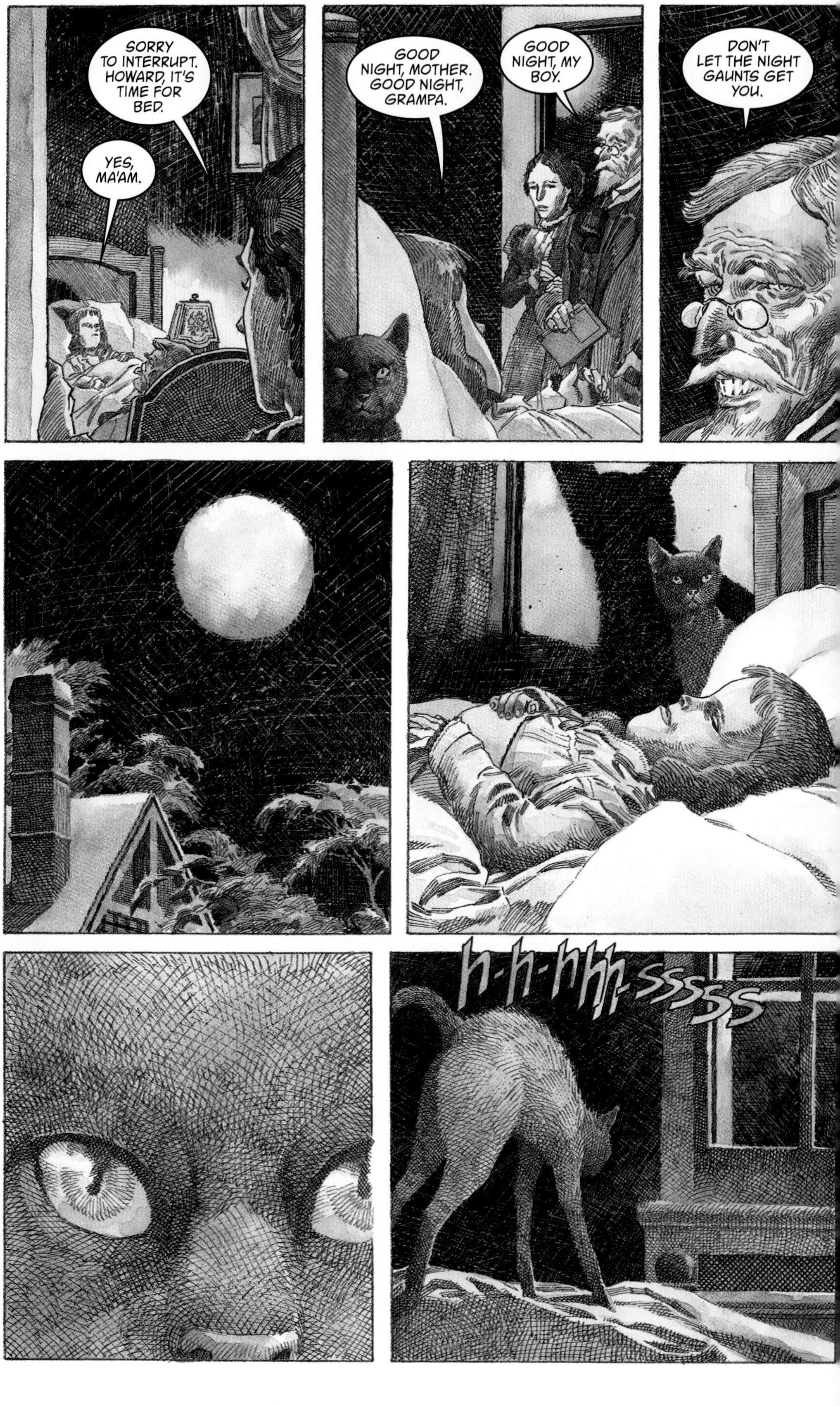
SORRY TO INTERRUPT. HOWARD, IT'S TIME FOR BED.
YES, MA'AM.
GOOD NIGHT, MOTHER. GOOD NIGHT, GRAMPA.
GOOD NIGHT, MY BOY.
DON'T LET THE NIGHT GAUNTS GET YOU.
h-h-hhh-SSSSSS

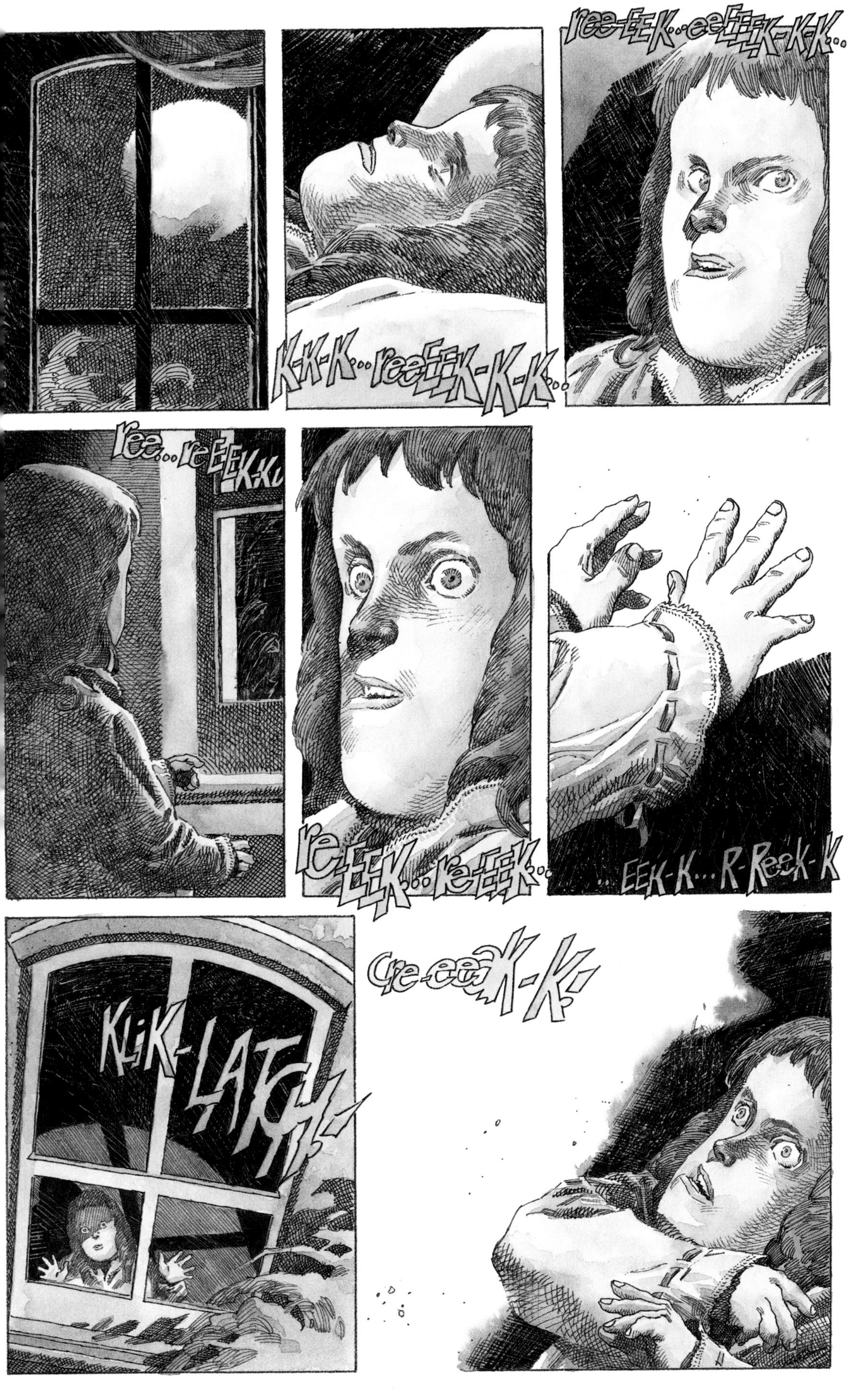

K-K-K...reeEEK-K-K...
ree-EEK...eeEEK-K-K...
ree...reEEK-K
re-EEK...re-EEK...
...EEK-K...R-Reek-K
KLIK-LATCH
Cre-eeeK-K

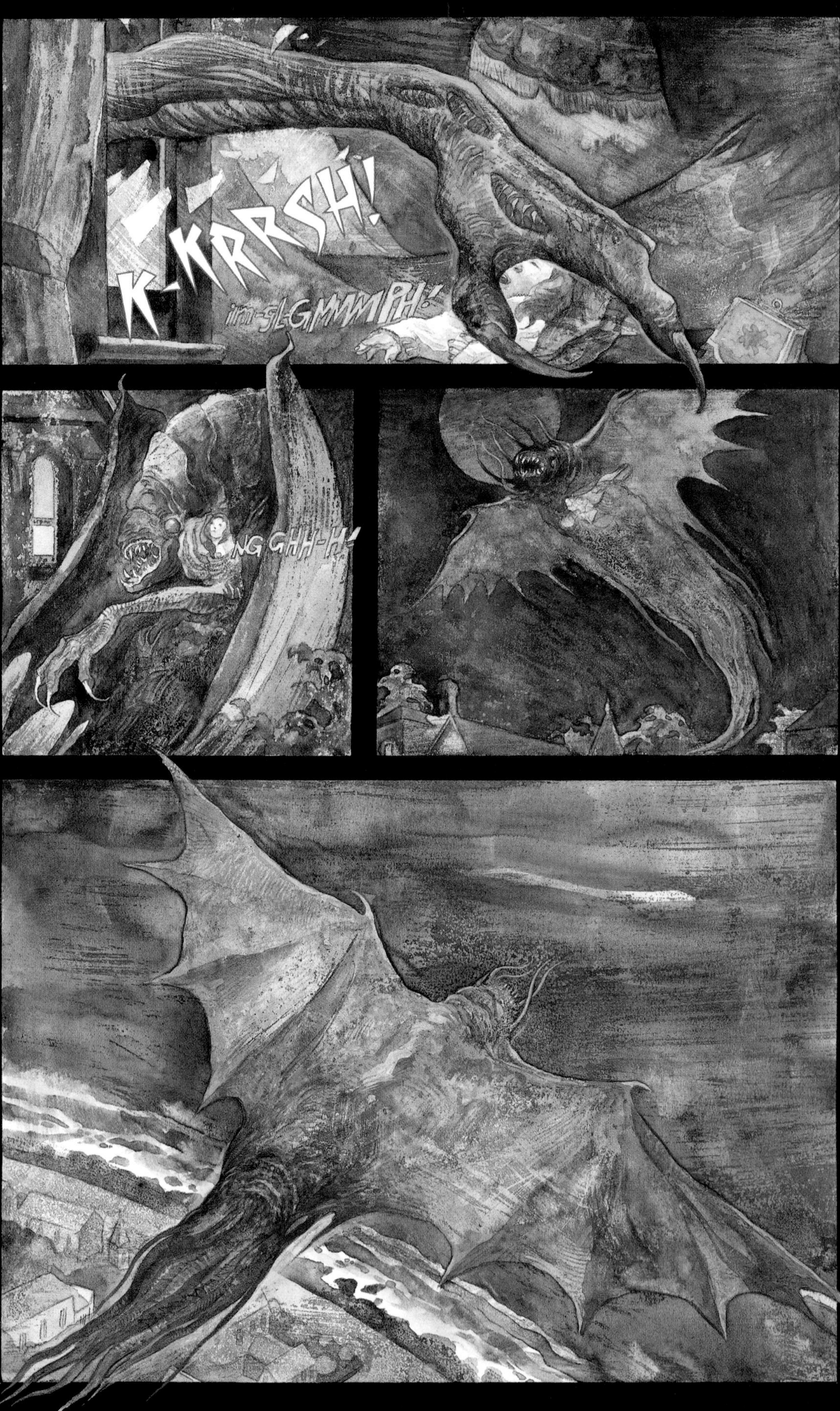
K-KRRSH!
MM-SLGMMMPH!
NG GHH-H!

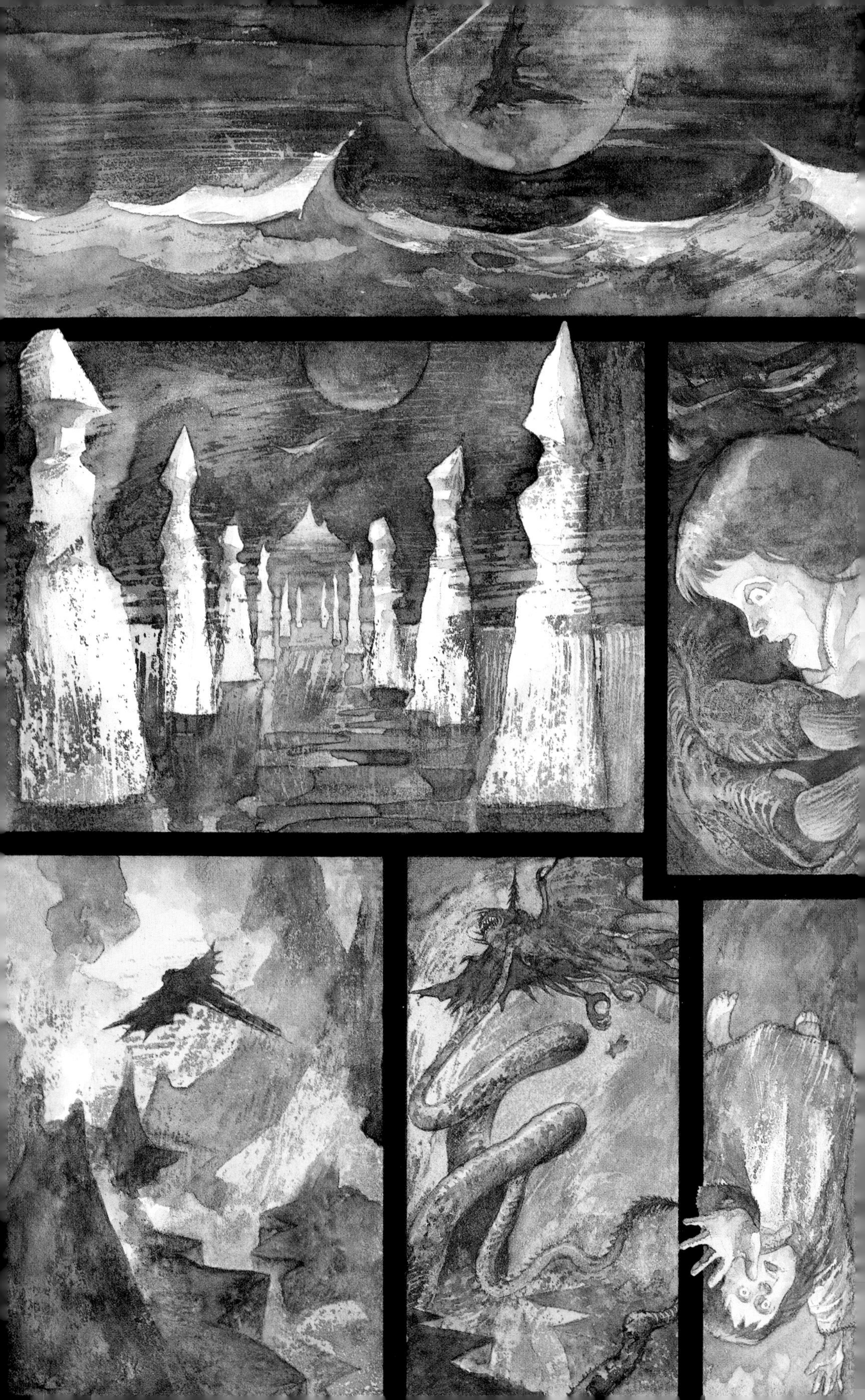

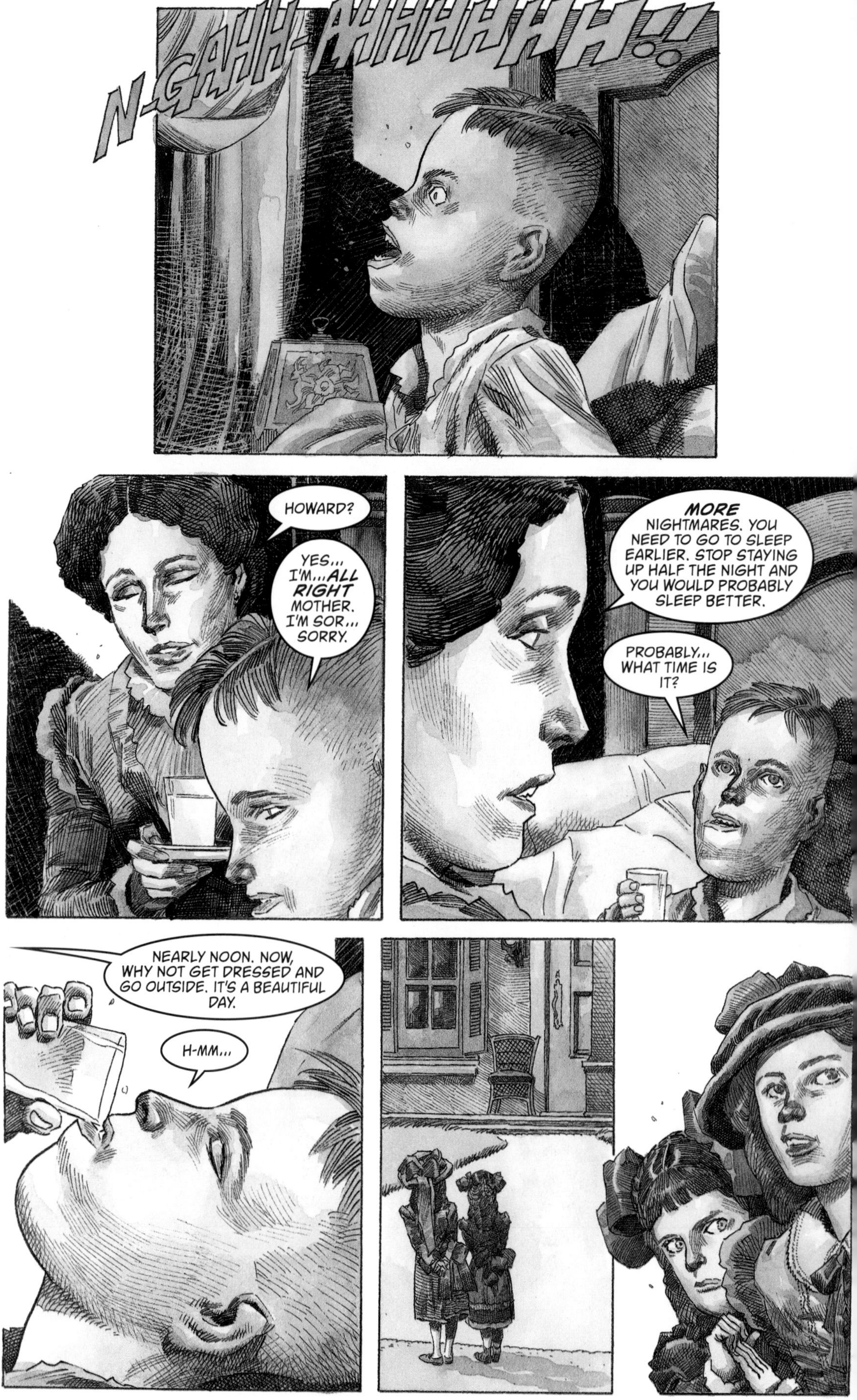
N-GAHH-AHHHHHHH!!
HOWARD?
YES... I'M... ALL RIGHT MOTHER. I'M SOR... SORRY.
MORE NIGHTMARES. YOU NEED TO GO TO SLEEP EARLIER. STOP STAYING UP HALF THE NIGHT AND YOU WOULD PROBABLY SLEEP BETTER.
PROBABLY... WHAT TIME IS IT?
NEARLY NOON. NOW, WHY NOT GET DRESSED AND GO OUTSIDE. IT'S A BEAUTIFUL DAY.
H-MM...

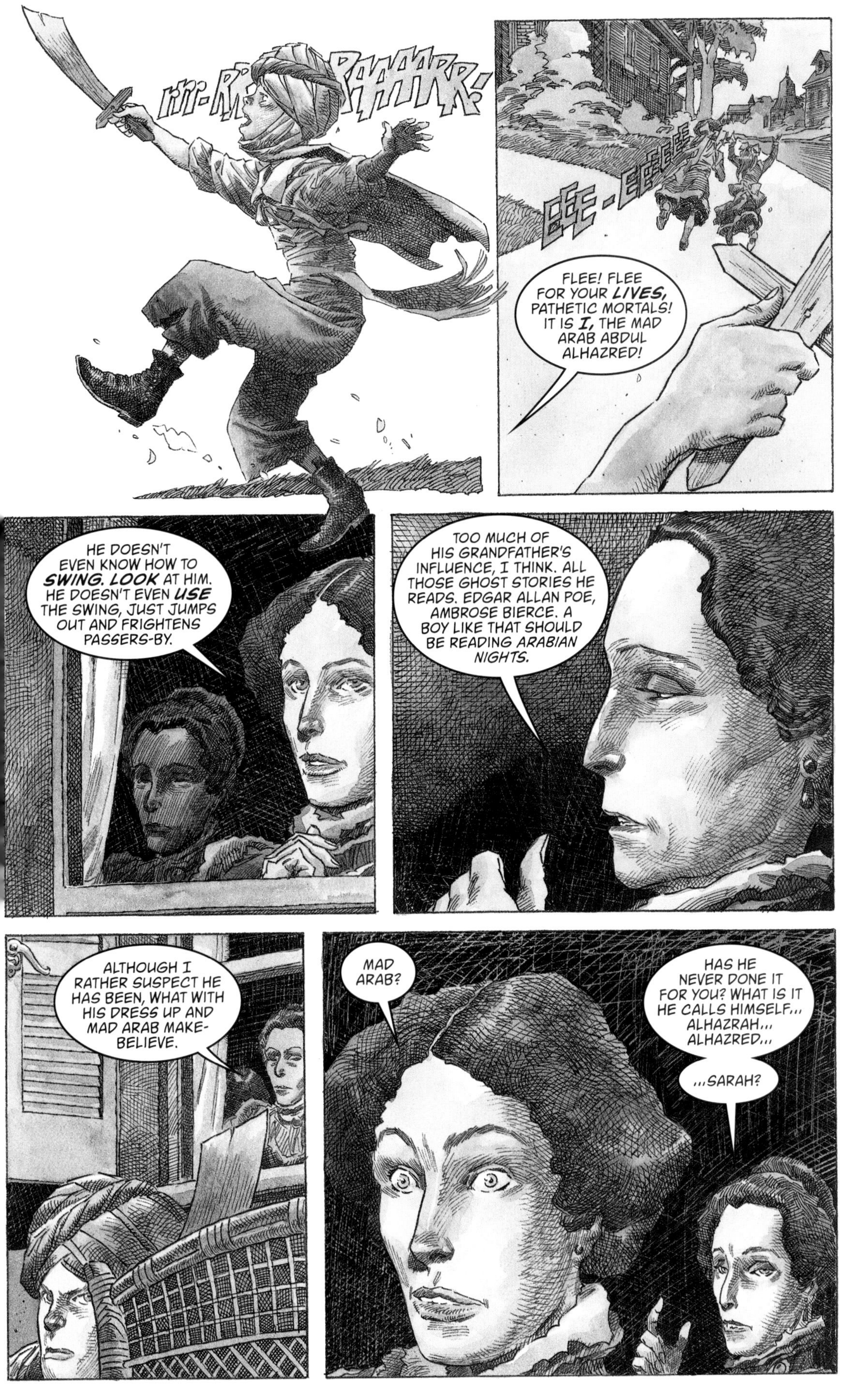

RRR-RRRAAAARR!
EEE-EEEEE
FLEE! FLEE FOR YOUR LIVES, PATHETIC MORTALS! IT IS I, THE MAD ARAB ABDUL ALHAZRED!
HE DOESN'T EVEN KNOW HOW TO SWING. LOOK AT HIM. HE DOESN'T EVEN USE THE SWING, JUST JUMPS OUT AND FRIGHTENS PASSERS-BY.
TOO MUCH OF HIS GRANDFATHER'S INFLUENCE, I THINK. ALL THOSE GHOST STORIES HE READS. EDGAR ALLAN POE, AMBROSE BIERCE. A BOY LIKE THAT SHOULD BE READING ARABIAN NIGHTS.
ALTHOUGH I RATHER SUSPECT HE HAS BEEN, WHAT WITH HIS DRESS UP AND MAD ARAB MAKE-BELIEVE.
MAD ARAB?
HAS HE NEVER DONE IT FOR YOU? WHAT IS IT HE CALLS HIMSELF... ALHAZRAH... ALHAZRED...
...SARAH?

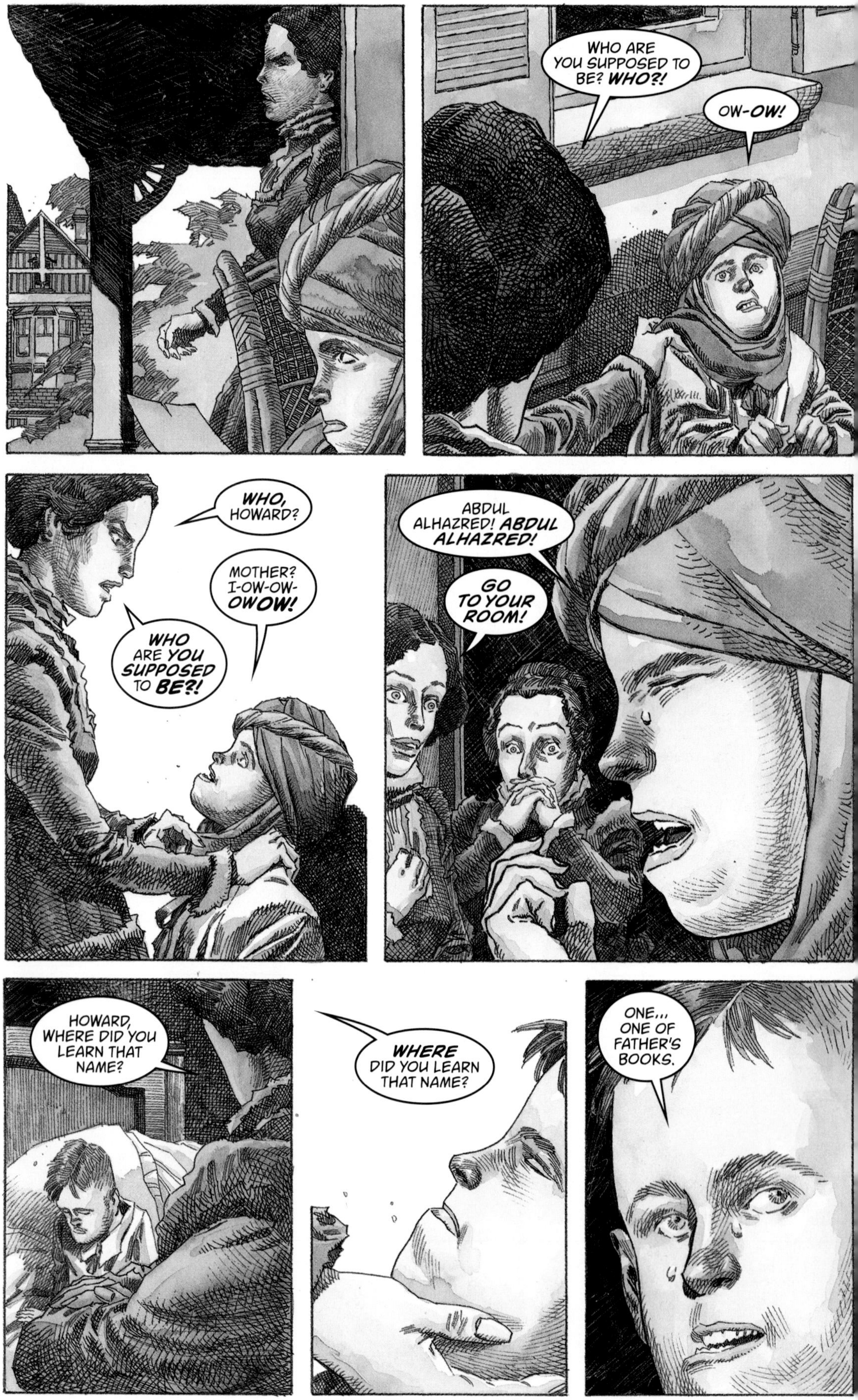
WHO ARE YOU SUPPOSED TO BE? WHO?!
OW-OW!
WHO, HOWARD?
WHO ARE YOU SUPPOSED TO BE?!
MOTHER? I-OW-OW-OWOW!
ABDUL ALHAZRED! ABDUL ALHAZRED!
GO TO YOUR ROOM!
HOWARD, WHERE DID YOU LEARN THAT NAME?
WHERE DID YOU LEARN THAT NAME?
ONE... ONE OF FATHER'S BOOKS.

WHICH ONE? **WHICH** BOOK OF YOUR FATHER'S?

IT'S CALLED AL AZIF, I THINK. IT WAS WRITTEN BY ABDUL ALHAZRED.

THE **NECRONOMICON.** OH GOD, HOWARD, **PLEASE** SAY IT WASN'T THE NECRONOMICON.

BUT MOTHER, WHY? I THOUGHT I WAS ALLOWED TO READ **ANYTHING** IN FATHER'S LIBRARY.

OH GOD...GOD, NO. YOUR FATHER DIDN'T **KEEP** THAT BOOK IN THE LI...

WHERE IS IT, HOWARD? WHERE IS THE BOOK **NOW?**

UNDER THE BED. IT... IT LIVES UNDER THE BED.

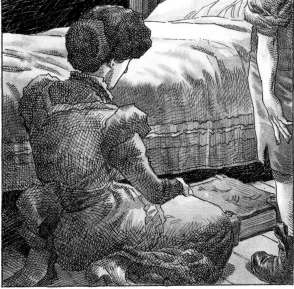

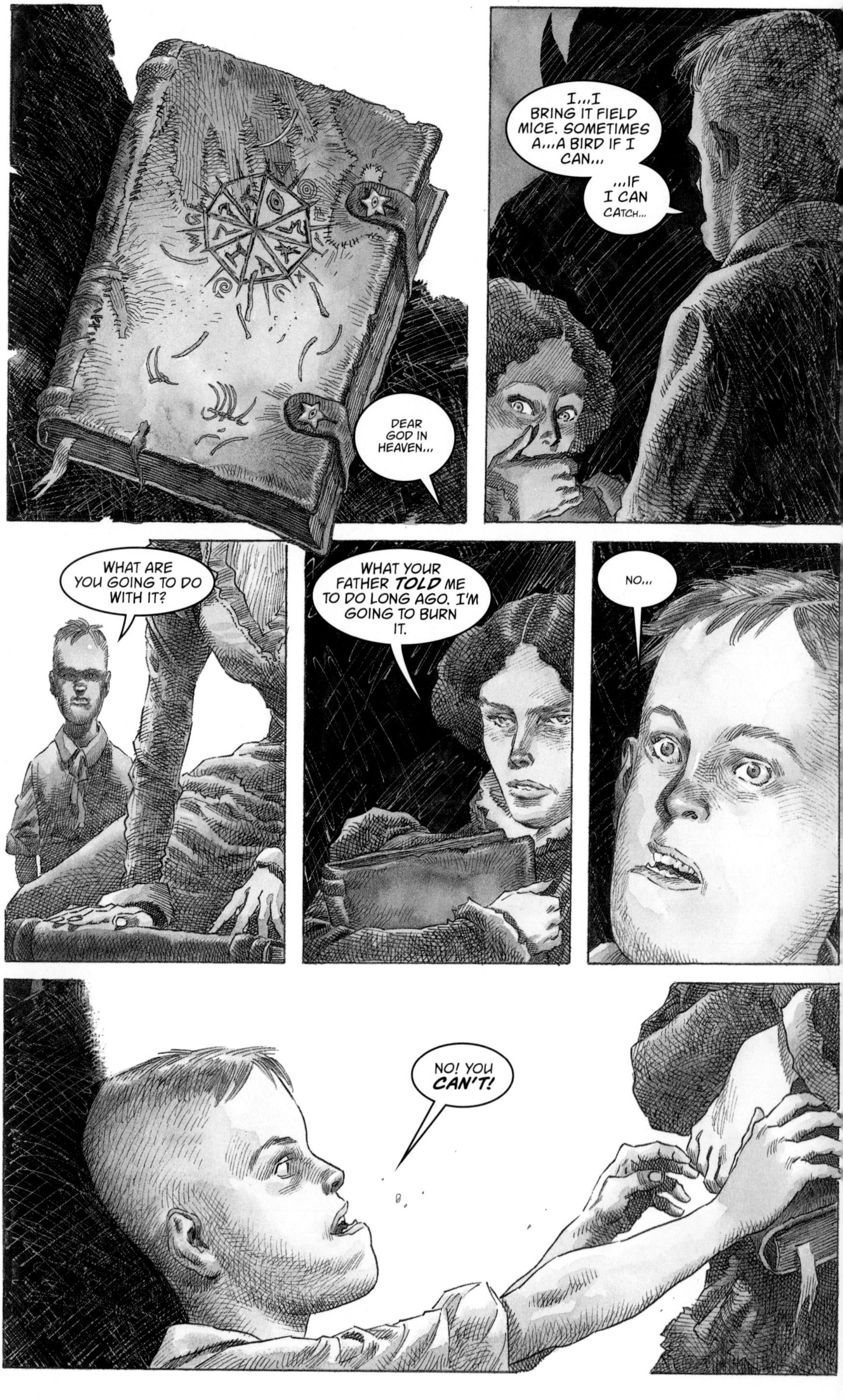
DEAR GOD IN HEAVEN...
I...I BRING IT FIELD MICE. SOMETIMES A...A BIRD IF I CAN...
...IF I CAN CATCH...
WHAT ARE YOU GOING TO DO WITH IT?
WHAT YOUR FATHER TOLD ME TO DO LONG AGO. I'M GOING TO BURN IT.
NO...
NO! YOU CAN'T!

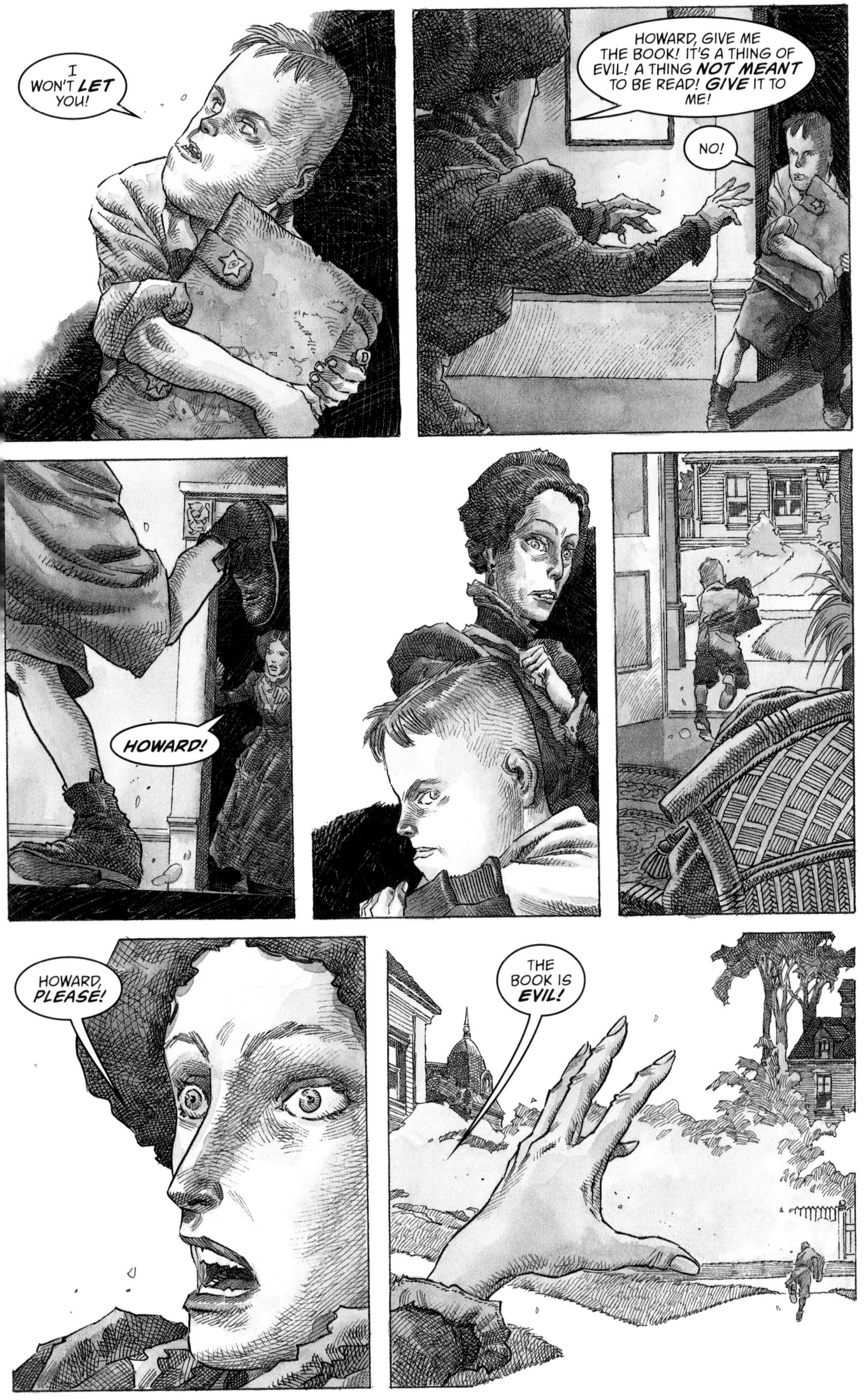
I WON'T LET YOU!
HOWARD, GIVE ME THE BOOK! IT'S A THING OF EVIL! A THING NOT MEANT TO BE READ! GIVE IT TO ME!
NO!
HOWARD!
HOWARD, PLEASE!
THE BOOK IS EVIL!

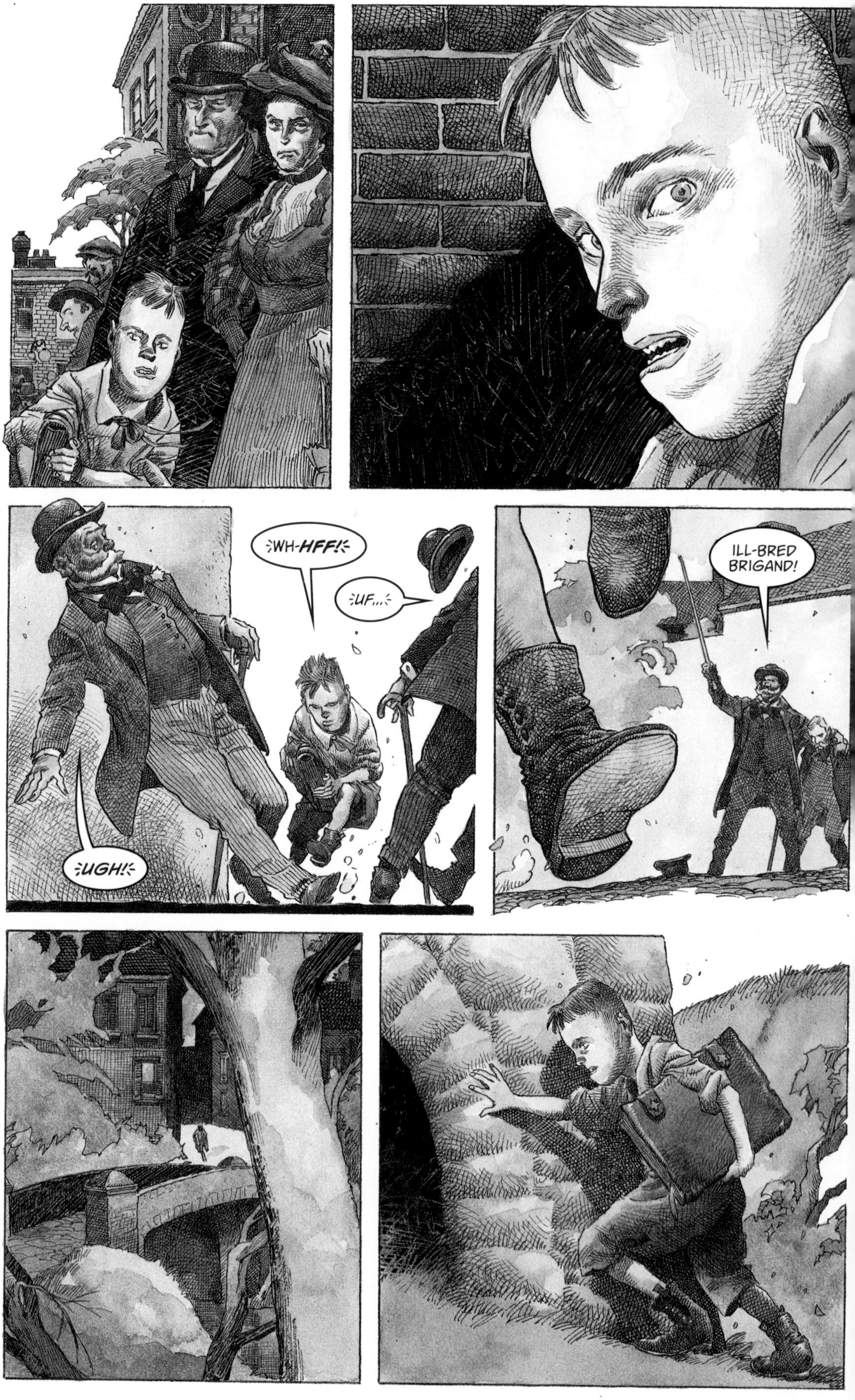
WH-HFF!
UF...
UGH!
ILL-BRED BRIGAND!

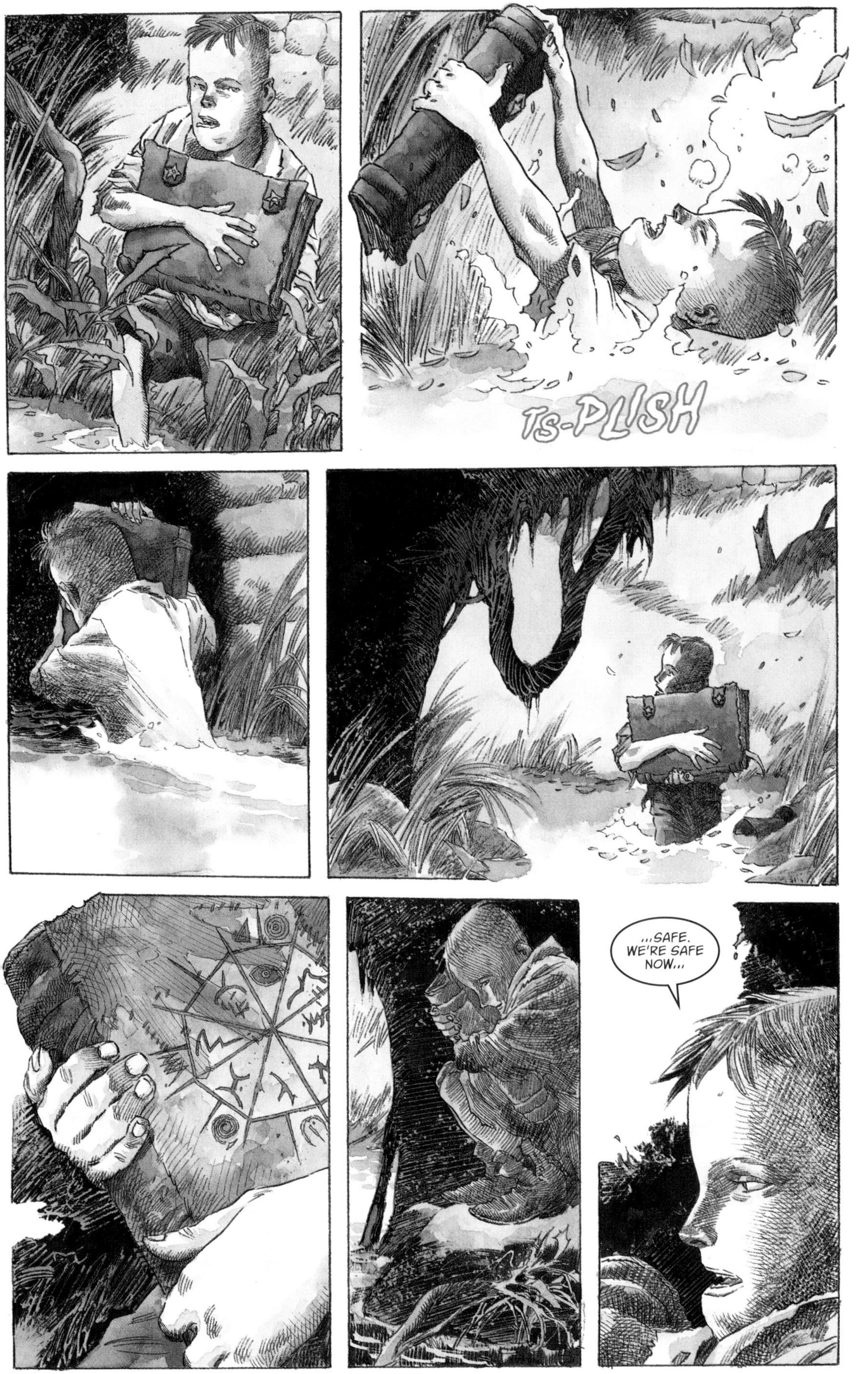
TS-PLISH
...SAFE. WE'RE SAFE NOW...

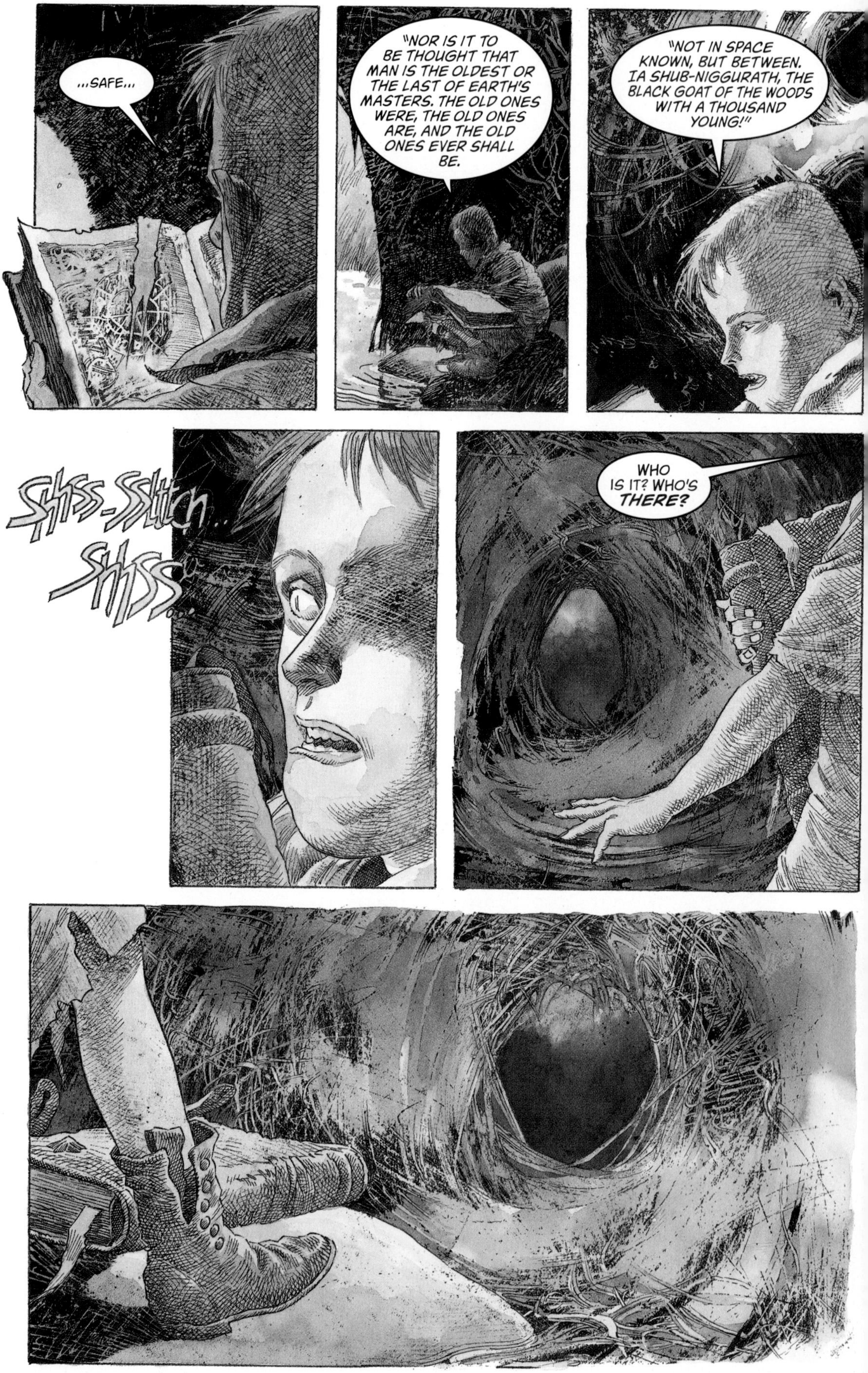
...SAFE...
"NOR IS IT TO BE THOUGHT THAT MAN IS THE OLDEST OR THE LAST OF EARTH'S MASTERS. THE OLD ONES WERE, THE OLD ONES ARE, AND THE OLD ONES EVER SHALL BE.
"NOT IN SPACE KNOWN, BUT BETWEEN. IA SHUB-NIGGURATH, THE BLACK GOAT OF THE WOODS WITH A THOUSAND YOUNG!"
SHHSS-SSLITCH...
SHHSS...
WHO IS IT? WHO'S THERE?

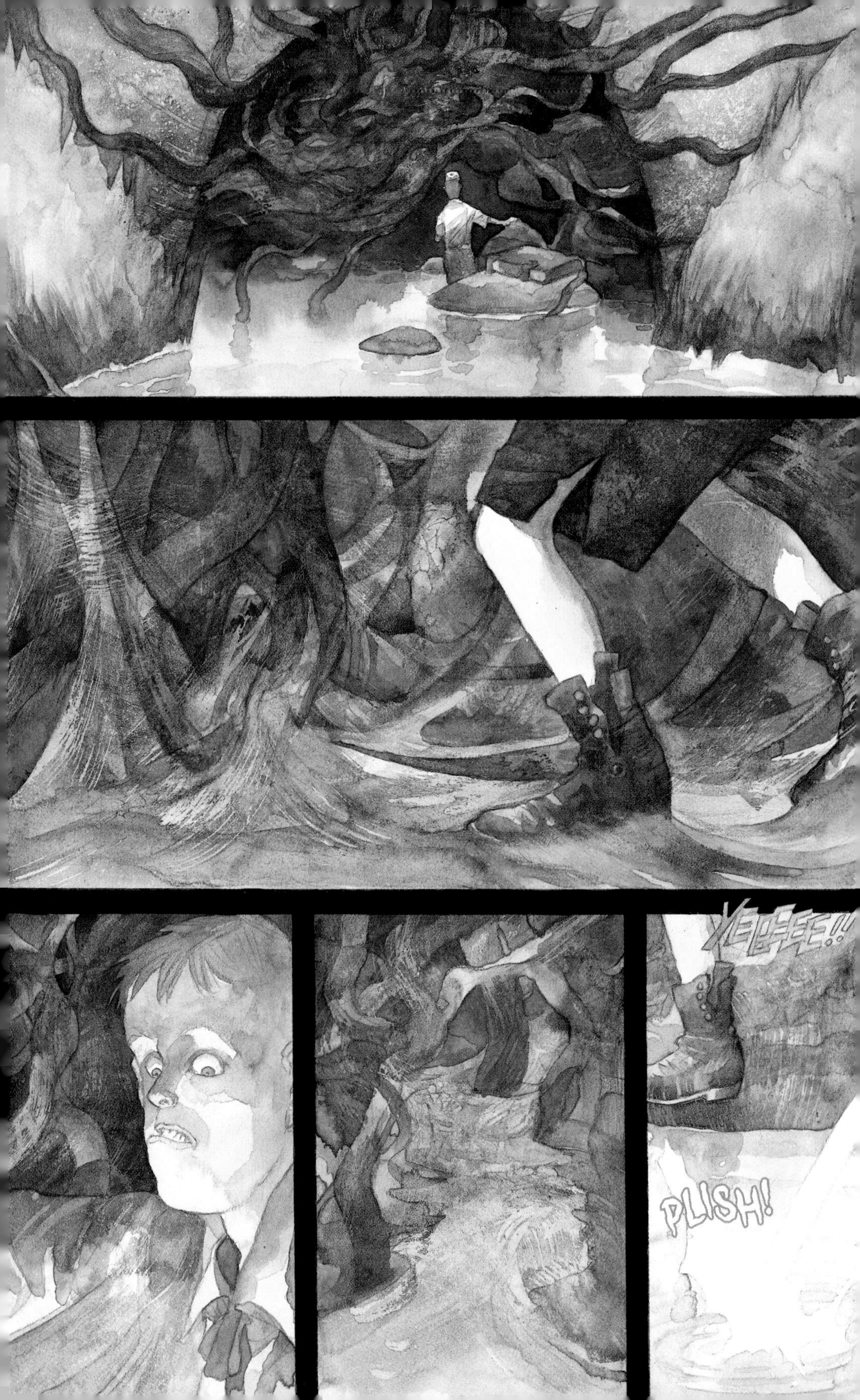
PLISH!

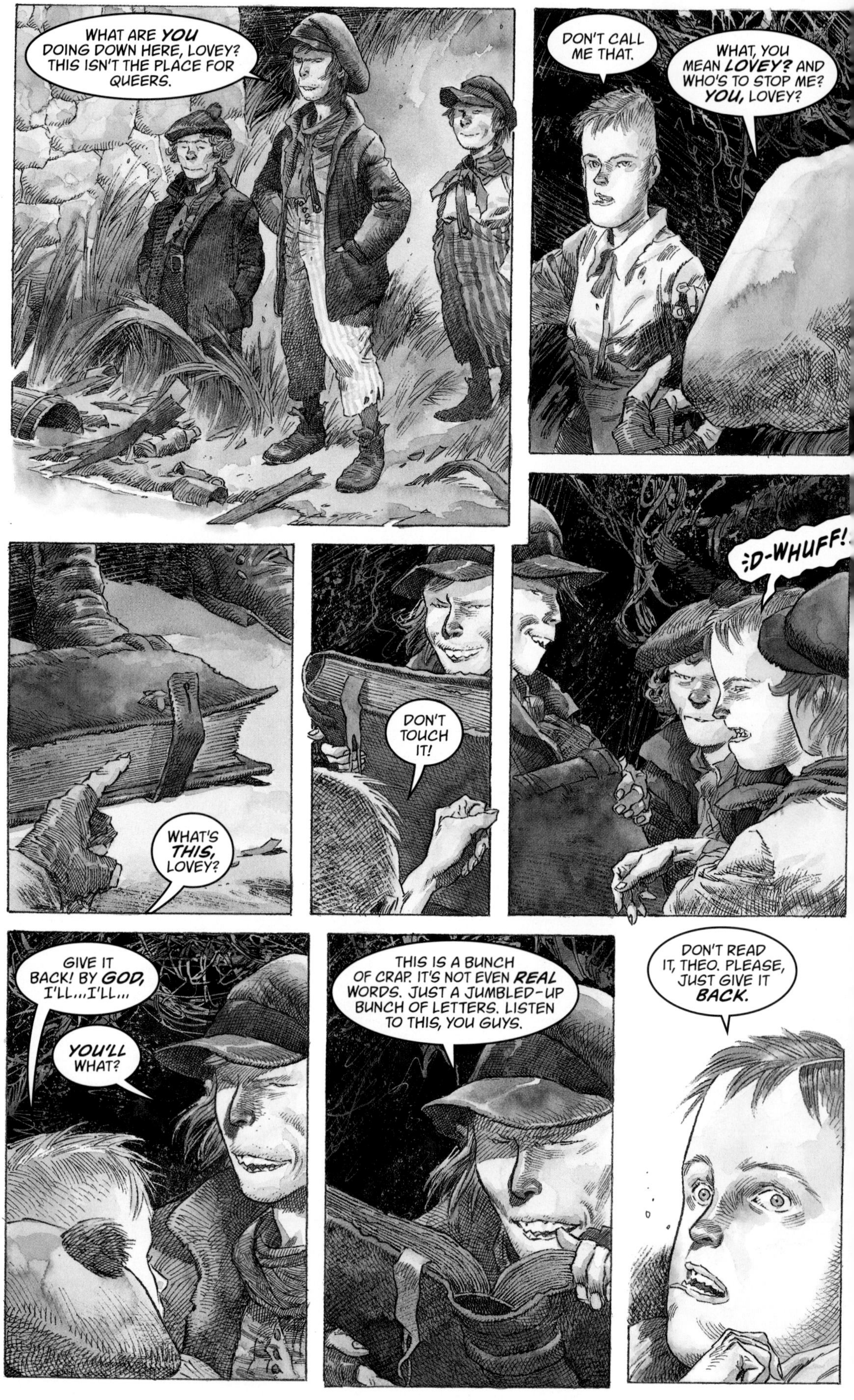

WHAT ARE YOU DOING DOWN HERE, LOVEY? THIS ISN'T THE PLACE FOR QUEERS.
DON'T CALL ME THAT.
WHAT, YOU MEAN LOVEY? AND WHO'S TO STOP ME? YOU, LOVEY?
WHAT'S THIS, LOVEY?
DON'T TOUCH IT!
¡D-WHUFF!
GIVE IT BACK! BY GOD, I'LL...I'LL...
YOU'LL WHAT?
THIS IS A BUNCH OF CRAP. IT'S NOT EVEN REAL WORDS. JUST A JUMBLED-UP BUNCH OF LETTERS. LISTEN TO THIS, YOU GUYS.
DON'T READ IT, THEO. PLEASE, JUST GIVE IT BACK.

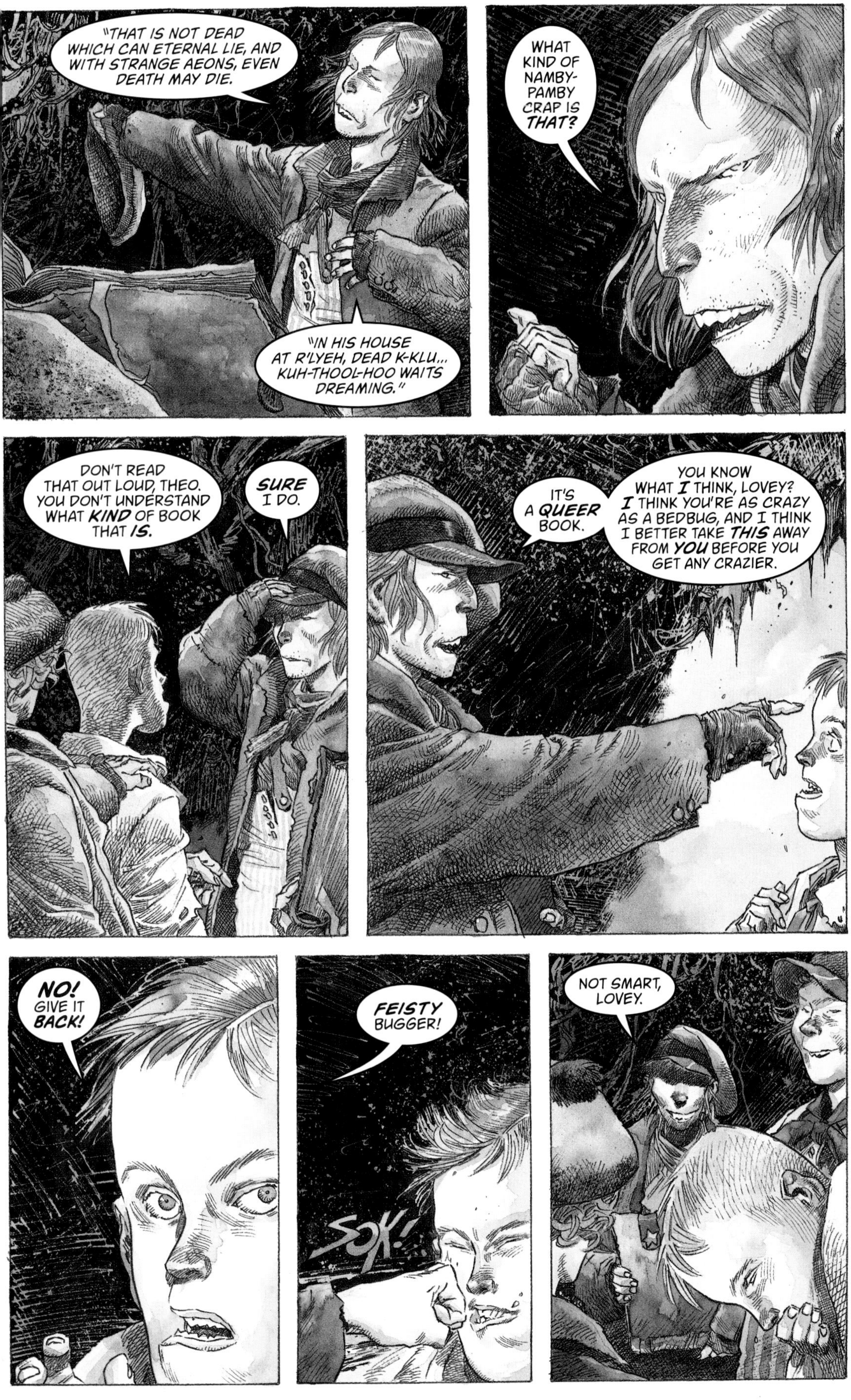
"THAT IS NOT DEAD WHICH CAN ETERNAL LIE, AND WITH STRANGE AEONS, EVEN DEATH MAY DIE.
"IN HIS HOUSE AT R'LYEH, DEAD K-KLU... KUH-THOOL-HOO WAITS DREAMING."
WHAT KIND OF NAMBY-PAMBY CRAP IS **THAT?**
DON'T READ THAT OUT LOUD, THEO. YOU DON'T UNDERSTAND WHAT **KIND** OF BOOK THAT **IS.**
SURE I DO.
IT'S A **QUEER** BOOK.
YOU KNOW WHAT **I** THINK, LOVEY? **I** THINK YOU'RE AS CRAZY AS A BEDBUG, AND I THINK I BETTER TAKE **THIS** AWAY FROM **YOU** BEFORE YOU GET ANY CRAZIER.
NO! GIVE IT **BACK!**
FEISTY BUGGER!
SOK!
NOT SMART, LOVEY.

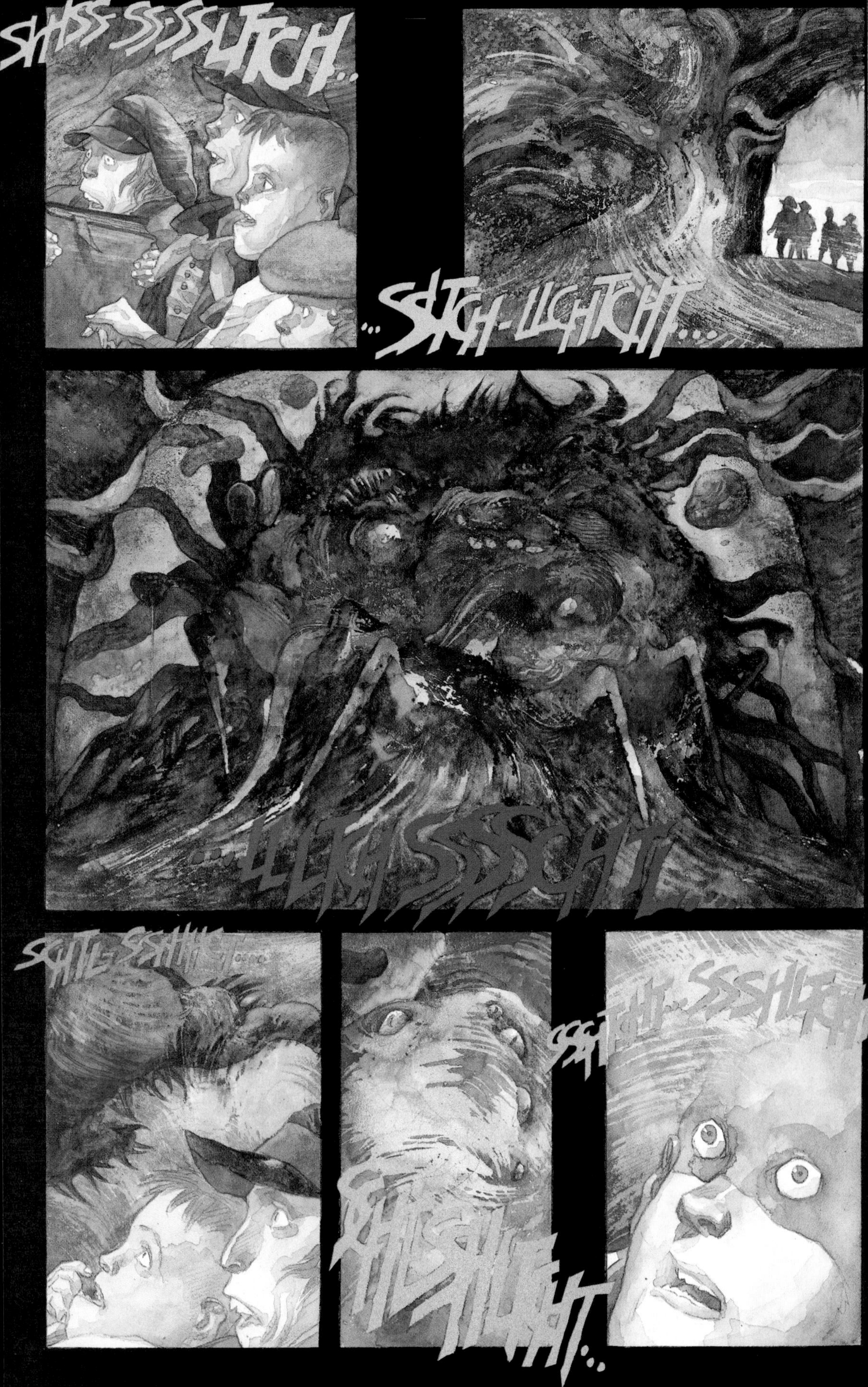
SHSS-SS-SSLTCH..
...SSLTCH-LLCHTCHT....

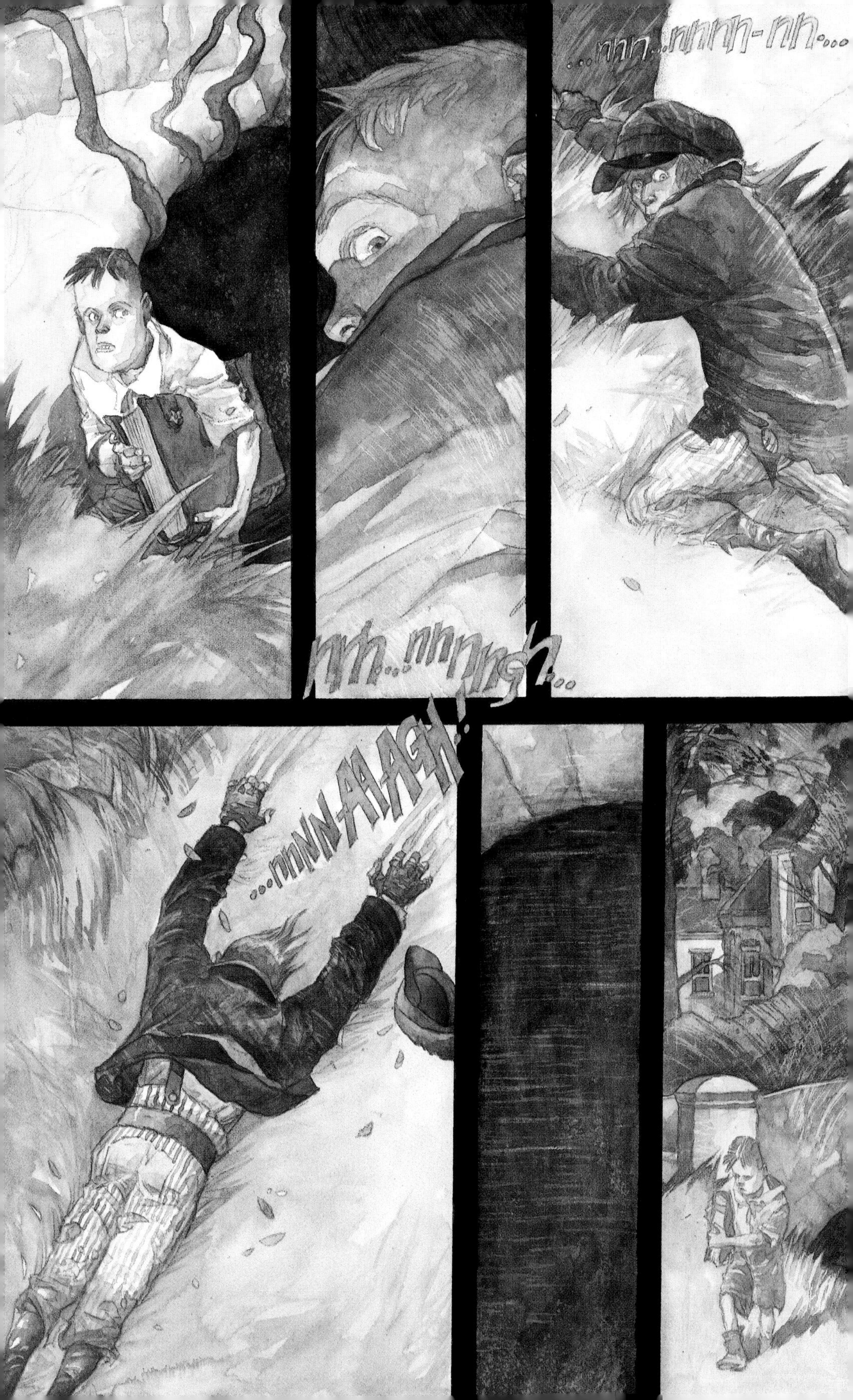
...nnn...nnnh-nh...
nnh...nhhnngh...
...nnnNN-AAAGH!!

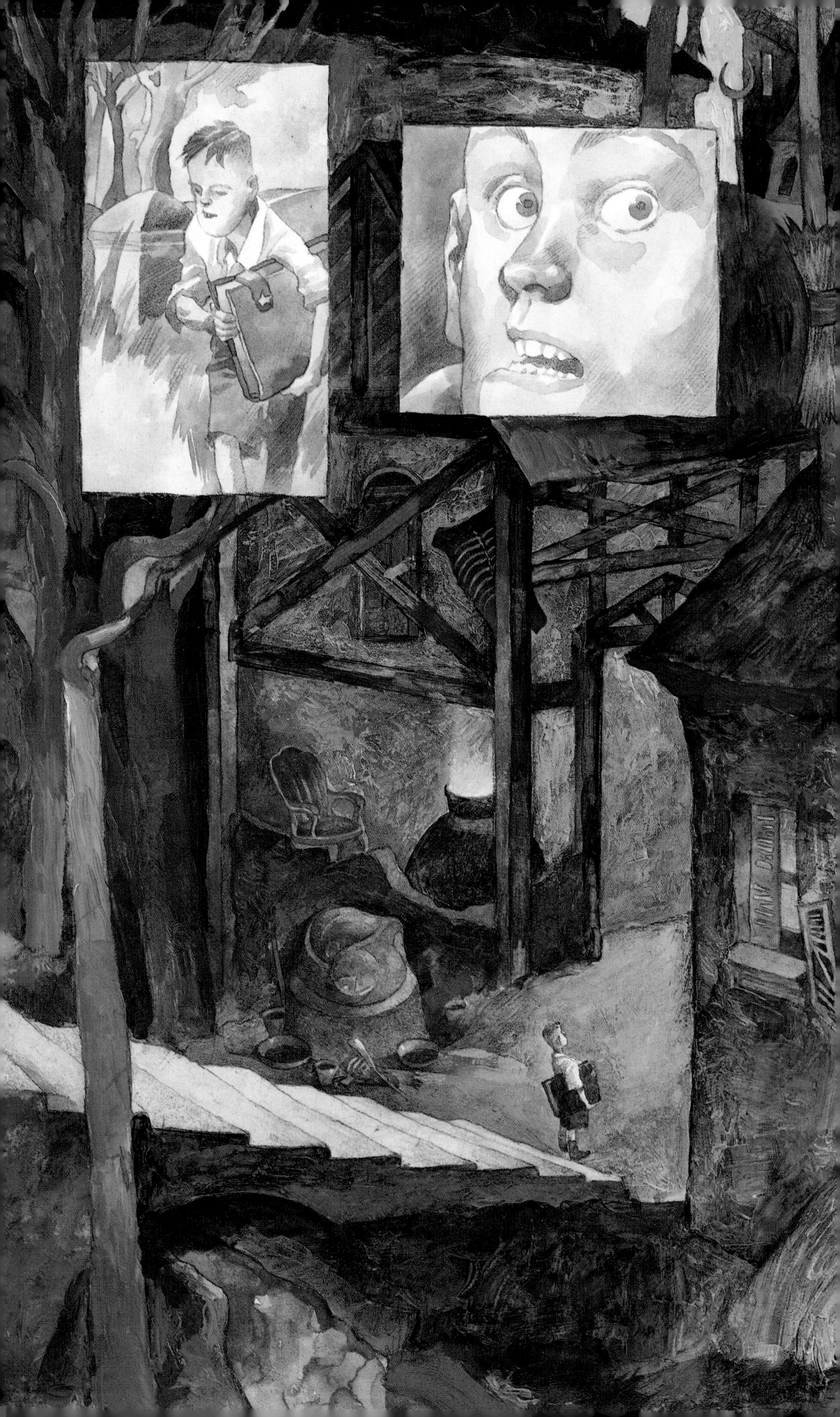

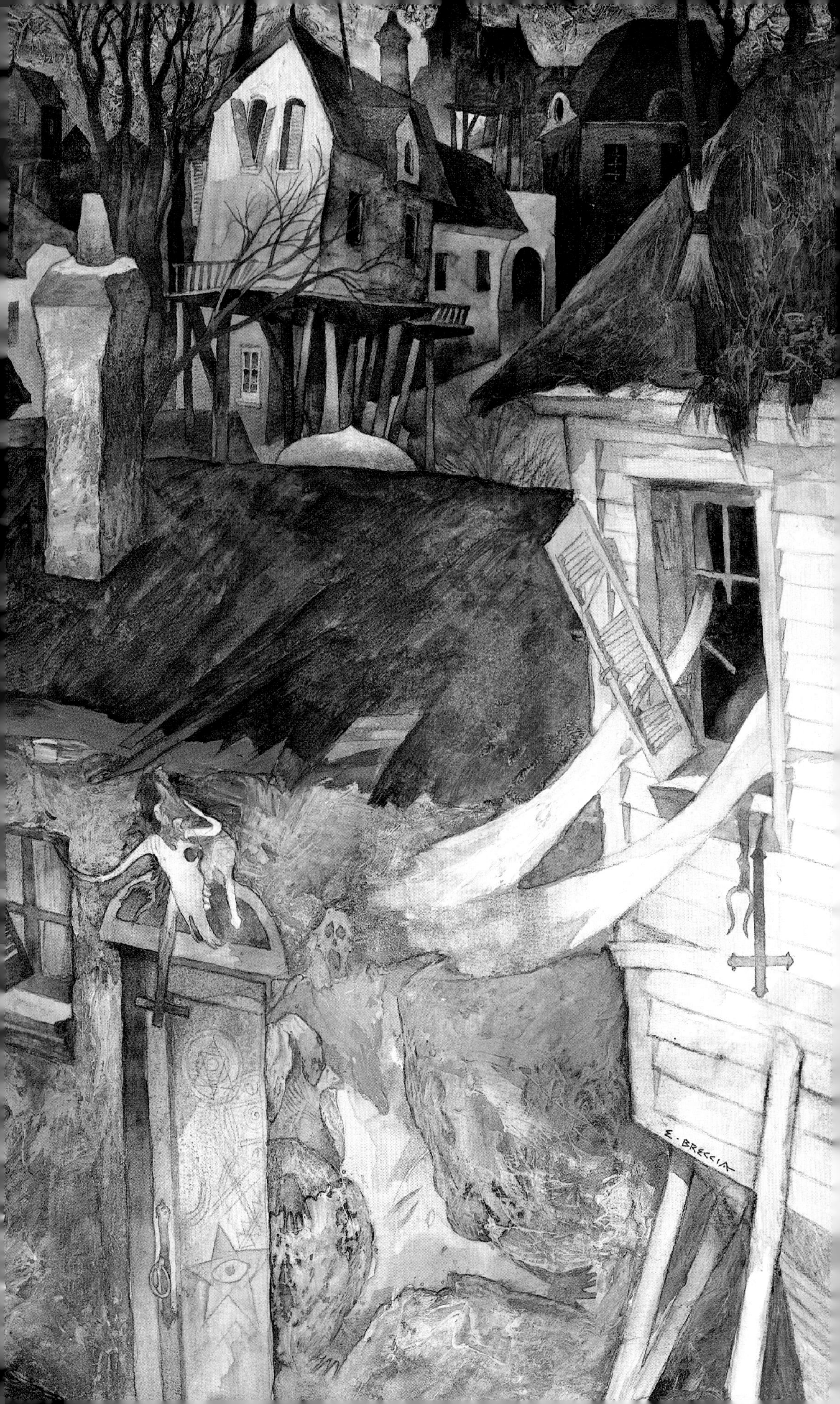

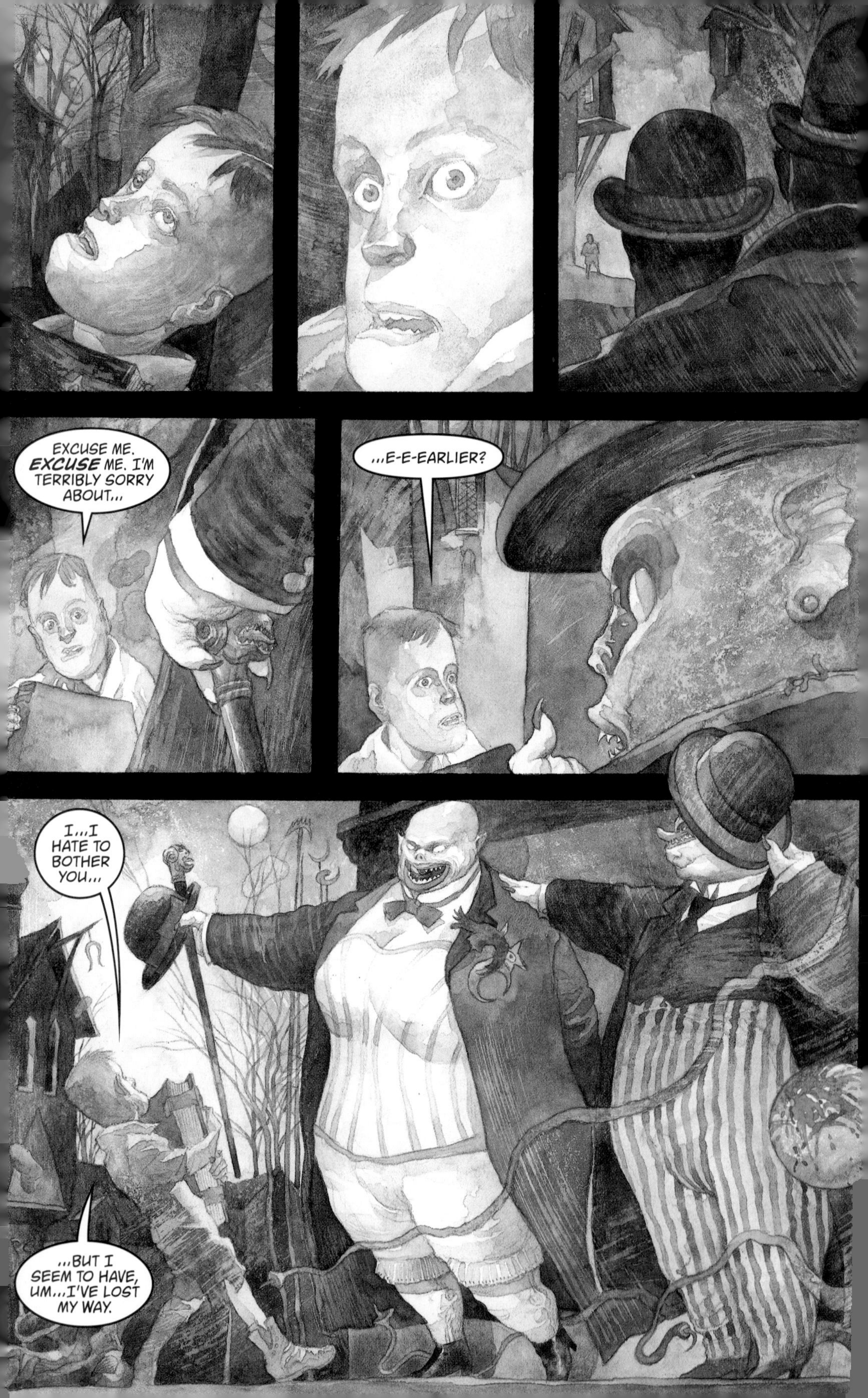

EXCUSE ME. **EXCUSE** ME. I'M TERRIBLY SORRY ABOUT...
...E-E-EARLIER?
I...I HATE TO BOTHER YOU...
...BUT I SEEM TO HAVE, UM...I'VE LOST MY WAY.

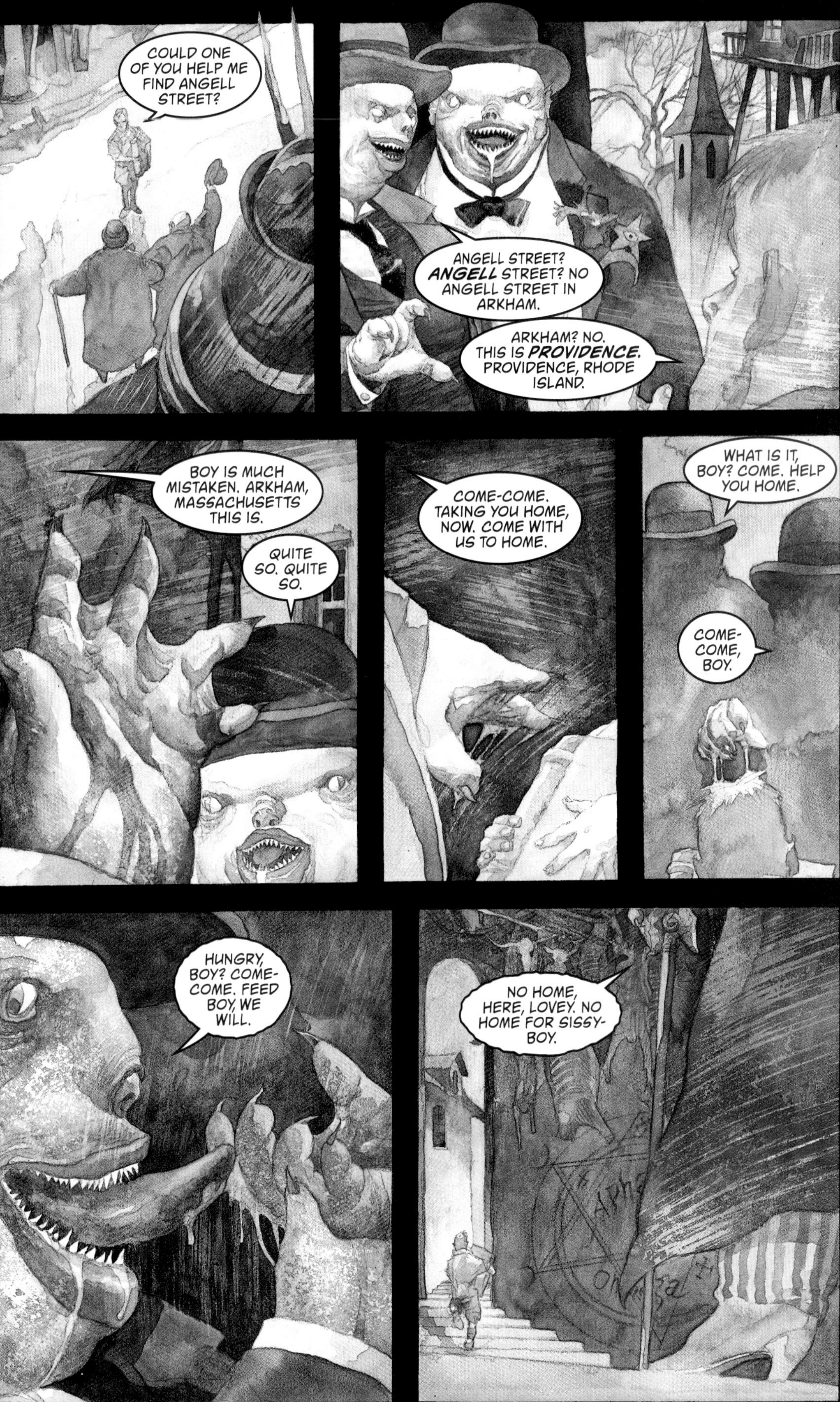

COULD ONE OF YOU HELP ME FIND ANGELL STREET?
ANGELL STREET? ANGELL STREET? NO ANGELL STREET IN ARKHAM.
ARKHAM? NO. THIS IS PROVIDENCE. PROVIDENCE, RHODE ISLAND.
BOY IS MUCH MISTAKEN. ARKHAM, MASSACHUSETTS THIS IS.
QUITE SO. QUITE SO.
COME-COME. TAKING YOU HOME, NOW. COME WITH US TO HOME.
WHAT IS IT, BOY? COME. HELP YOU HOME.
COME-COME, BOY.
HUNGRY, BOY? COME-COME. FEED BOY, WE WILL.
NO HOME, HERE, LOVEY. NO HOME FOR SISSY-BOY.

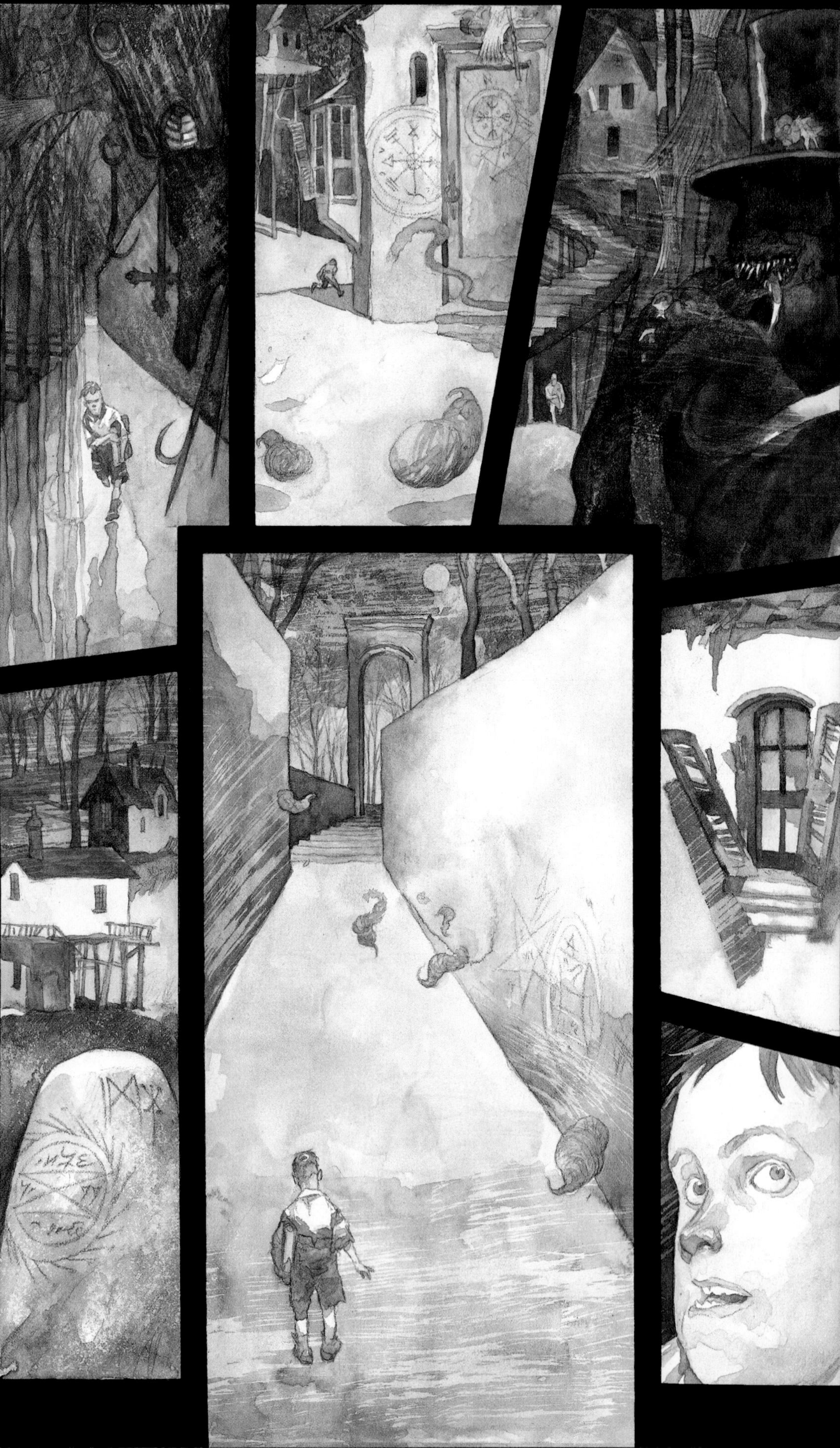

ch-KLAT!
SCREEEEEEE-EEEE

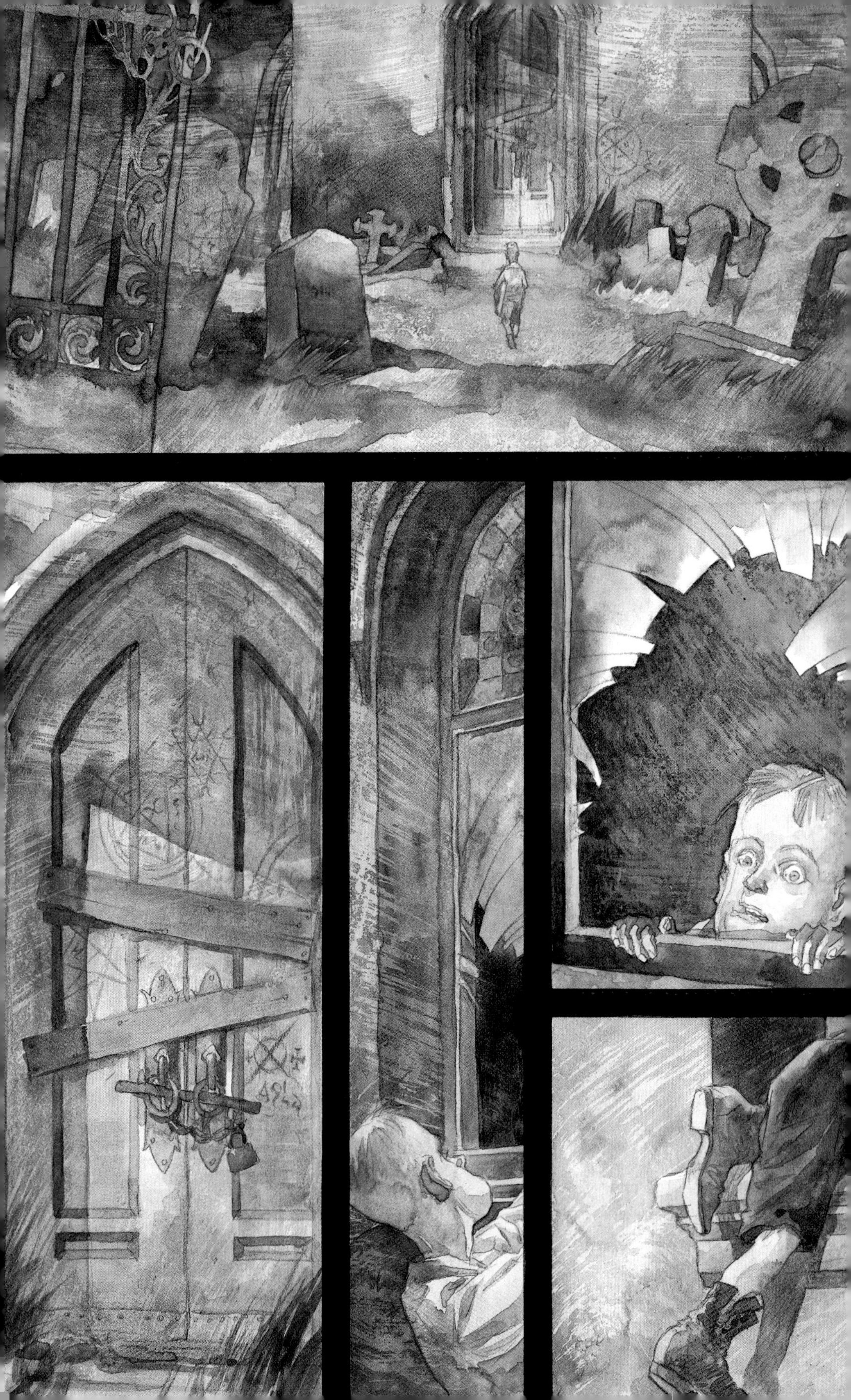

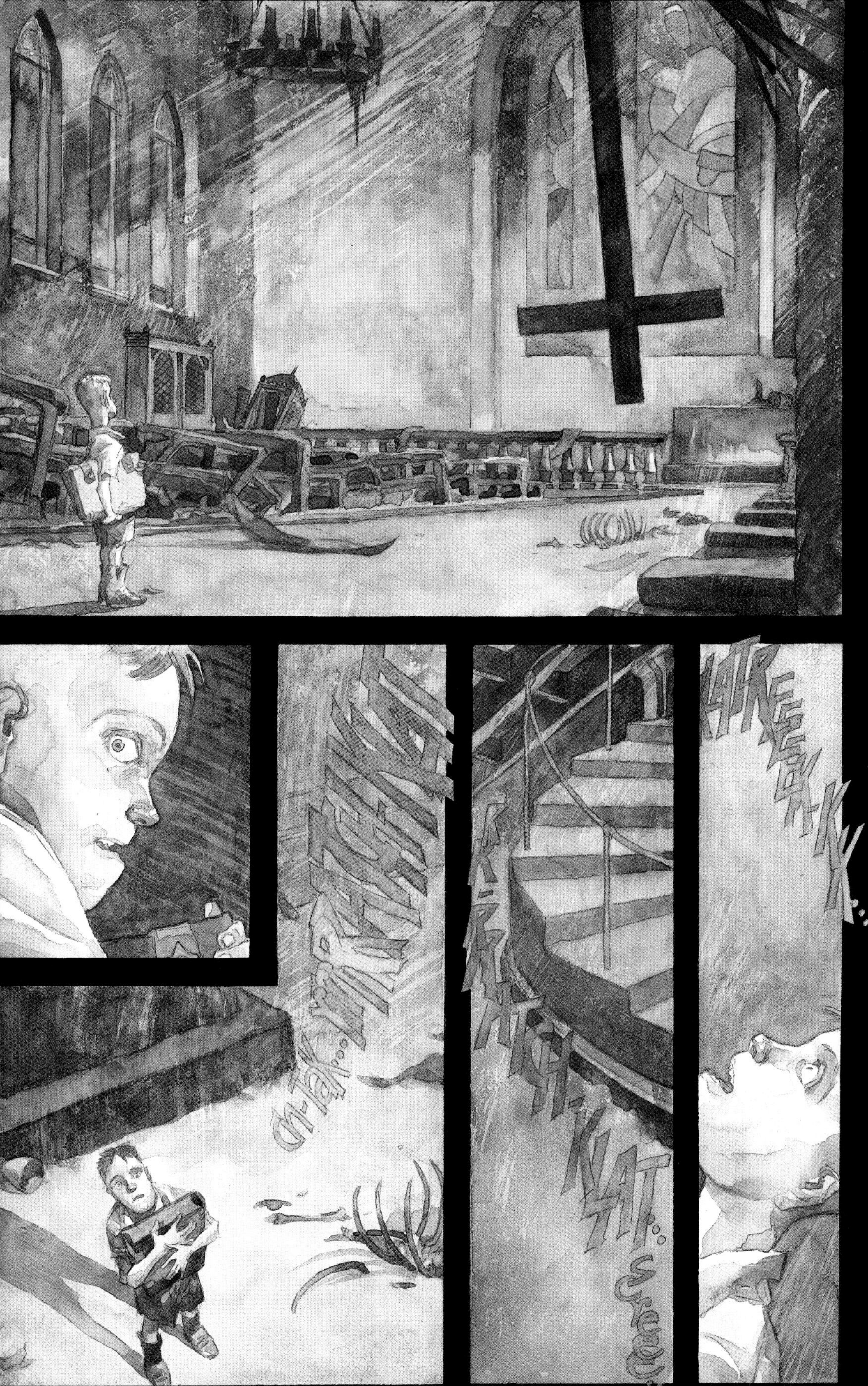
KLAT...

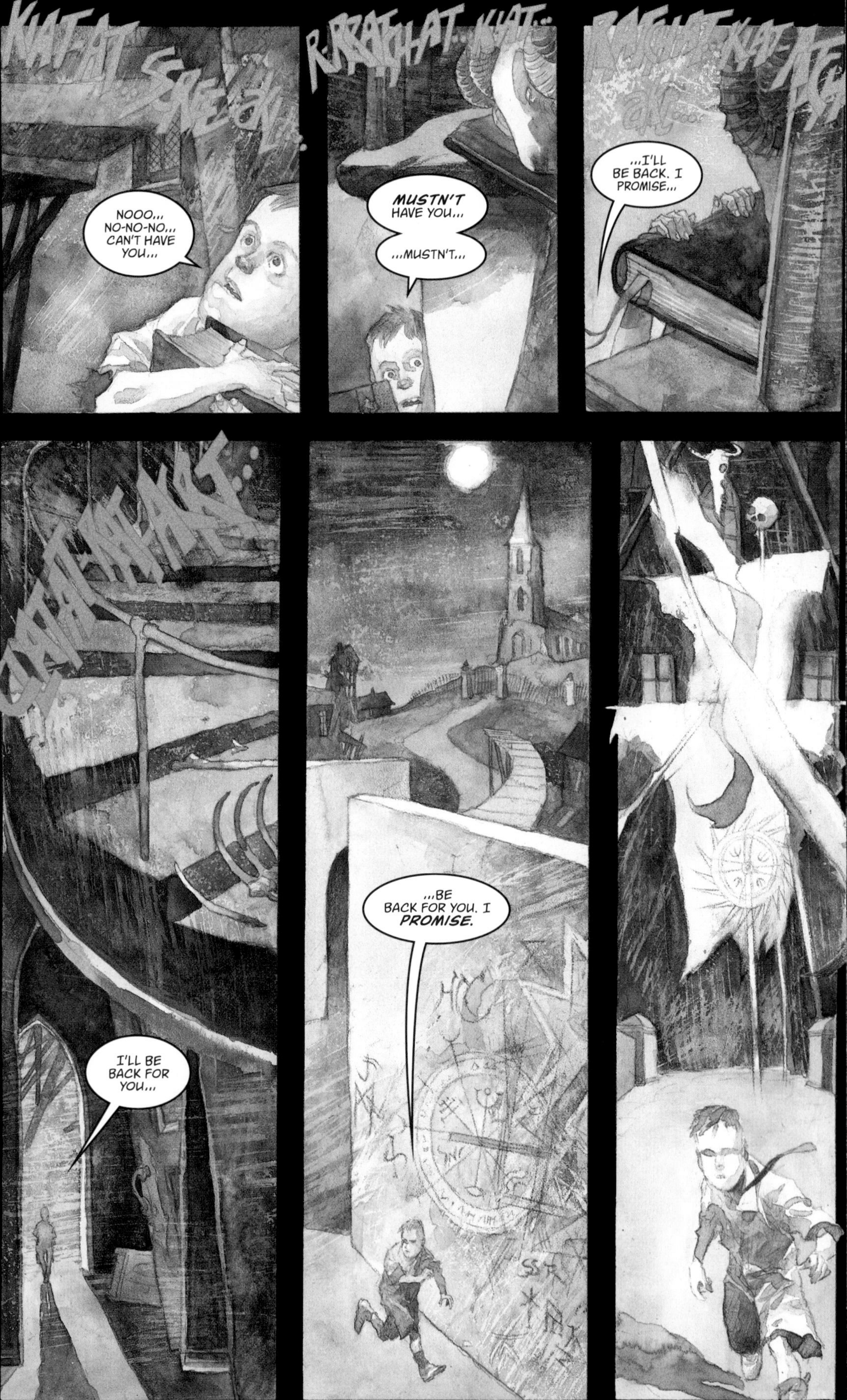
NOOO... NO-NO-NO... CAN'T HAVE YOU...
MUSTN'T HAVE YOU...
...MUSTN'T...
...I'LL BE BACK. I PROMISE...
I'LL BE BACK FOR YOU...
...BE BACK FOR YOU. I PROMISE.

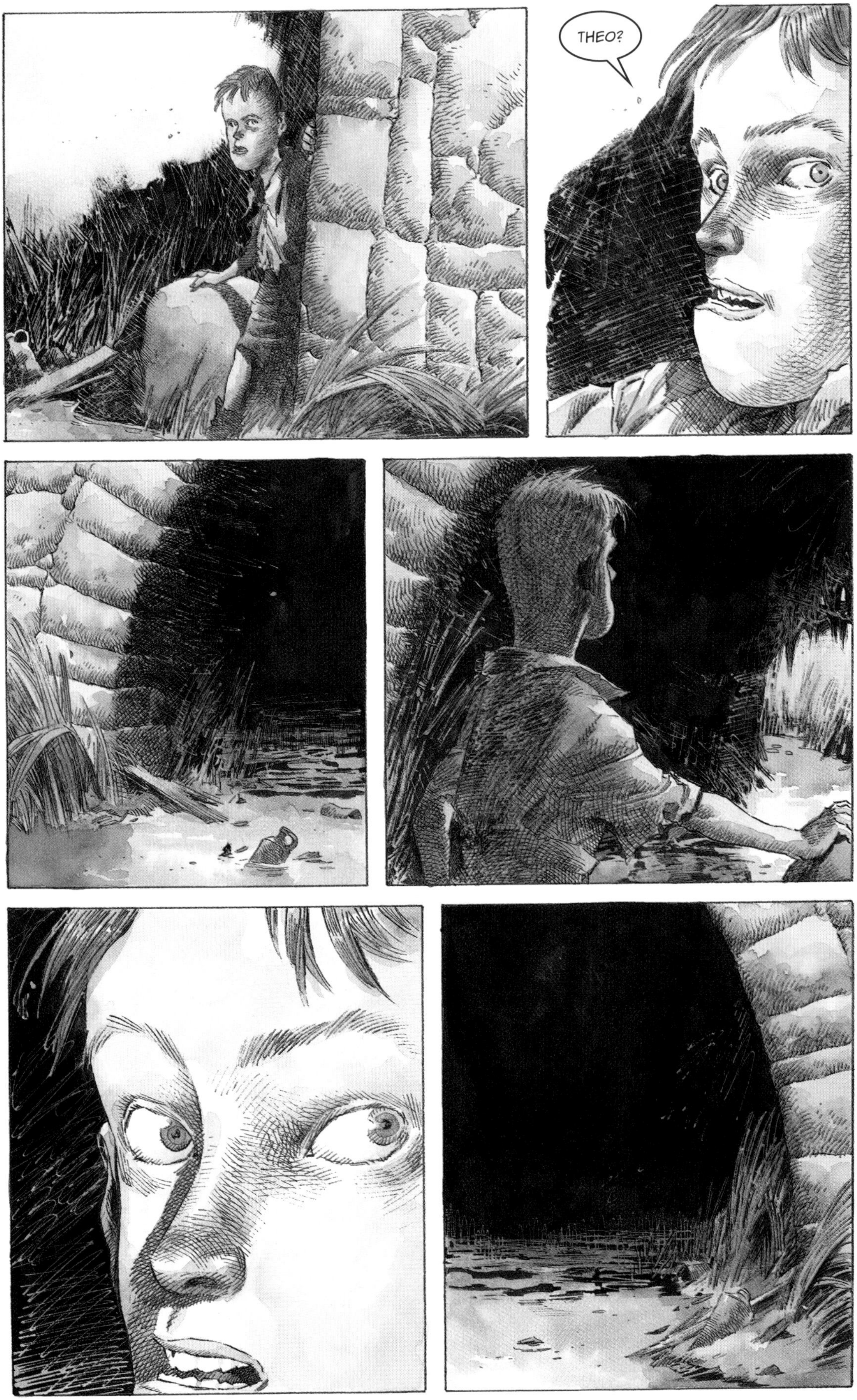
THEO?

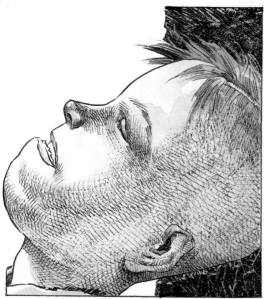

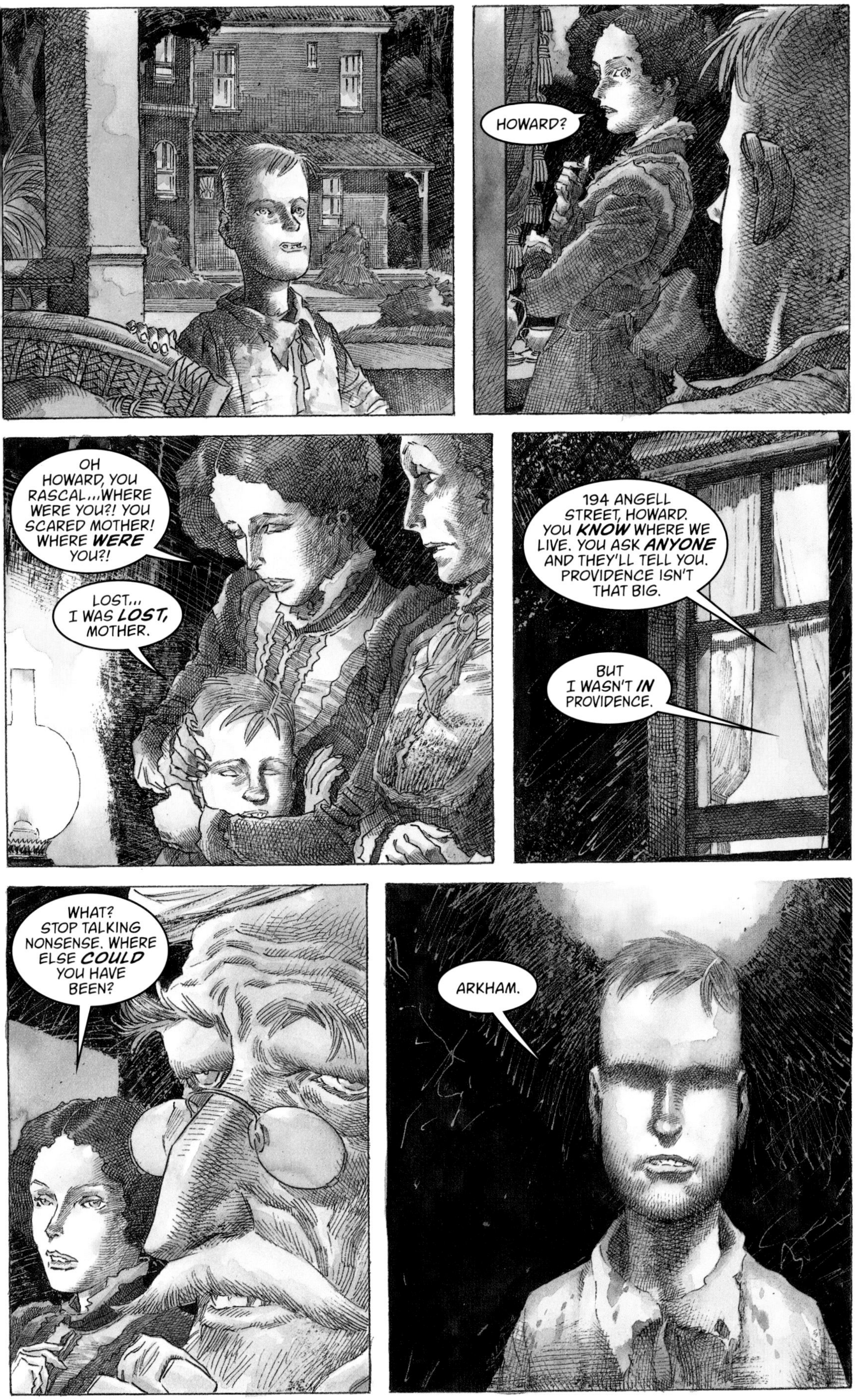
HOWARD?
OH HOWARD, YOU RASCAL...WHERE WERE YOU?! YOU SCARED MOTHER! WHERE **WERE** YOU?!
LOST... I WAS **LOST,** MOTHER.
194 ANGELL STREET, HOWARD. YOU **KNOW** WHERE WE LIVE. YOU ASK **ANYONE** AND THEY'LL TELL YOU. PROVIDENCE ISN'T THAT BIG.
BUT I WASN'T **IN** PROVIDENCE.
WHAT? STOP TALKING NONSENSE. WHERE ELSE **COULD** YOU HAVE BEEN?
ARKHAM.

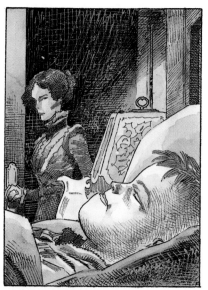

DO YOU SEE *NOW?* DO YOU SEE THE DAMAGE THAT YOUR HORRIBLE STORIES DO?

DON'T BE SUCH A WORRYWART, SARAH. HE'S A BOY, TAKEN TO FLIGHTS OF FANCY AND IMAGINATION.

THERE'S NO HARM IN IT.

NO *HARM?!* DISAPPEARING FOR THE BETTER PART OF AN *ENTIRE DAY?*

PROBABLY OFF IN HIS BELOVED CHURCHYARD PLAYING THE MAD ARAB.

HE SAID HE WAS IN A PLACE CALLED *ARKHAM.*

ARKHAM IS A TOWN THAT I USE IN MY STORIES. IT'S NO MORE REAL THAN THE *NIGHT GAUNTS,* FOR GOODNESS' SAKE.

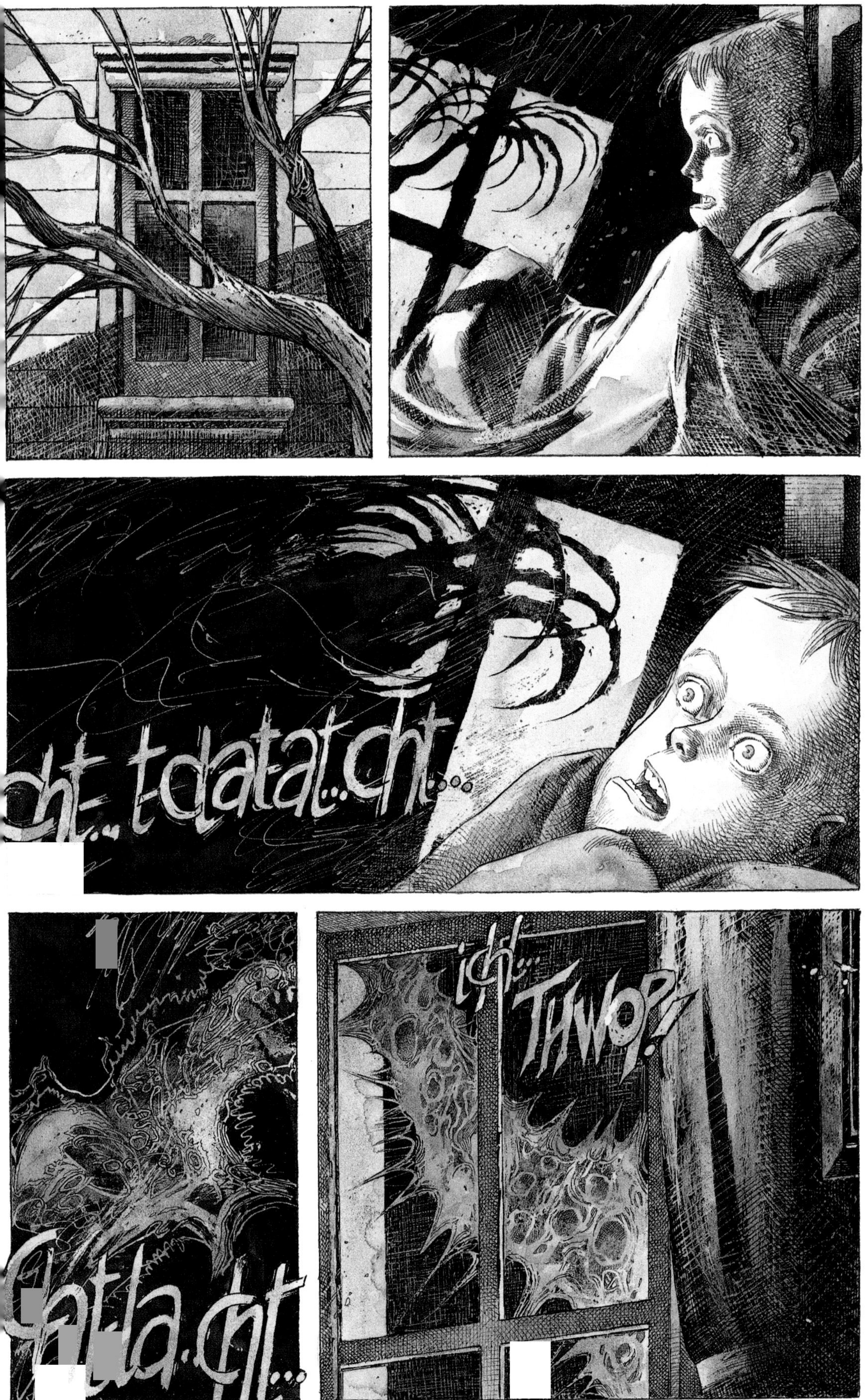
cht... tclatat..cht...
chtla.cht...
ichl...
THWOP!

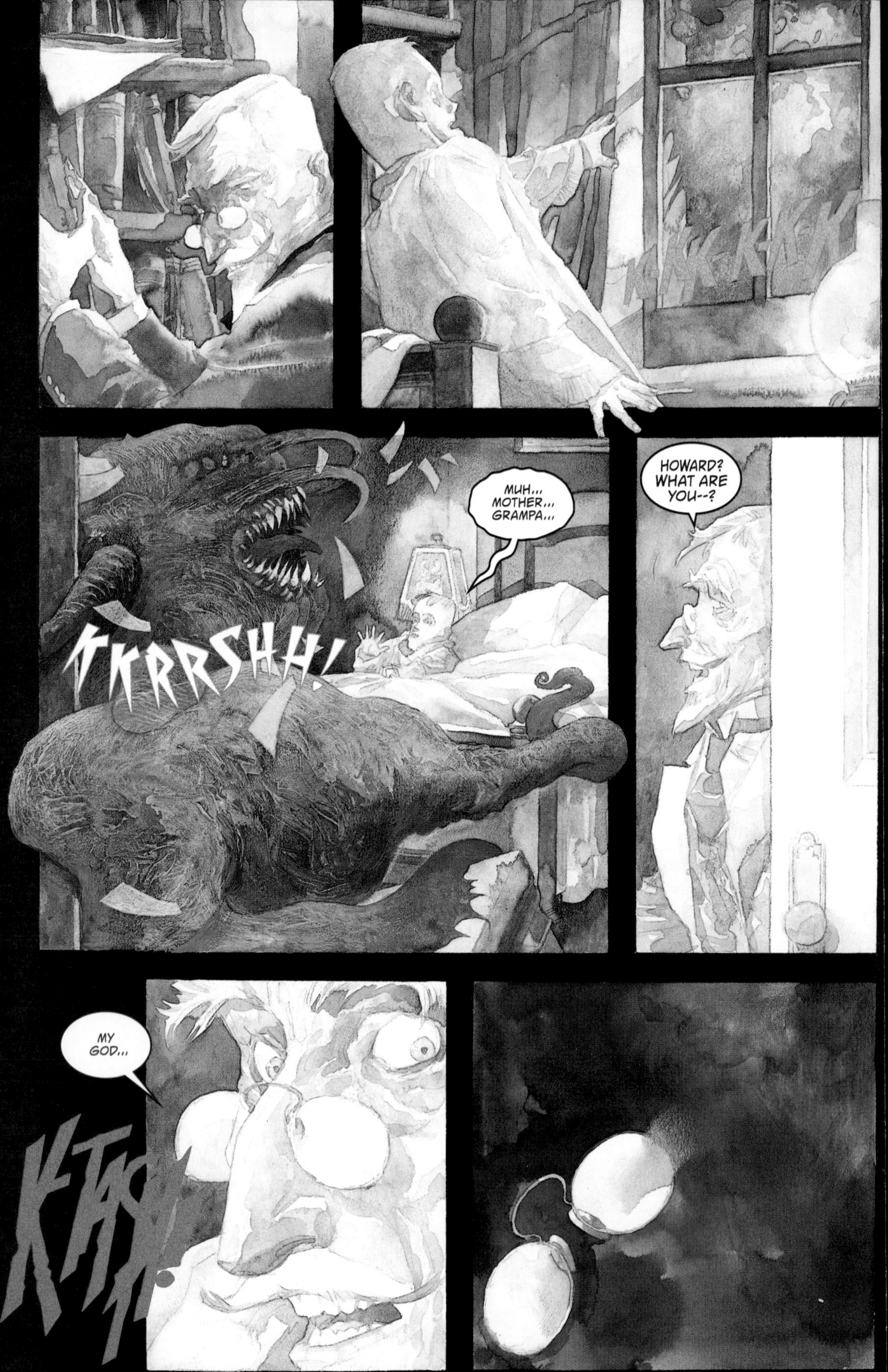
K-K-K-KAK
KKRRSHH!
MUH... MOTHER... GRAMPA...
HOWARD? WHAT ARE YOU--?
MY GOD...

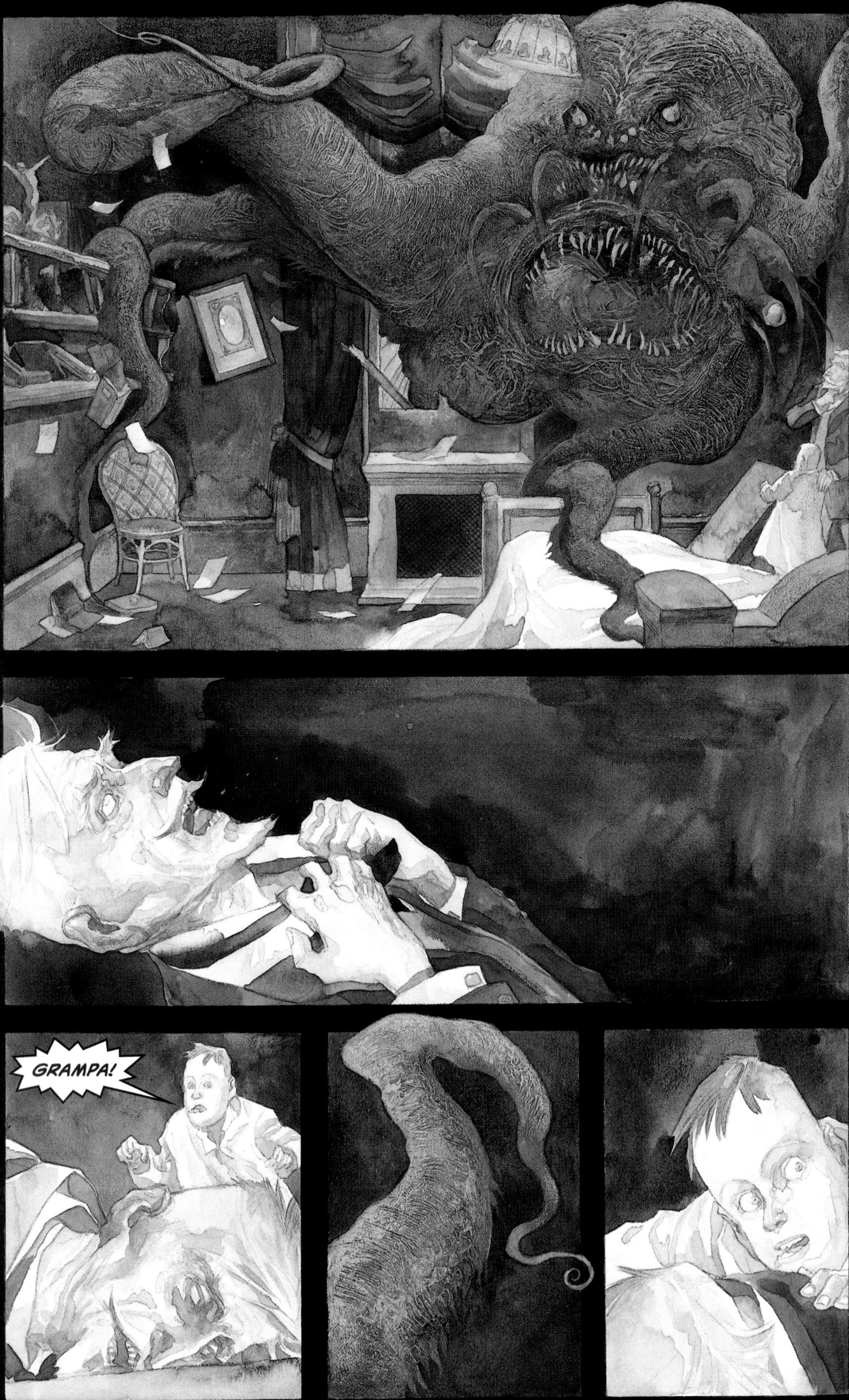
GRAMPA!

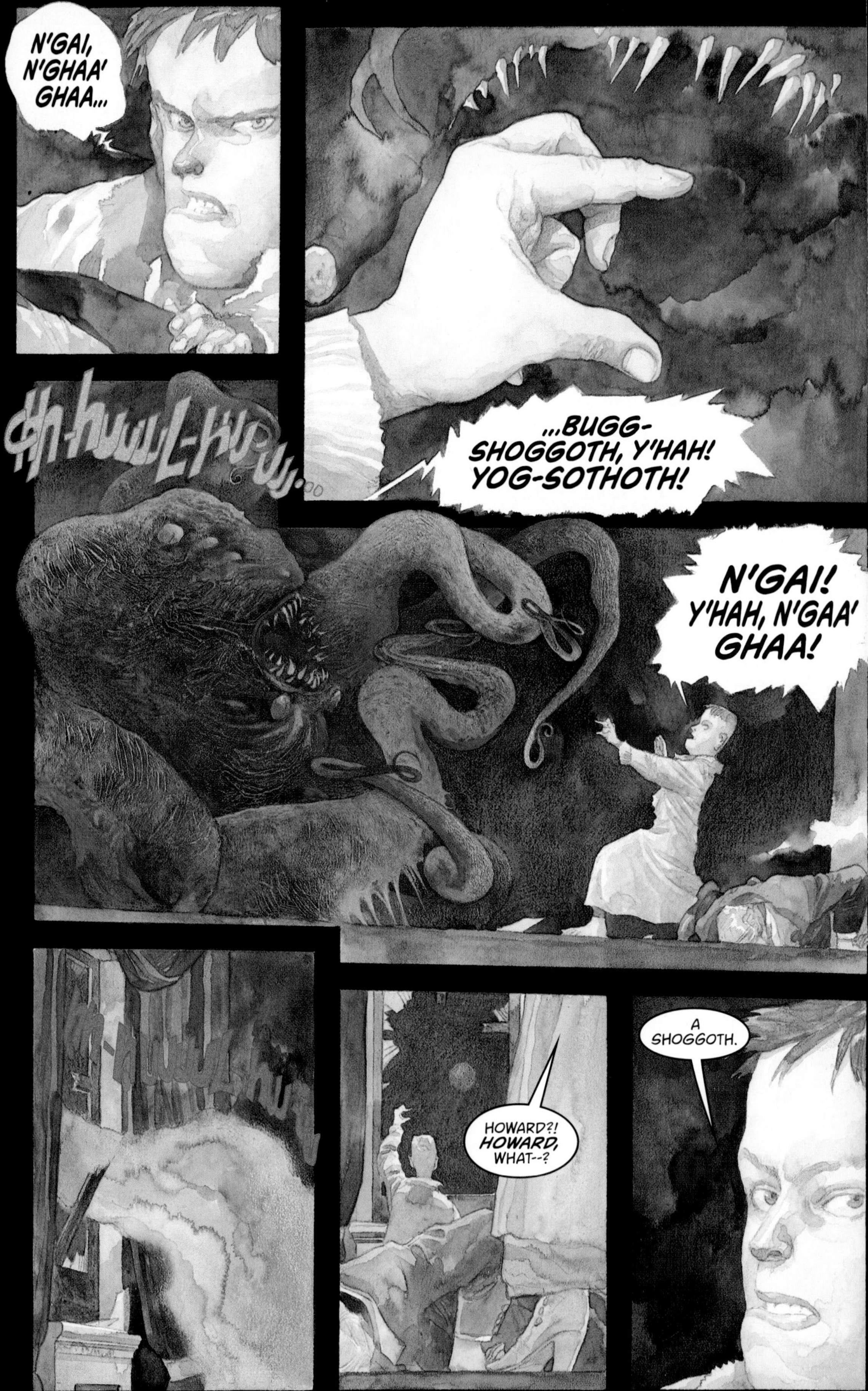
N'GAI, N'GHAA' GHAA...
...BUGG-SHOGGOTH, Y'HAH! YOG-SOTHOTH!
N'GAI! Y'HAH, N'GAA' GHAA!
HOWARD?! HOWARD, WHAT--?
A SHOGGOTH.

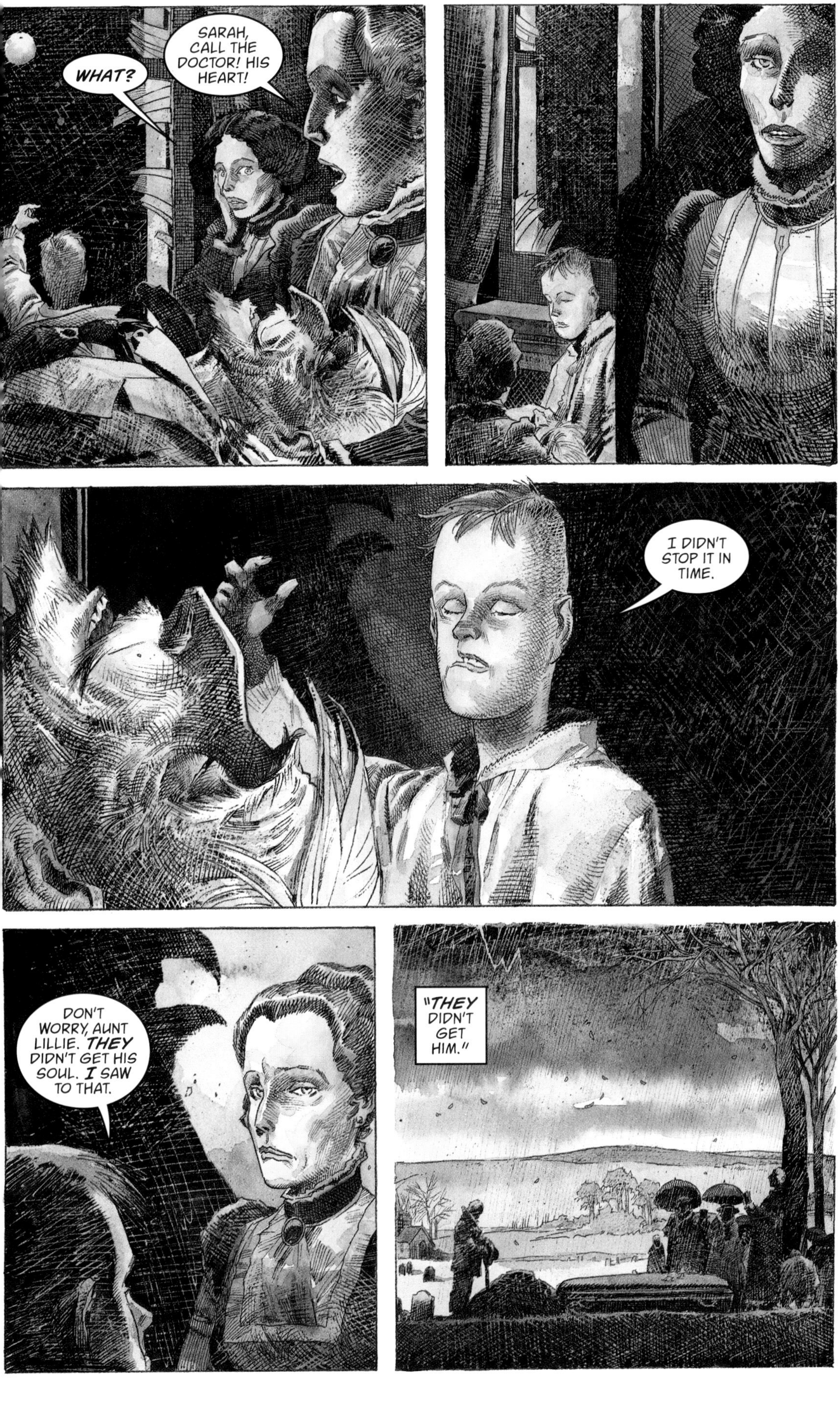
SARAH, CALL THE DOCTOR! HIS HEART!
WHAT?
I DIDN'T STOP IT IN TIME.
DON'T WORRY, AUNT LILLIE. THEY DIDN'T GET HIS SOUL. I SAW TO THAT.
"THEY DIDN'T GET HIM."

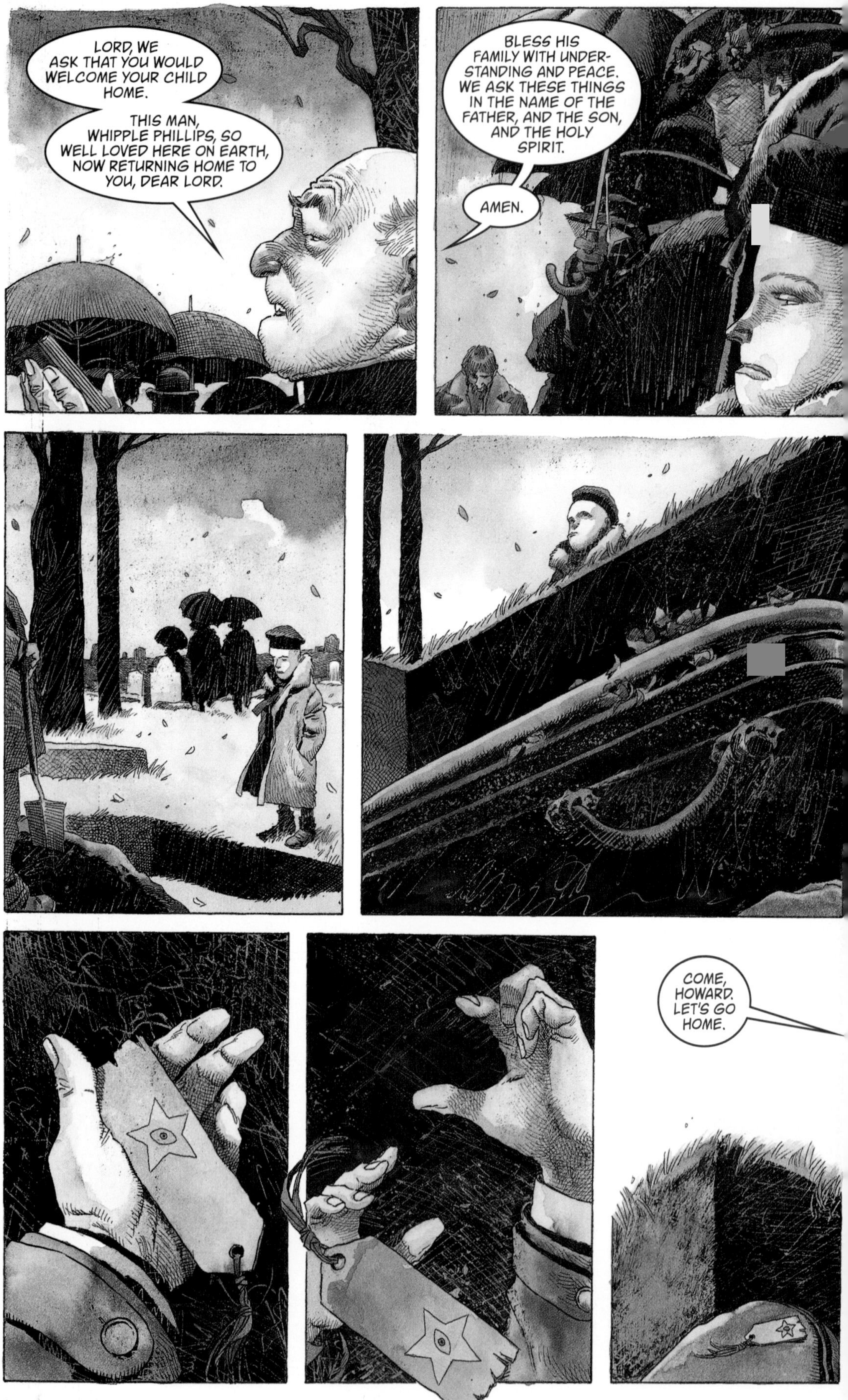
LORD, WE ASK THAT YOU WOULD WELCOME YOUR CHILD HOME.
THIS MAN, WHIPPLE PHILLIPS, SO WELL LOVED HERE ON EARTH, NOW RETURNING HOME TO YOU, DEAR LORD.
BLESS HIS FAMILY WITH UNDER-STANDING AND PEACE. WE ASK THESE THINGS IN THE NAME OF THE FATHER, AND THE SON, AND THE HOLY SPIRIT.
AMEN.
COME, HOWARD. LET'S GO HOME.

I'M SORRY, LILLIAN. I SIMPLY *CAN'T* TALK ABOUT THIS NOW.

WHEN, SARAH? WHEN IT'S TOO LATE?

WITH FATHER GONE WE WON'T BE ABLE TO SUPPORT OURSELVES. WE HAVE TO MOVE TO A SMALLER HOUSE OR WE STAND TO LOSE *EVERYTHING.*

THIS *IS* EVERYTHING. THIS IS ALL I HAVE LEFT, LILLIAN. MY BELOVED WINFIELD DIED IN THAT HORRIBLE ASYLUM, NOW *FATHER* IS DEAD.

"YOU AND HOWARD AND THIS HOME. THAT'S *ALL I HAVE LEFT.*

"IF I LOSE ANYTHING MORE, I MAY GO MAD MYSELF."

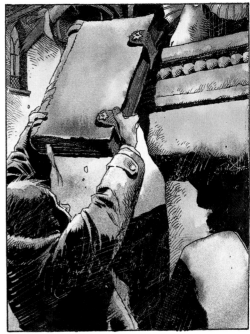

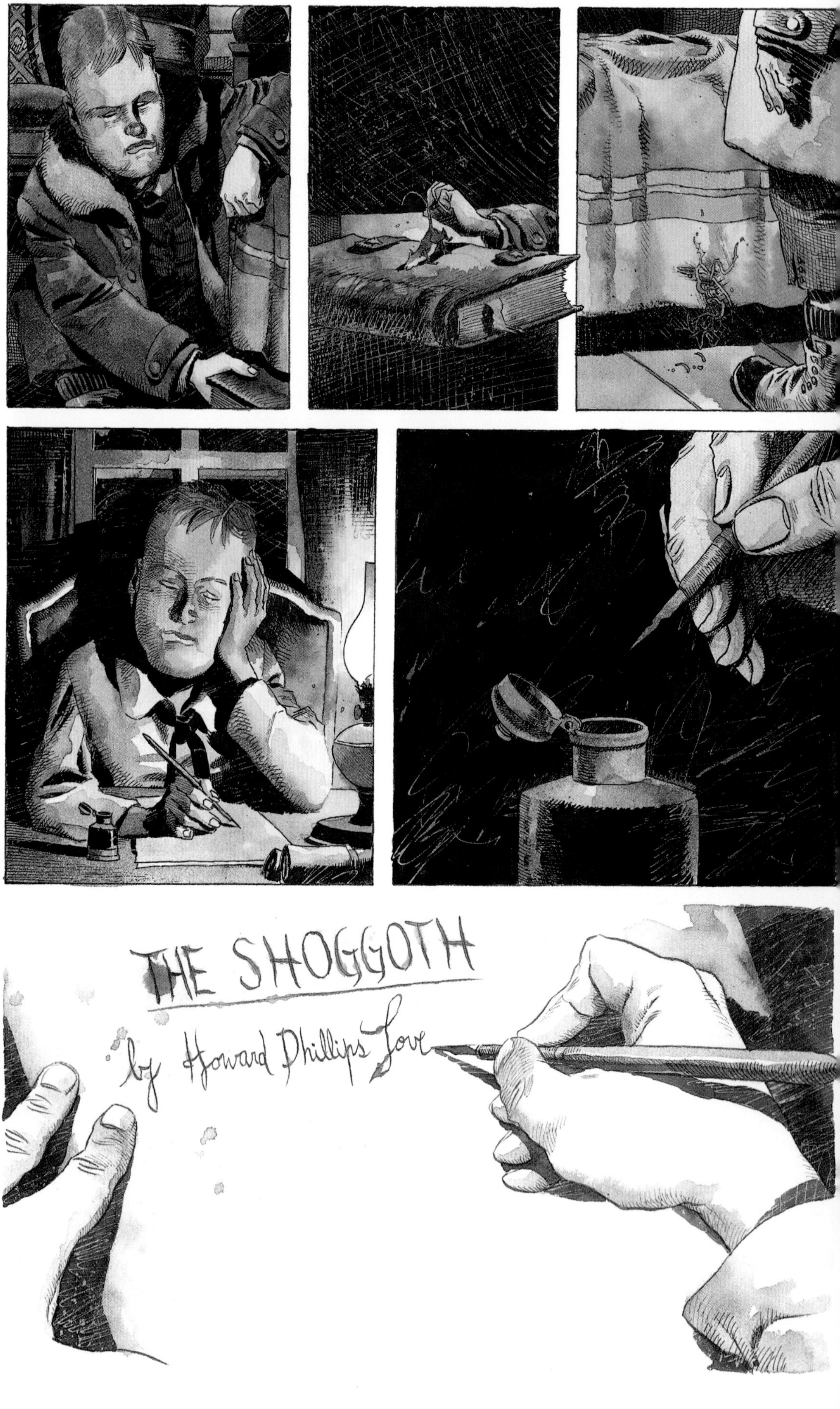
THE SHOGGOTH
by Howard Phillips Love

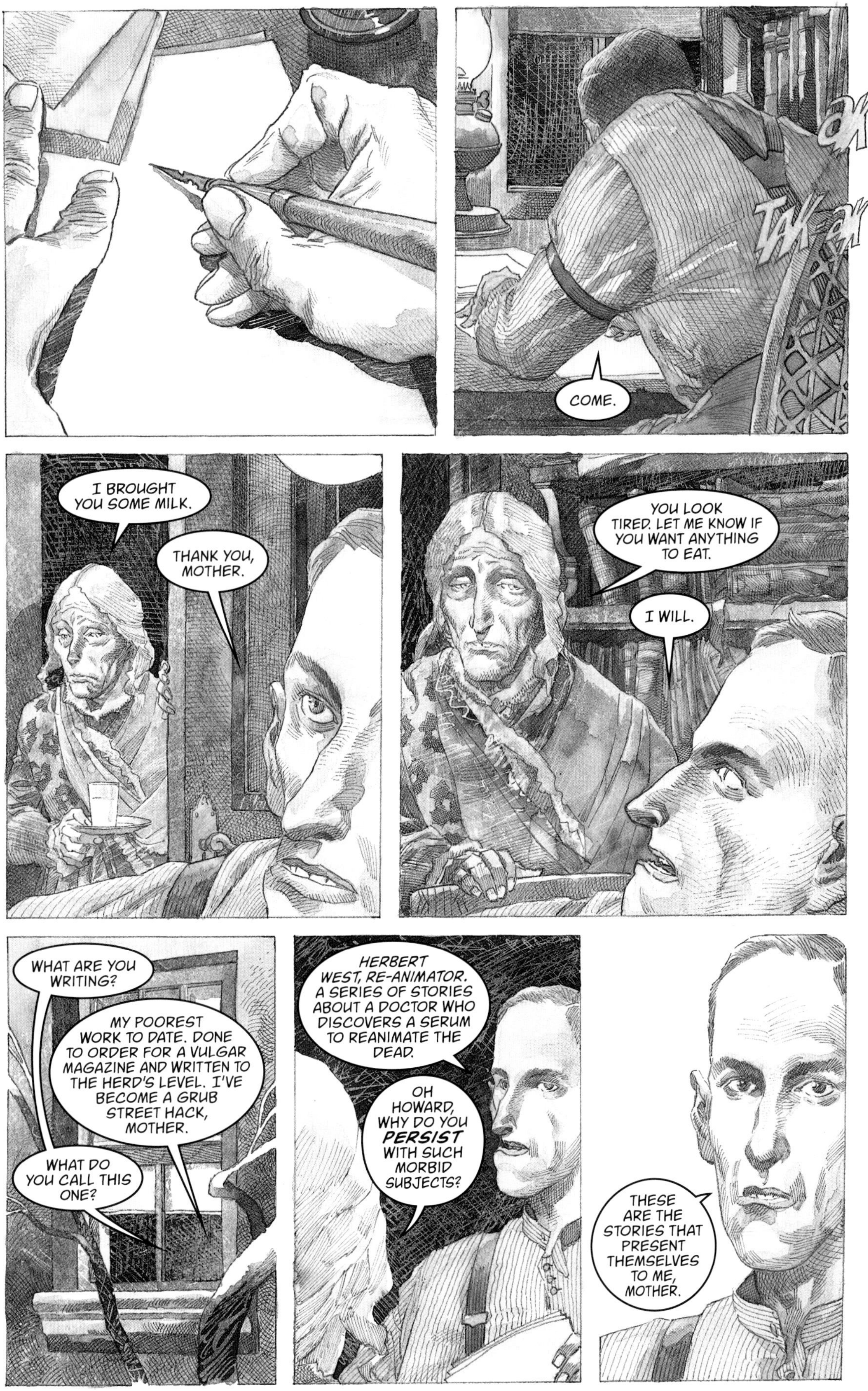
TAK TAK
COME.
I BROUGHT YOU SOME MILK.
THANK YOU, MOTHER.
YOU LOOK TIRED. LET ME KNOW IF YOU WANT ANYTHING TO EAT.
I WILL.
WHAT ARE YOU WRITING?
MY POOREST WORK TO DATE. DONE TO ORDER FOR A VULGAR MAGAZINE AND WRITTEN TO THE HERD'S LEVEL. I'VE BECOME A GRUB STREET HACK, MOTHER.
WHAT DO YOU CALL THIS ONE?
HERBERT WEST, RE-ANIMATOR. A SERIES OF STORIES ABOUT A DOCTOR WHO DISCOVERS A SERUM TO REANIMATE THE DEAD.
OH HOWARD, WHY DO YOU PERSIST WITH SUCH MORBID SUBJECTS?
THESE ARE THE STORIES THAT PRESENT THEMSELVES TO ME, MOTHER.

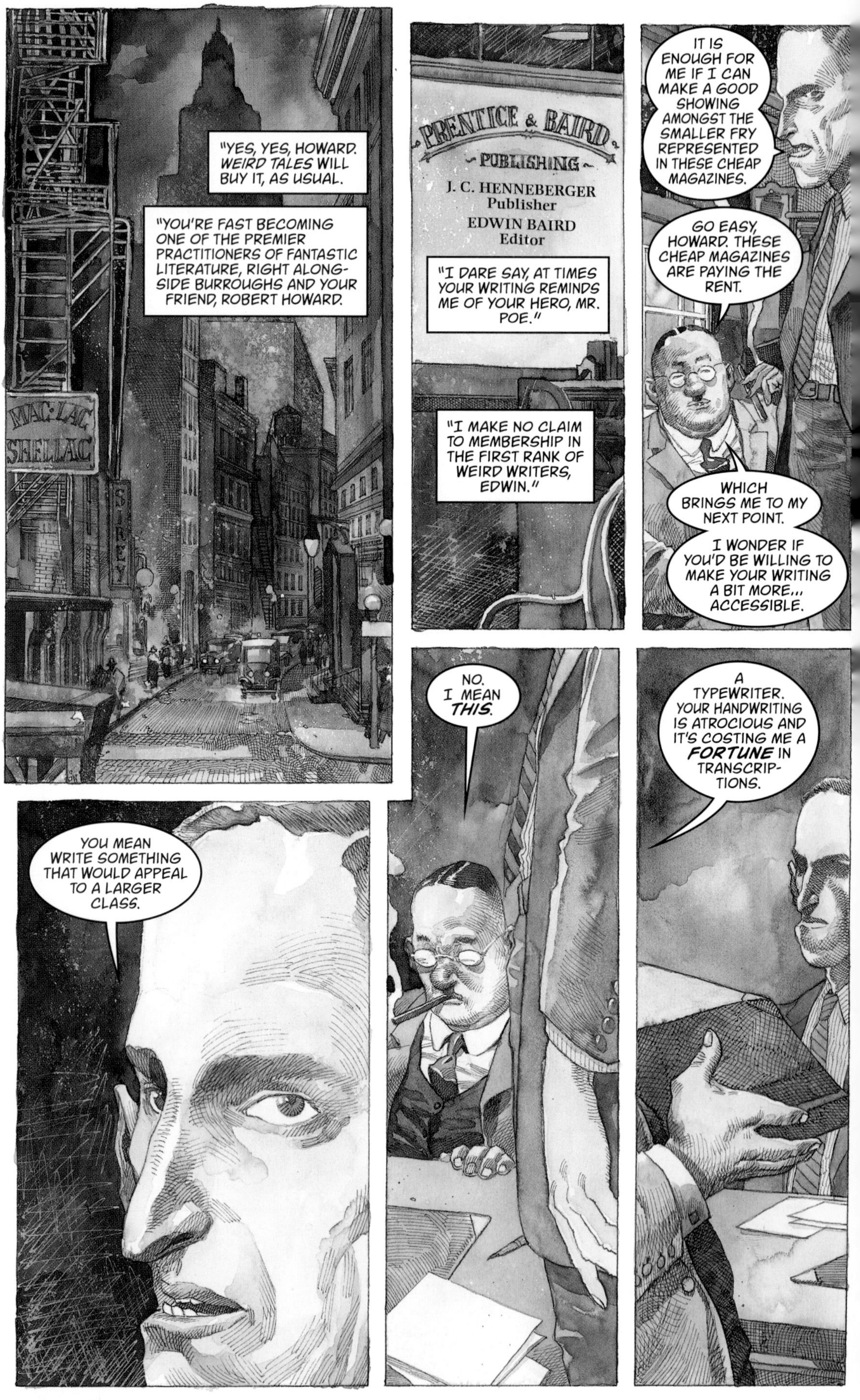
"YES, YES, HOWARD. *WEIRD TALES* WILL BUY IT, AS USUAL.
"YOU'RE FAST BECOMING ONE OF THE PREMIER PRACTITIONERS OF FANTASTIC LITERATURE, RIGHT ALONG-SIDE BURROUGHS AND YOUR FRIEND, ROBERT HOWARD.
MAC-LAC SHELLAC
PRENTICE & BAIRD PUBLISHING
J. C. HENNEBERGER Publisher
EDWIN BAIRD Editor
"I DARE SAY, AT TIMES YOUR WRITING REMINDS ME OF YOUR HERO, MR. POE."
"I MAKE NO CLAIM TO MEMBERSHIP IN THE FIRST RANK OF WEIRD WRITERS, EDWIN."
IT IS ENOUGH FOR ME IF I CAN MAKE A GOOD SHOWING AMONGST THE SMALLER FRY REPRESENTED IN THESE CHEAP MAGAZINES.
GO EASY, HOWARD. THESE CHEAP MAGAZINES ARE PAYING THE RENT.
WHICH BRINGS ME TO MY NEXT POINT.
I WONDER IF YOU'D BE WILLING TO MAKE YOUR WRITING A BIT MORE... ACCESSIBLE.
YOU MEAN WRITE SOMETHING THAT WOULD APPEAL TO A LARGER CLASS.
NO. I MEAN ***THIS***.
A TYPEWRITER. YOUR HANDWRITING IS ATROCIOUS AND IT'S COSTING ME A ***FORTUNE*** IN TRANSCRIP-TIONS.

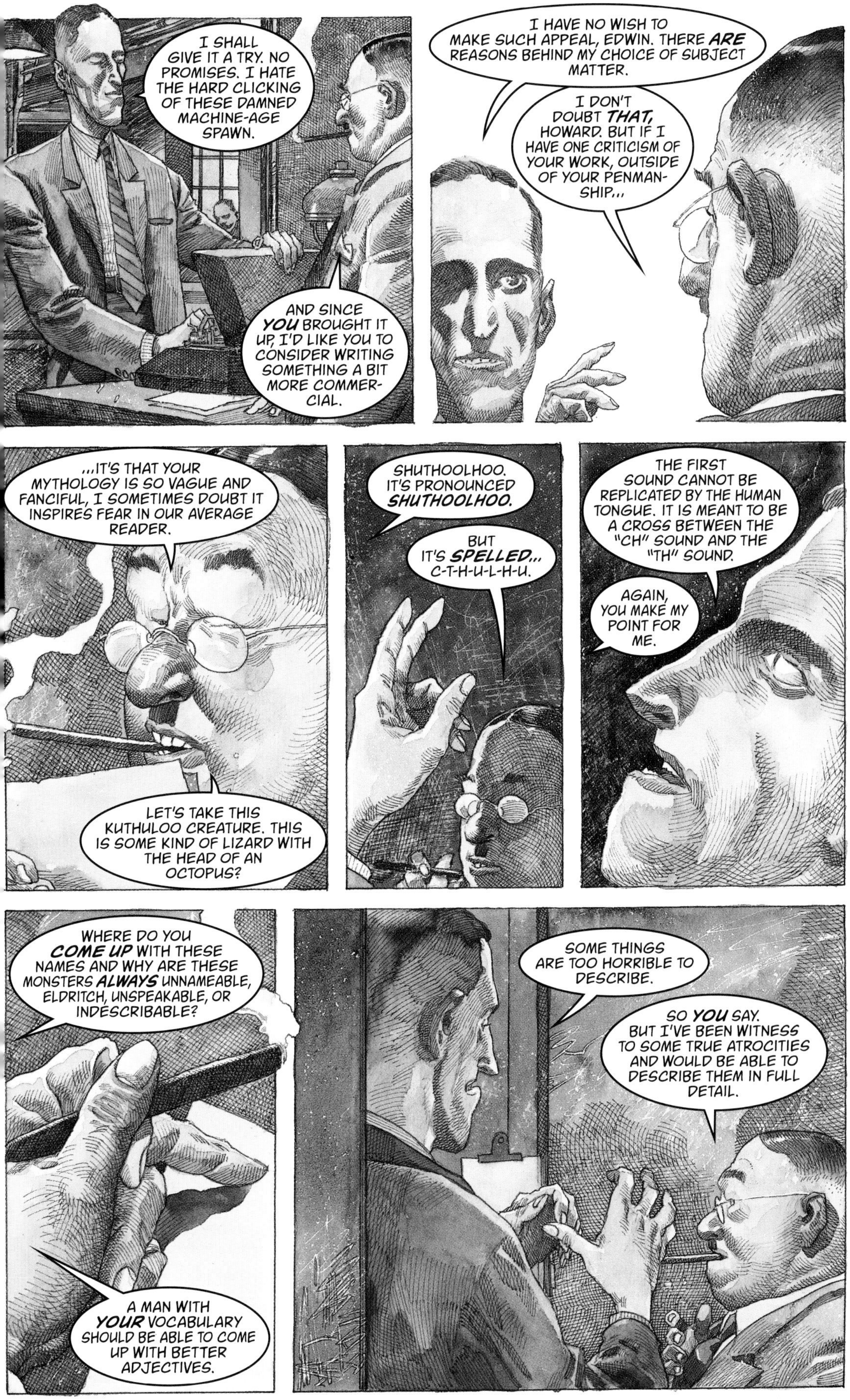
I SHALL GIVE IT A TRY. NO PROMISES. I HATE THE HARD CLICKING OF THESE DAMNED MACHINE-AGE SPAWN.
AND SINCE YOU BROUGHT IT UP, I'D LIKE YOU TO CONSIDER WRITING SOMETHING A BIT MORE COMMERCIAL.
I HAVE NO WISH TO MAKE SUCH APPEAL, EDWIN. THERE ARE REASONS BEHIND MY CHOICE OF SUBJECT MATTER.
I DON'T DOUBT THAT, HOWARD. BUT IF I HAVE ONE CRITICISM OF YOUR WORK, OUTSIDE OF YOUR PENMANSHIP...
...IT'S THAT YOUR MYTHOLOGY IS SO VAGUE AND FANCIFUL, I SOMETIMES DOUBT IT INSPIRES FEAR IN OUR AVERAGE READER.
LET'S TAKE THIS KUTHULOO CREATURE. THIS IS SOME KIND OF LIZARD WITH THE HEAD OF AN OCTOPUS?
SHUTHOOLHOO. IT'S PRONOUNCED SHUTHOOLHOO.
BUT IT'S SPELLED... C-T-H-U-L-H-U.
THE FIRST SOUND CANNOT BE REPLICATED BY THE HUMAN TONGUE. IT IS MEANT TO BE A CROSS BETWEEN THE "CH" SOUND AND THE "TH" SOUND.
AGAIN, YOU MAKE MY POINT FOR ME.
WHERE DO YOU COME UP WITH THESE NAMES AND WHY ARE THESE MONSTERS ALWAYS UNNAMEABLE, ELDRITCH, UNSPEAKABLE, OR INDESCRIBABLE?
A MAN WITH YOUR VOCABULARY SHOULD BE ABLE TO COME UP WITH BETTER ADJECTIVES.
SOME THINGS ARE TOO HORRIBLE TO DESCRIBE.
SO YOU SAY. BUT I'VE BEEN WITNESS TO SOME TRUE ATROCITIES AND WOULD BE ABLE TO DESCRIBE THEM IN FULL DETAIL.

EVIDENTLY, WE'VE WITNESSED DIFFERENT **KINDS** OF ATROCITIES.

YOU'RE A STUBBORN MAN, HOWARD. STUBBORN AS A MULE. WHICH IS WHY I THINK YOU'LL BE PERFECT FOR THIS ASSIGNMENT.

WHAT ASSIGNMENT?

HAVE YOU HEARD OF HARRY HOUDINI?

YES. THE ILLUSIONIST.

WELL, HE'S EXPRESSED INTEREST IN PUTTING TOGETHER A FEW STORIES FOR WEIRD TALES.

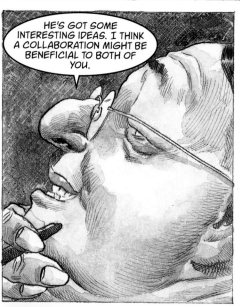

HE'S GOT SOME INTERESTING IDEAS. I THINK A COLLABORATION MIGHT BE BENEFICIAL TO BOTH OF YOU.

I DON'T WANT TO **COLLABORATE** WITH **ANYONE**, AND I DON'T WANT TO STAY IN NEW YORK ANY LONGER THAN IS **ABSOLUTELY NECESSARY.** I NEED TO GET BACK HOME.

ONE DAY, HOWARD. IT WON'T **KILL** YOU. MEET MR. HOUDINI THIS EVENING. YOU CAN CATCH A TRAIN BACK TO YOUR BELOVED PROVIDENCE IN THE MORNING.

I'LL ARRANGE A GOOD ROOM FOR YOU.

I'D REALLY RATHER NOT.

DID I MENTION THE GOURMET ICE CREAM SHOP AROUND THE CORNER?

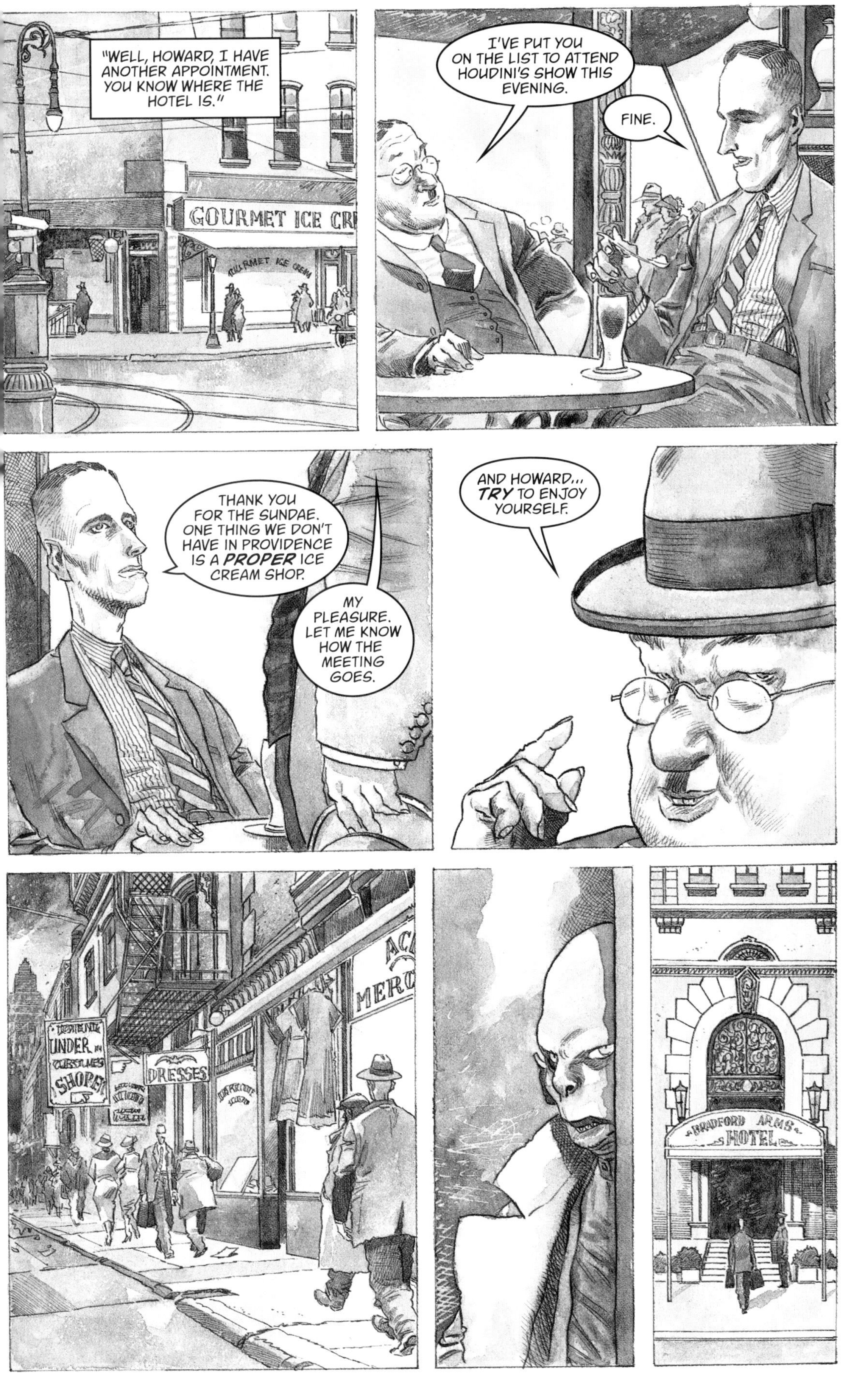
"WELL, HOWARD, I HAVE ANOTHER APPOINTMENT. YOU KNOW WHERE THE HOTEL IS."
GOURMET ICE CR
GOURMET ICE CREAM
I'VE PUT YOU ON THE LIST TO ATTEND HOUDINI'S SHOW THIS EVENING.
FINE.
THANK YOU FOR THE SUNDAE. ONE THING WE DON'T HAVE IN PROVIDENCE IS A *PROPER* ICE CREAM SHOP.
MY PLEASURE. LET ME KNOW HOW THE MEETING GOES.
AND HOWARD... *TRY* TO ENJOY YOURSELF.
UNDER
SHOPPE
DRESSES
MERC
BRADFORD ARMS
HOTEL

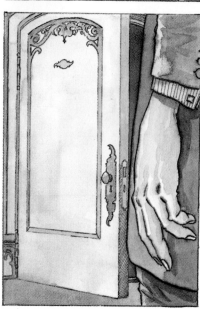

TAK...

CHIK...

HELLO?

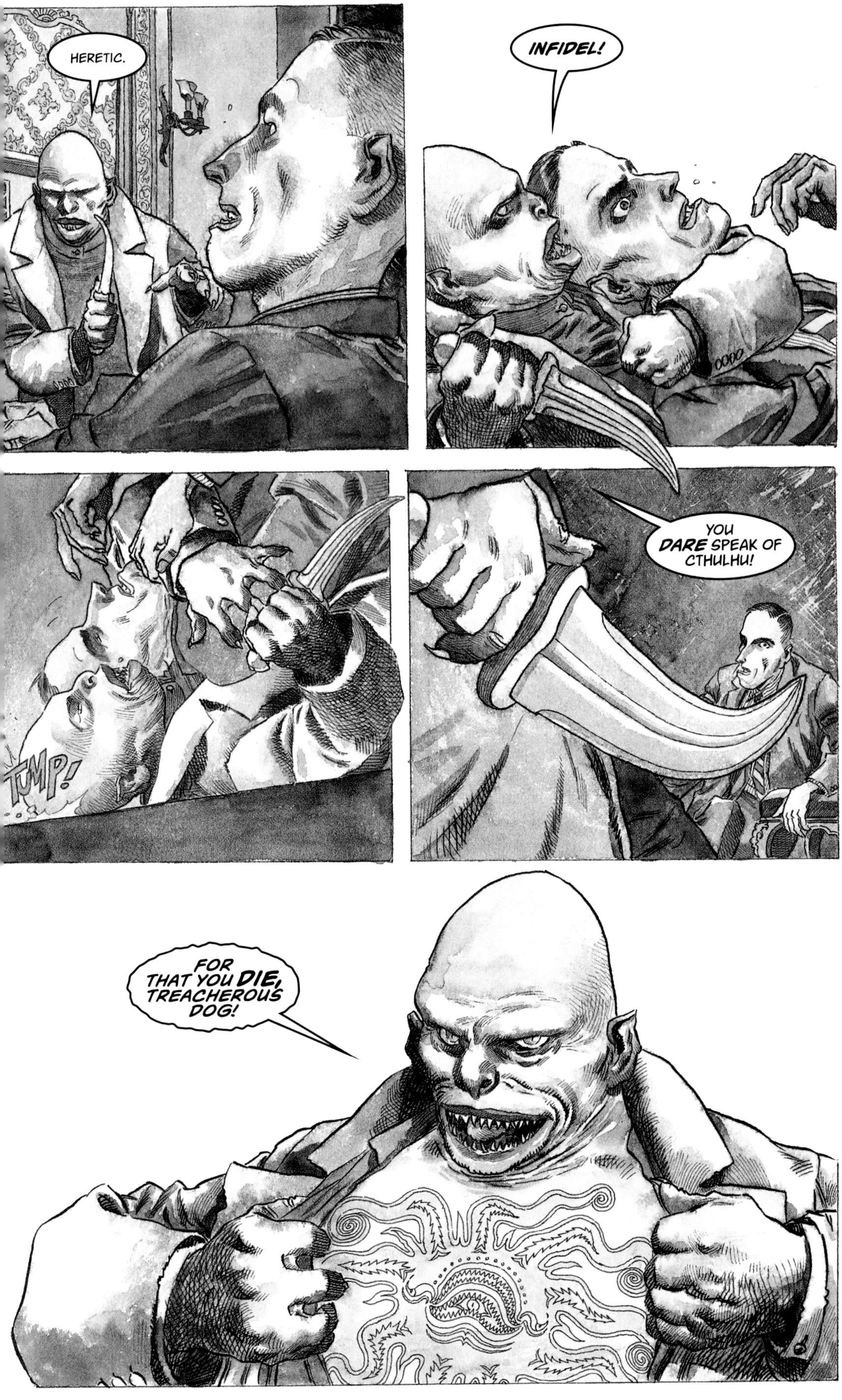
HERETIC.
INFIDEL!
TUMP!
YOU DARE SPEAK OF CTHULHU!
FOR THAT YOU DIE, TREACHEROUS DOG!

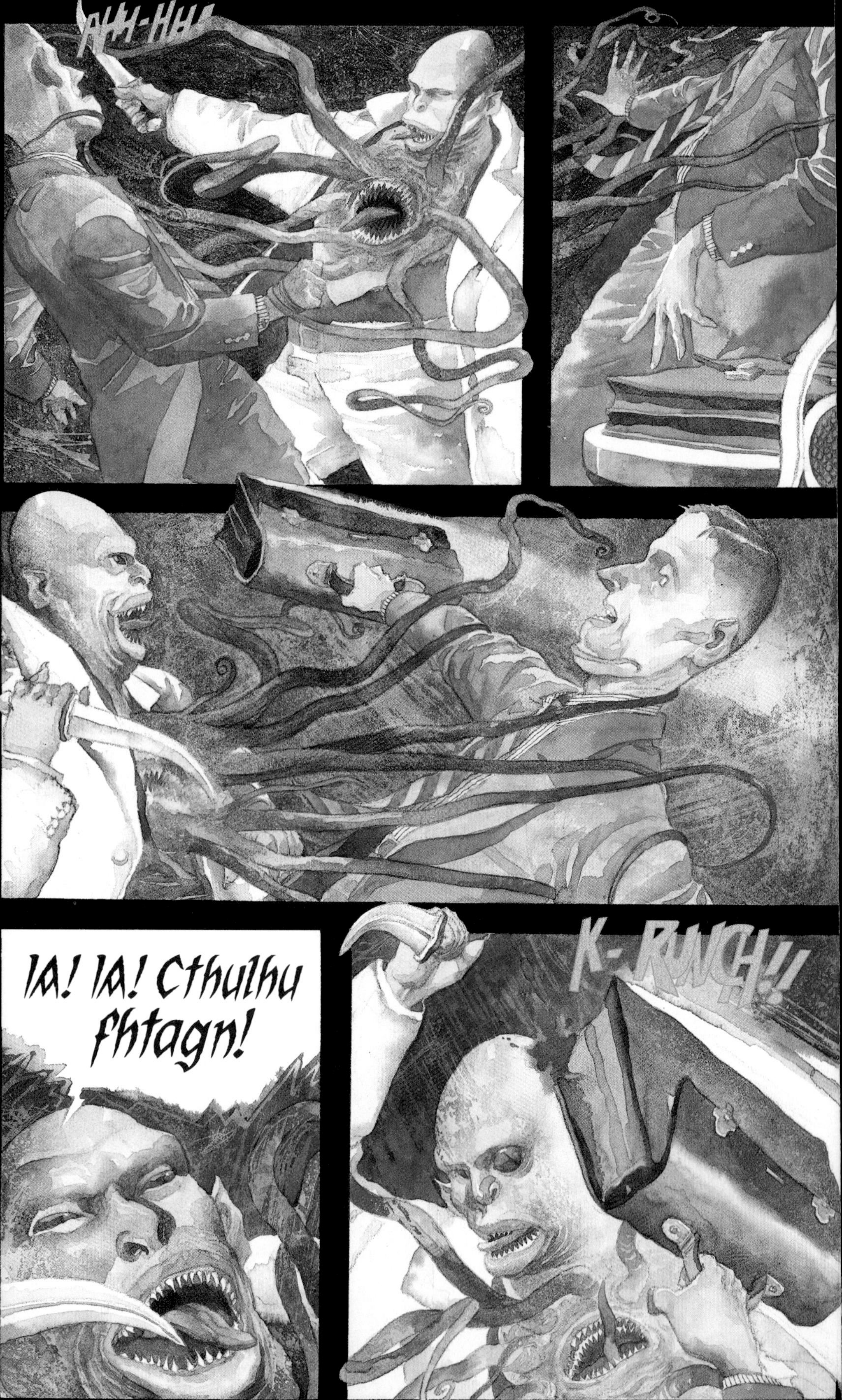
AHH-HHH
IA! IA! Cthulhu fhtagn!
K-RUNCH!!

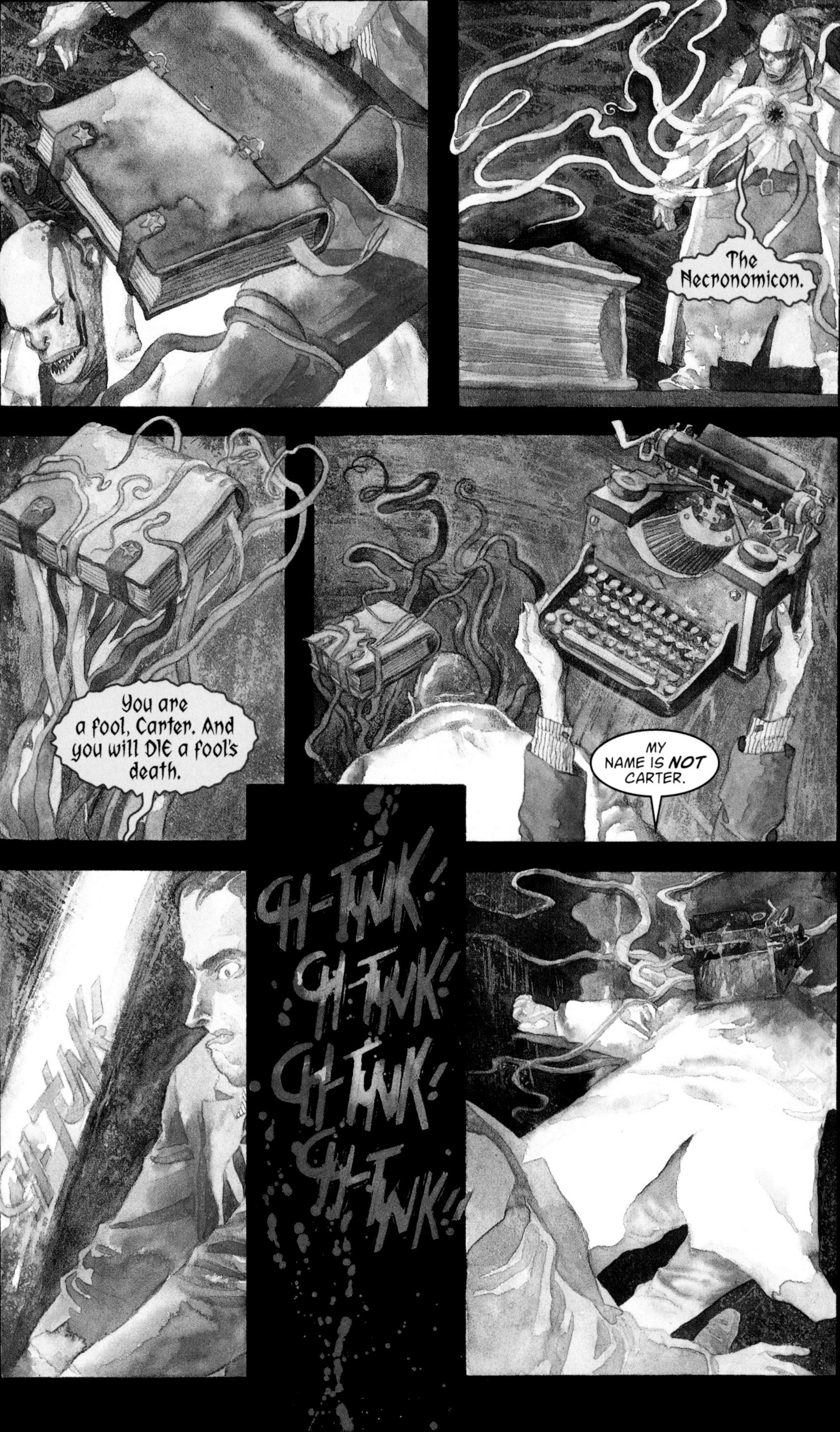
The Necronomicon.
You are a fool, Carter. And you will DIE a fool's death.
MY NAME IS ***NOT*** CARTER.
CH-TUNK!
CH-TUNK!
CH-TUNK!
CH-TUNK!
CH-TUNK!!

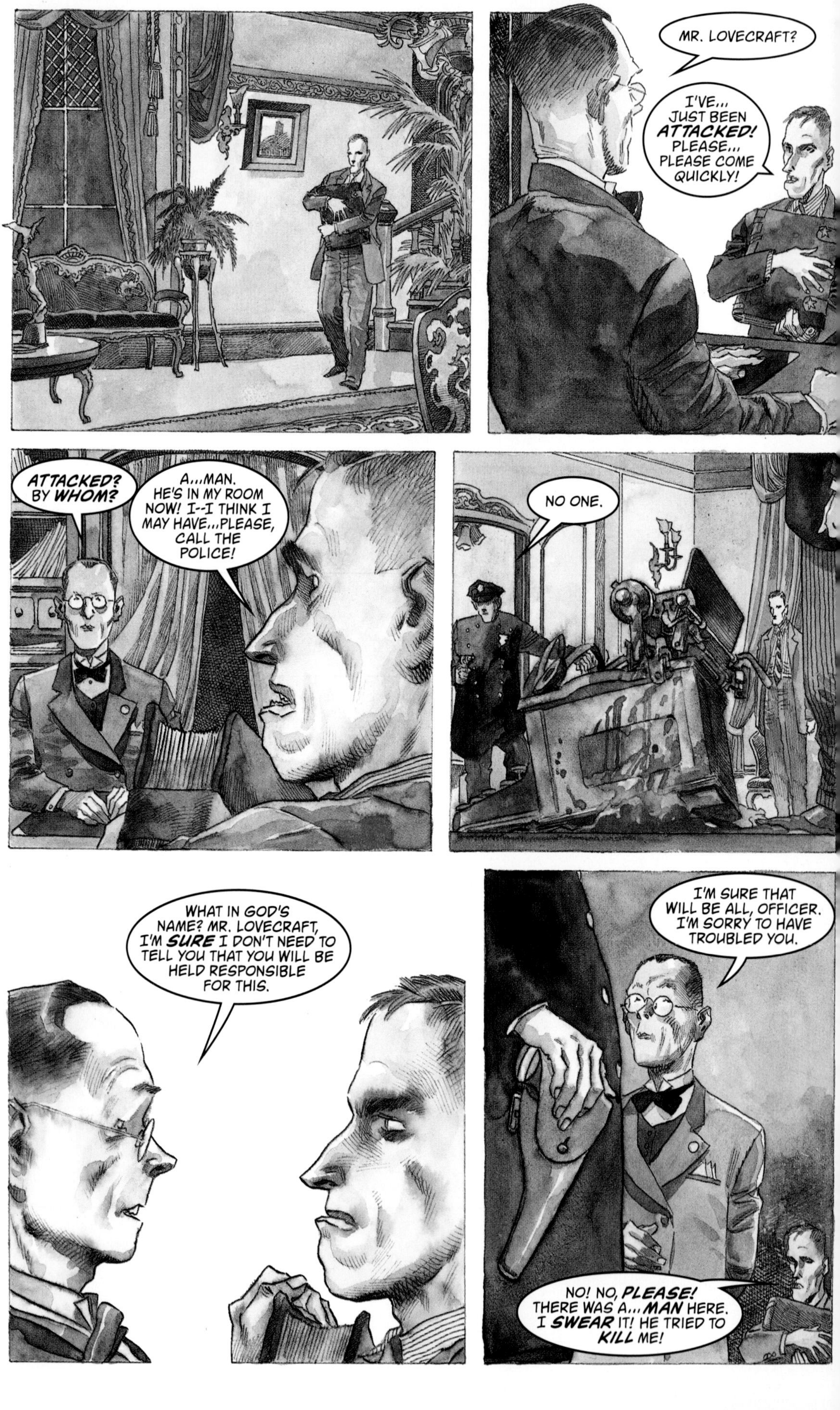
MR. LOVECRAFT?
I'VE... JUST BEEN ATTACKED! PLEASE... PLEASE COME QUICKLY!
ATTACKED? BY WHOM?
A...MAN. HE'S IN MY ROOM NOW! I--I THINK I MAY HAVE...PLEASE, CALL THE POLICE!
NO ONE.
WHAT IN GOD'S NAME? MR. LOVECRAFT, I'M SURE I DON'T NEED TO TELL YOU THAT YOU WILL BE HELD RESPONSIBLE FOR THIS.
I'M SURE THAT WILL BE ALL, OFFICER. I'M SORRY TO HAVE TROUBLED YOU.
NO! NO, PLEASE! THERE WAS A... MAN HERE. I SWEAR IT! HE TRIED TO KILL ME!

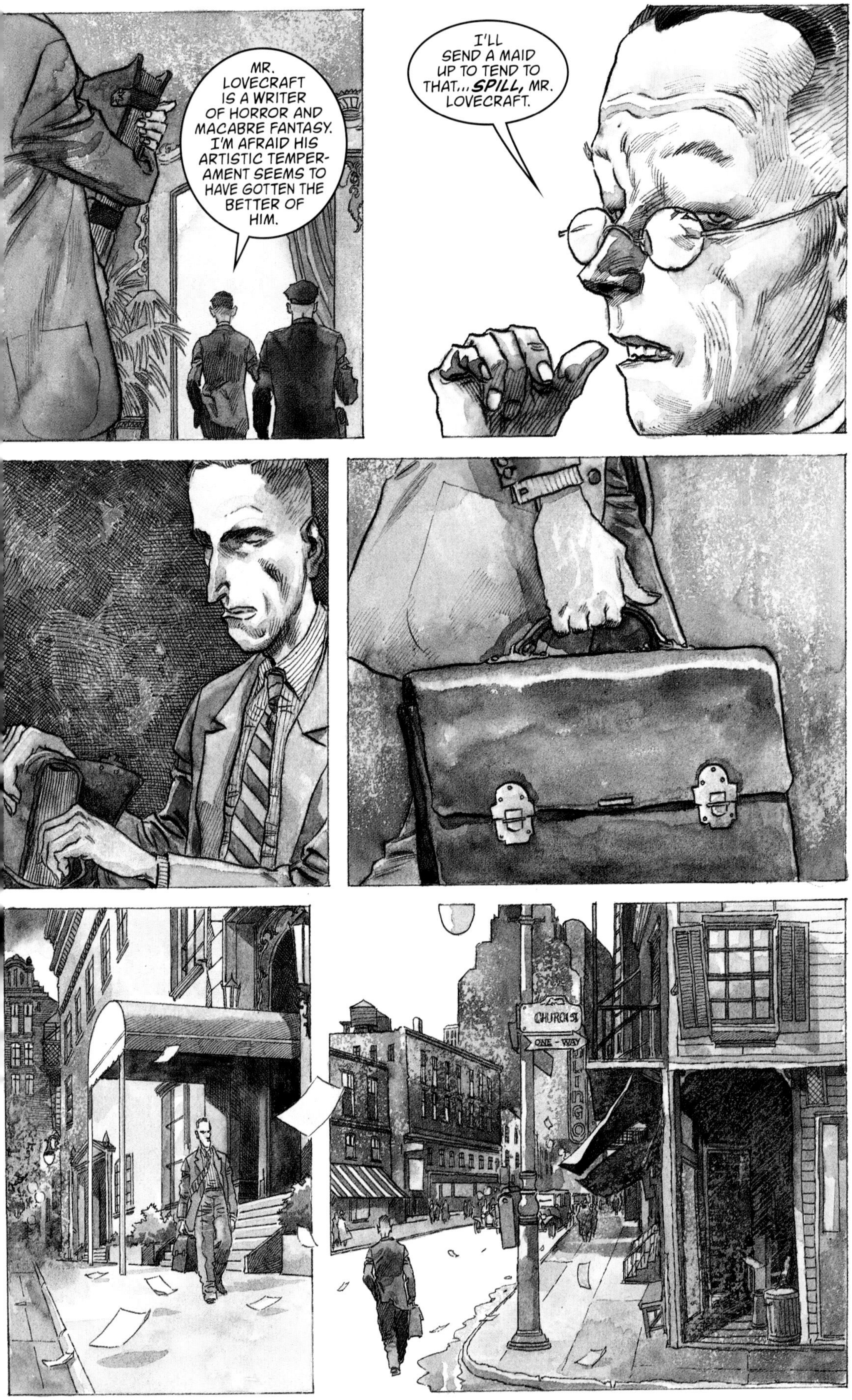
MR. LOVECRAFT IS A WRITER OF HORROR AND MACABRE FANTASY. I'M AFRAID HIS ARTISTIC TEMPER-AMENT SEEMS TO HAVE GOTTEN THE BETTER OF HIM.
I'LL SEND A MAID UP TO TEND TO THAT... SPILL, MR. LOVECRAFT.
CHURCH ST
ONE-WAY

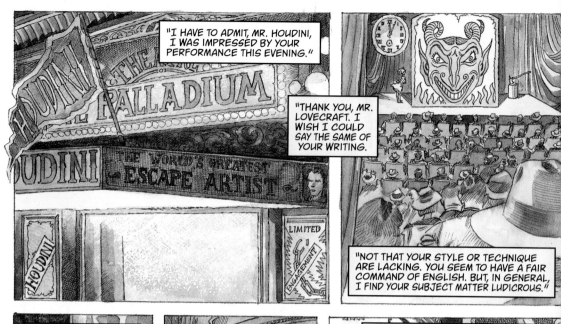

"I HAVE TO ADMIT, MR. HOUDINI, I WAS IMPRESSED BY YOUR PERFORMANCE THIS EVENING."
HOUDINI
THE PALLADIUM
HOUDINI
THE WORLD'S GREATEST ESCAPE ARTIST
HOUDINI
LIMITED ENGAGEMENT
"THANK YOU, MR. LOVECRAFT. I WISH I COULD SAY THE SAME OF YOUR WRITING.
"NOT THAT YOUR STYLE OR TECHNIQUE ARE LACKING. YOU SEEM TO HAVE A FAIR COMMAND OF ENGLISH. BUT, IN GENERAL, I FIND YOUR SUBJECT MATTER LUDICROUS."
"I APOLOGIZE FOR WASTING YOUR TIME."
"PLEASE, SIT. IT WAS NOT MY INTENTION TO OFFEND YOU. FORGIVE MY CANDOR.
"IT'S JUST THAT I'VE DEDICATED MY LIFE TO DISPELLING THE KIND OF SUPERNATURAL MUMBO-JUMBO THAT SEEMS TO BE THE CORNERSTONE OF YOUR STORIES.
"I UNDERSTAND YOU'VE BEEN TRAPPED IN THIS GENRE BY EDWIN'S MAGAZINE. MY GOAL, IS TO PULL YOU ***AND*** *WEIRD TALES* OUT OF THAT RUT. TO CREATE SOMETHING OF ***SUBSTANCE***.
"ARE YOU CERTAIN YOU WOULDN'T CARE TO STEP OUT FOR A BITE? MY TREAT.
"THEY'VE OPENED THE MOST ***MARVELOUS*** SEAFOOD EATERY NOT MORE THAN TWO BLOCKS AWAY..."
"NO THANK YOU. I... I DON'T CARE FOR SEAFOOD. CANNOT STOMACH IT."
"SUIT YOURSELF."

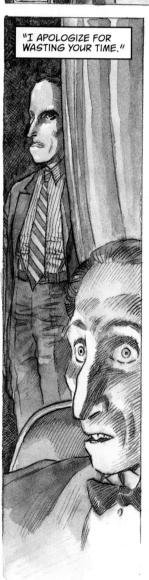

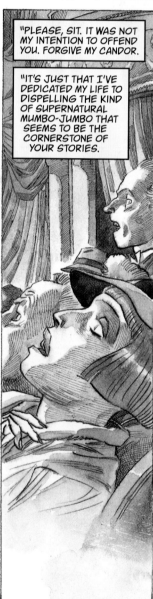

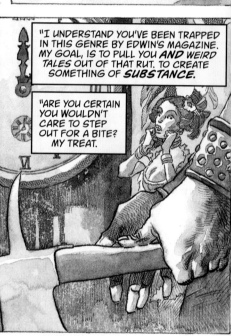

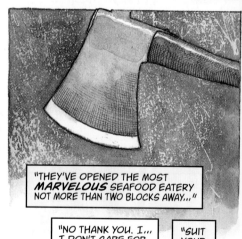

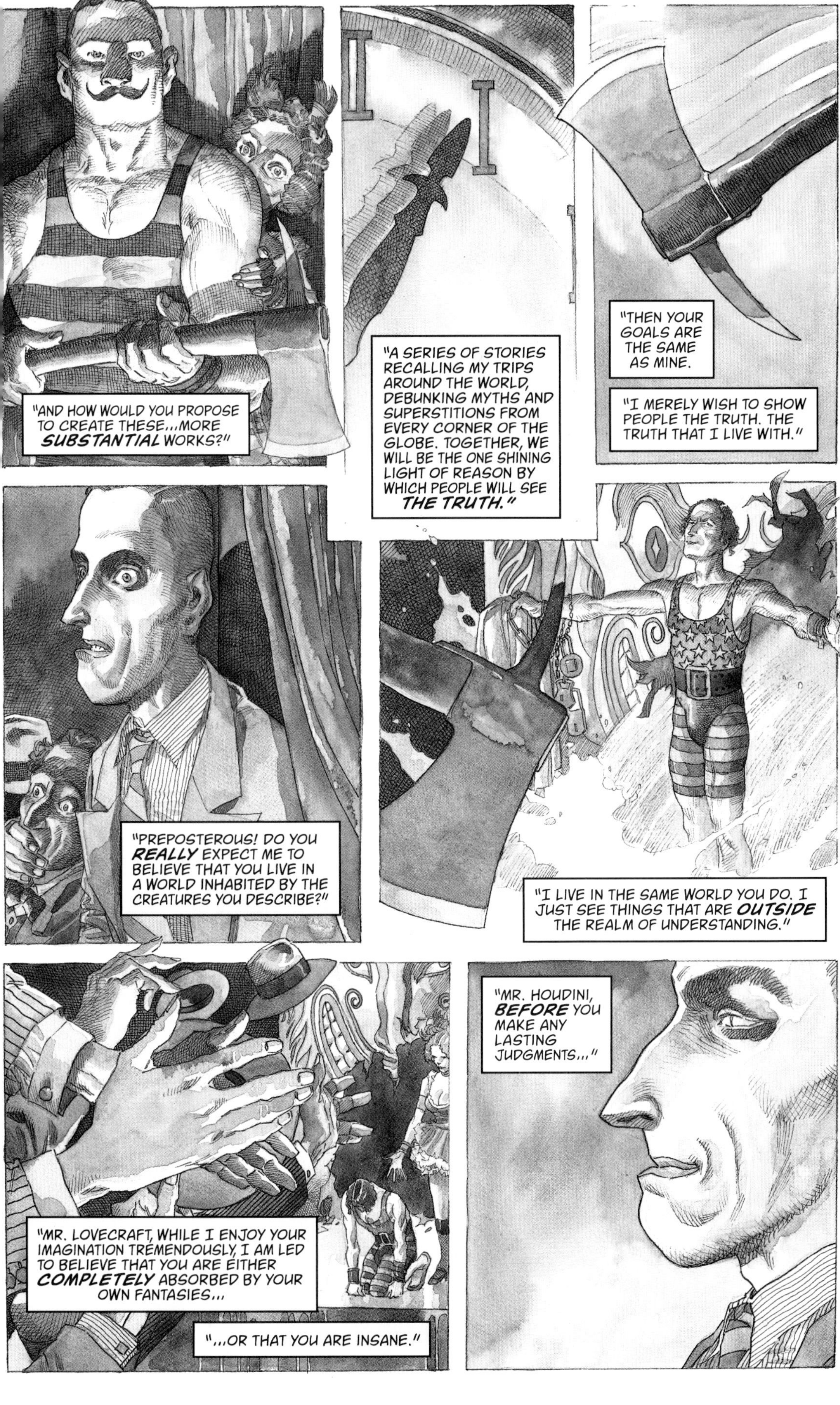
"AND HOW WOULD YOU PROPOSE TO CREATE THESE...MORE SUBSTANTIAL WORKS?"
"A SERIES OF STORIES RECALLING MY TRIPS AROUND THE WORLD, DEBUNKING MYTHS AND SUPERSTITIONS FROM EVERY CORNER OF THE GLOBE. TOGETHER, WE WILL BE THE ONE SHINING LIGHT OF REASON BY WHICH PEOPLE WILL SEE THE TRUTH."
"THEN YOUR GOALS ARE THE SAME AS MINE.
"I MERELY WISH TO SHOW PEOPLE THE TRUTH. THE TRUTH THAT I LIVE WITH."
"PREPOSTEROUS! DO YOU REALLY EXPECT ME TO BELIEVE THAT YOU LIVE IN A WORLD INHABITED BY THE CREATURES YOU DESCRIBE?"
"I LIVE IN THE SAME WORLD YOU DO. I JUST SEE THINGS THAT ARE OUTSIDE THE REALM OF UNDERSTANDING."
"MR. LOVECRAFT, WHILE I ENJOY YOUR IMAGINATION TREMENDOUSLY, I AM LED TO BELIEVE THAT YOU ARE EITHER COMPLETELY ABSORBED BY YOUR OWN FANTASIES...
"...OR THAT YOU ARE INSANE."
"MR. HOUDINI, BEFORE YOU MAKE ANY LASTING JUDGMENTS..."

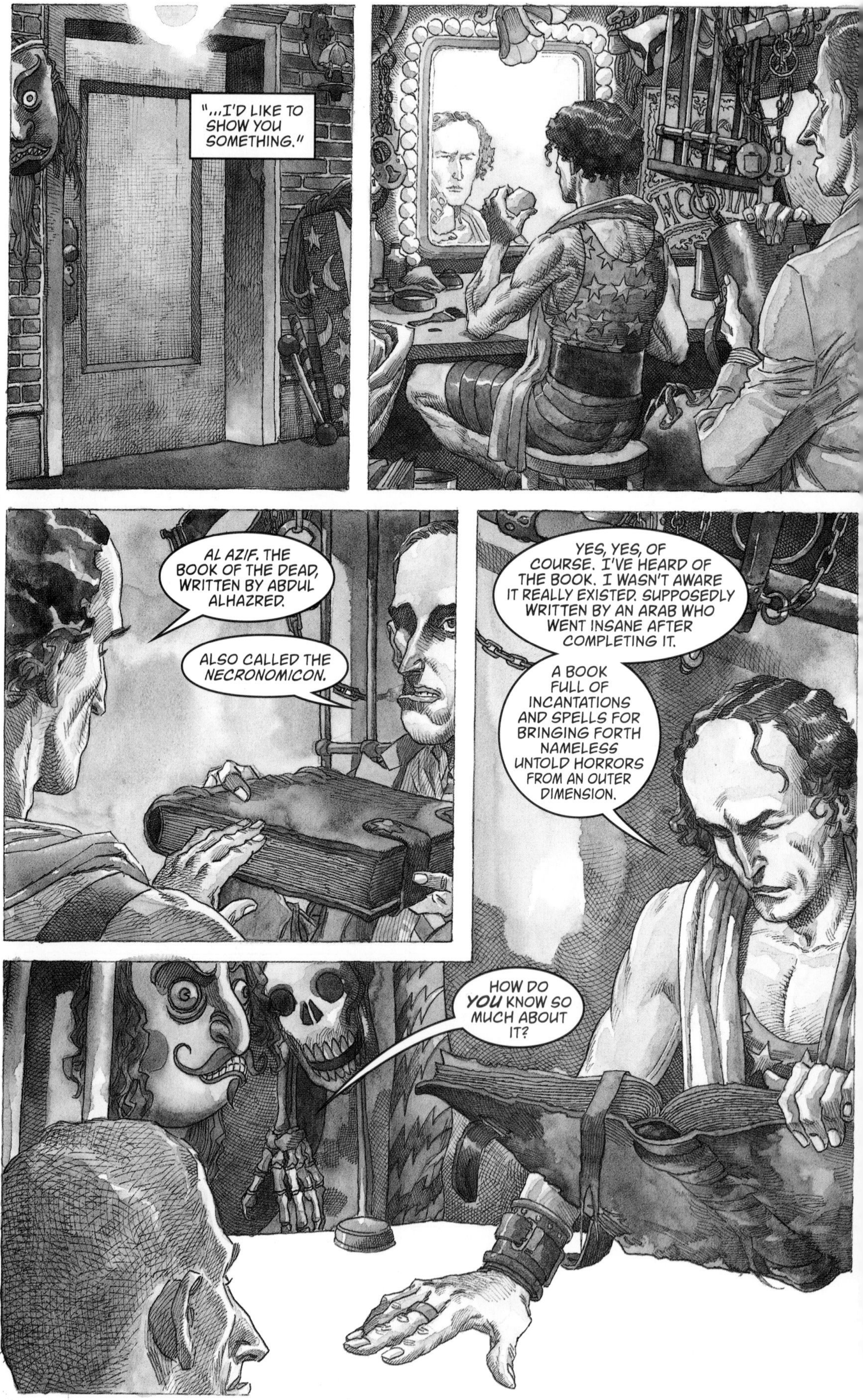
"...I'D LIKE TO SHOW YOU SOMETHING."
AL AZIF. THE BOOK OF THE DEAD, WRITTEN BY ABDUL ALHAZRED.
ALSO CALLED THE NECRONOMICON.
YES, YES, OF COURSE. I'VE HEARD OF THE BOOK. I WASN'T AWARE IT REALLY EXISTED. SUPPOSEDLY WRITTEN BY AN ARAB WHO WENT INSANE AFTER COMPLETING IT.
A BOOK FULL OF INCANTATIONS AND SPELLS FOR BRINGING FORTH NAMELESS UNTOLD HORRORS FROM AN OUTER DIMENSION.
HOW DO YOU KNOW SO MUCH ABOUT IT?

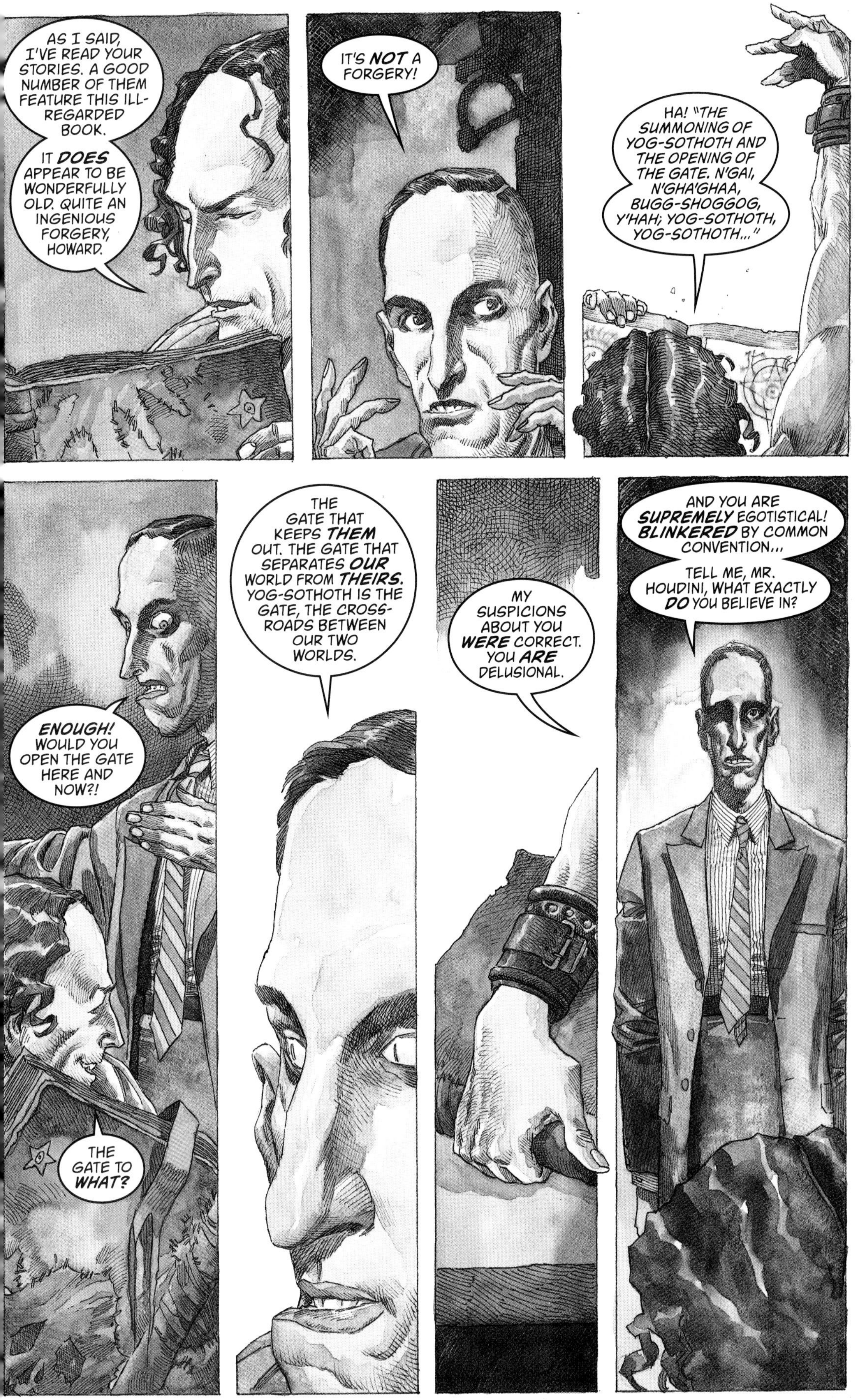
AS I SAID, I'VE READ YOUR STORIES. A GOOD NUMBER OF THEM FEATURE THIS ILL-REGARDED BOOK.
IT DOES APPEAR TO BE WONDERFULLY OLD. QUITE AN INGENIOUS FORGERY, HOWARD.
IT'S NOT A FORGERY!
HA! "THE SUMMONING OF YOG-SOTHOTH AND THE OPENING OF THE GATE. N'GAI, N'GHA'GHAA, BUGG-SHOGGOG, Y'HAH; YOG-SOTHOTH, YOG-SOTHOTH..."
ENOUGH! WOULD YOU OPEN THE GATE HERE AND NOW?!
THE GATE TO WHAT?
THE GATE THAT KEEPS THEM OUT. THE GATE THAT SEPARATES OUR WORLD FROM THEIRS. YOG-SOTHOTH IS THE GATE, THE CROSS-ROADS BETWEEN OUR TWO WORLDS.
MY SUSPICIONS ABOUT YOU WERE CORRECT. YOU ARE DELUSIONAL.
AND YOU ARE SUPREMELY EGOTISTICAL! BLINKERED BY COMMON CONVENTION...
TELL ME, MR. HOUDINI, WHAT EXACTLY DO YOU BELIEVE IN?

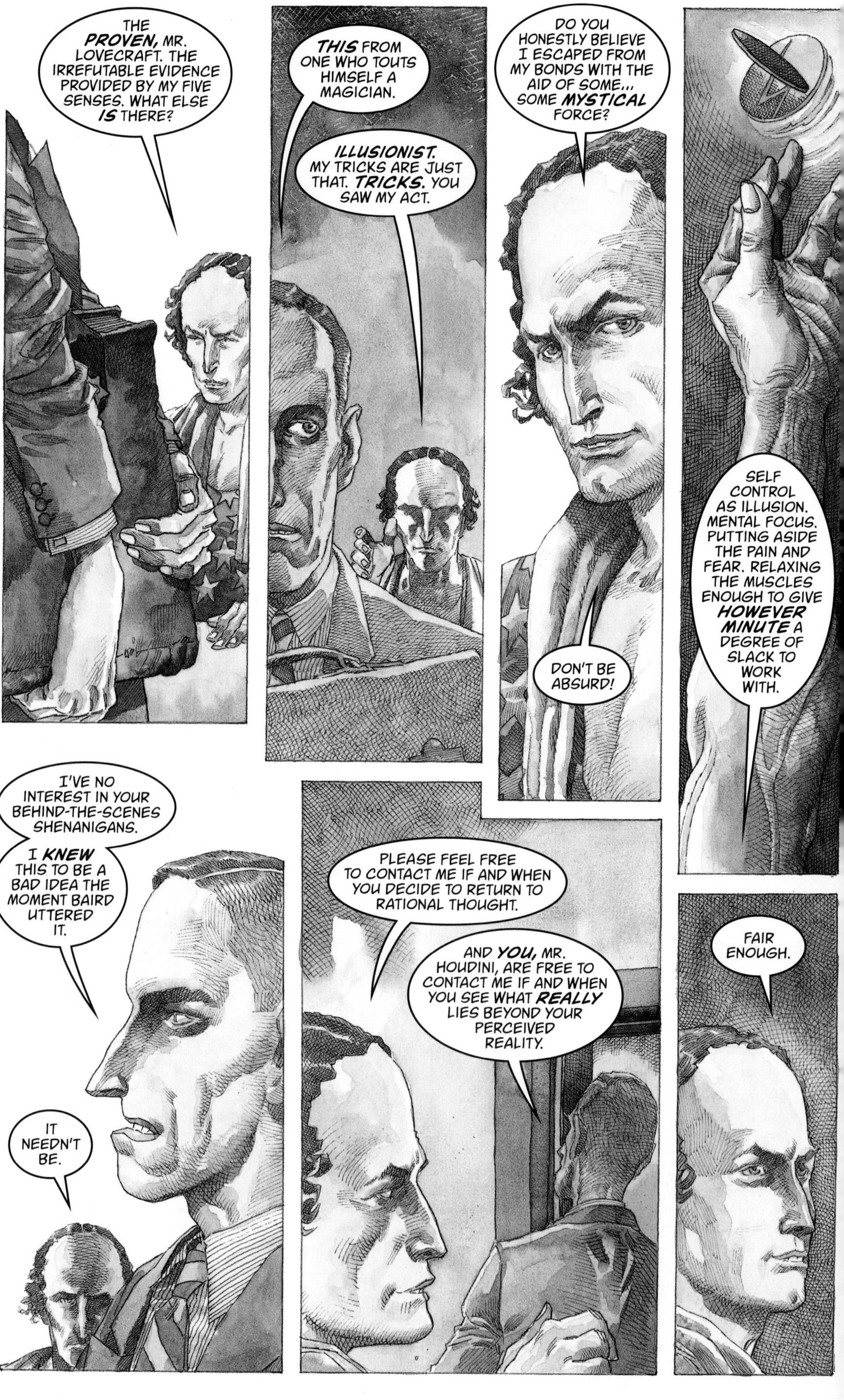
THE PROVEN, MR. LOVECRAFT. THE IRREFUTABLE EVIDENCE PROVIDED BY MY FIVE SENSES. WHAT ELSE IS THERE?
THIS FROM ONE WHO TOUTS HIMSELF A MAGICIAN.
ILLUSIONIST. MY TRICKS ARE JUST THAT. TRICKS. YOU SAW MY ACT.
DO YOU HONESTLY BELIEVE I ESCAPED FROM MY BONDS WITH THE AID OF SOME... SOME MYSTICAL FORCE?
DON'T BE ABSURD!
SELF CONTROL AS ILLUSION. MENTAL FOCUS. PUTTING ASIDE THE PAIN AND FEAR. RELAXING THE MUSCLES ENOUGH TO GIVE HOWEVER MINUTE A DEGREE OF SLACK TO WORK WITH.
I'VE NO INTEREST IN YOUR BEHIND-THE-SCENES SHENANIGANS.
I KNEW THIS TO BE A BAD IDEA THE MOMENT BAIRD UTTERED IT.
IT NEEDN'T BE.
PLEASE FEEL FREE TO CONTACT ME IF AND WHEN YOU DECIDE TO RETURN TO RATIONAL THOUGHT.
AND YOU, MR. HOUDINI, ARE FREE TO CONTACT ME IF AND WHEN YOU SEE WHAT REALLY LIES BEYOND YOUR PERCEIVED REALITY.
FAIR ENOUGH.

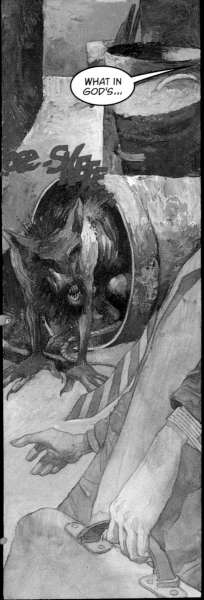

WHAT IN
GOD'S...

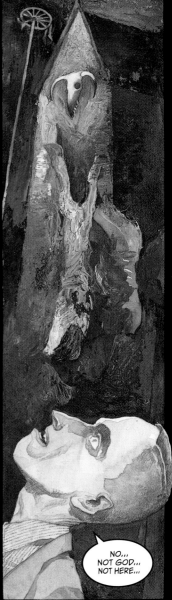

NO...
NOT GOD...
NOT HERE...

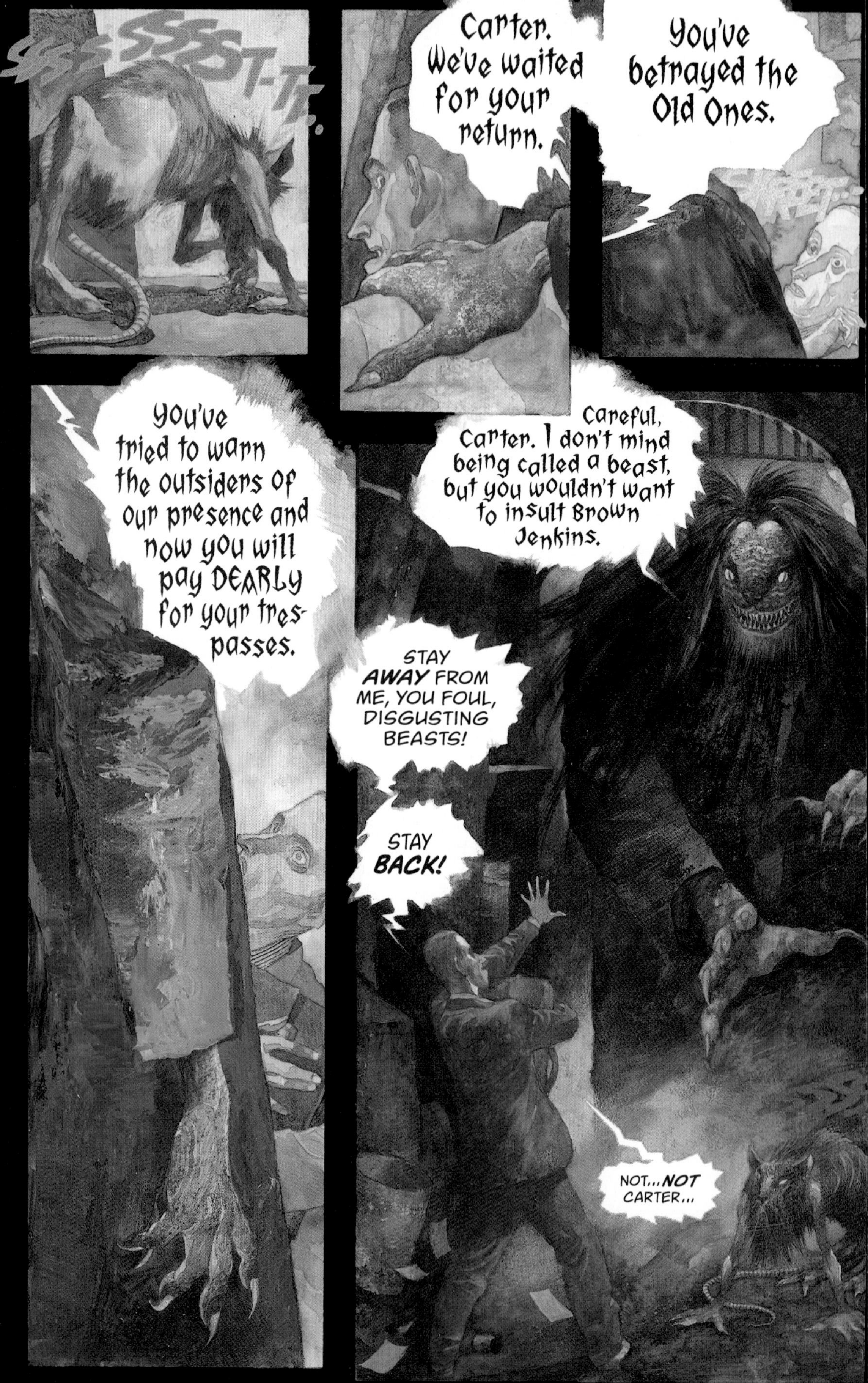
SSSSSST-TT..
Carter. We've waited for your return.
You've betrayed the Old Ones.
You've tried to warn the outsiders of our presence and now you will pay DEARLY for your tres-passes.
Careful, Carter. I don't mind being called a beast, but you wouldn't want to insult Brown Jenkins.
STAY AWAY FROM ME, YOU FOUL, DISGUSTING BEASTS!
STAY BACK!
NOT...NOT CARTER...

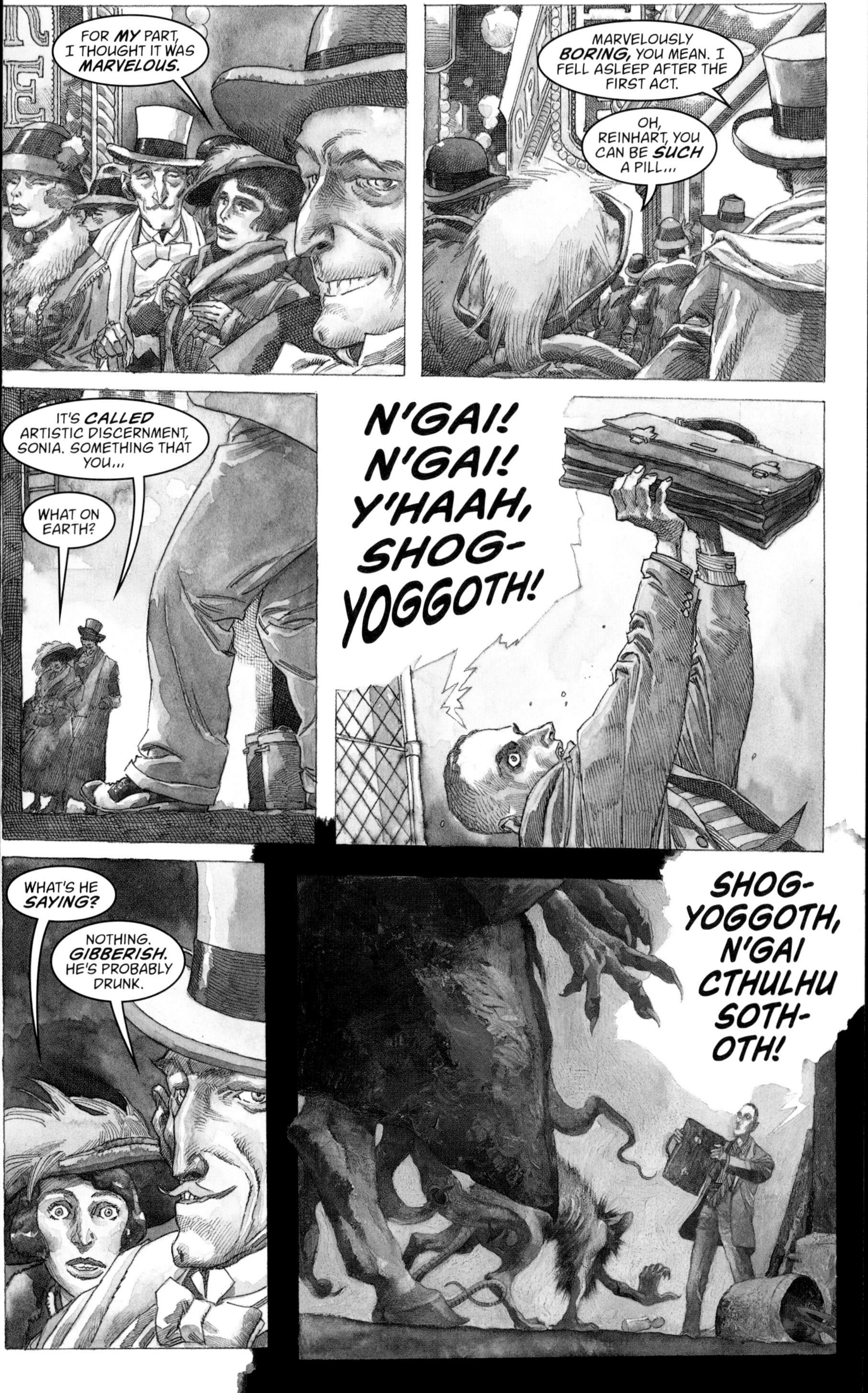
FOR MY PART, I THOUGHT IT WAS MARVELOUS.
MARVELOUSLY BORING, YOU MEAN. I FELL ASLEEP AFTER THE FIRST ACT.
OH, REINHART, YOU CAN BE SUCH A PILL...
IT'S CALLED ARTISTIC DISCERNMENT, SONIA. SOMETHING THAT YOU...
WHAT ON EARTH?
N'GAI! N'GAI! Y'HAAH, SHOG-YOGGOTH!
WHAT'S HE SAYING?
NOTHING. GIBBERISH. HE'S PROBABLY DRUNK.
SHOG-YOGGOTH, N'GAI CTHULHU SOTH-OTH!

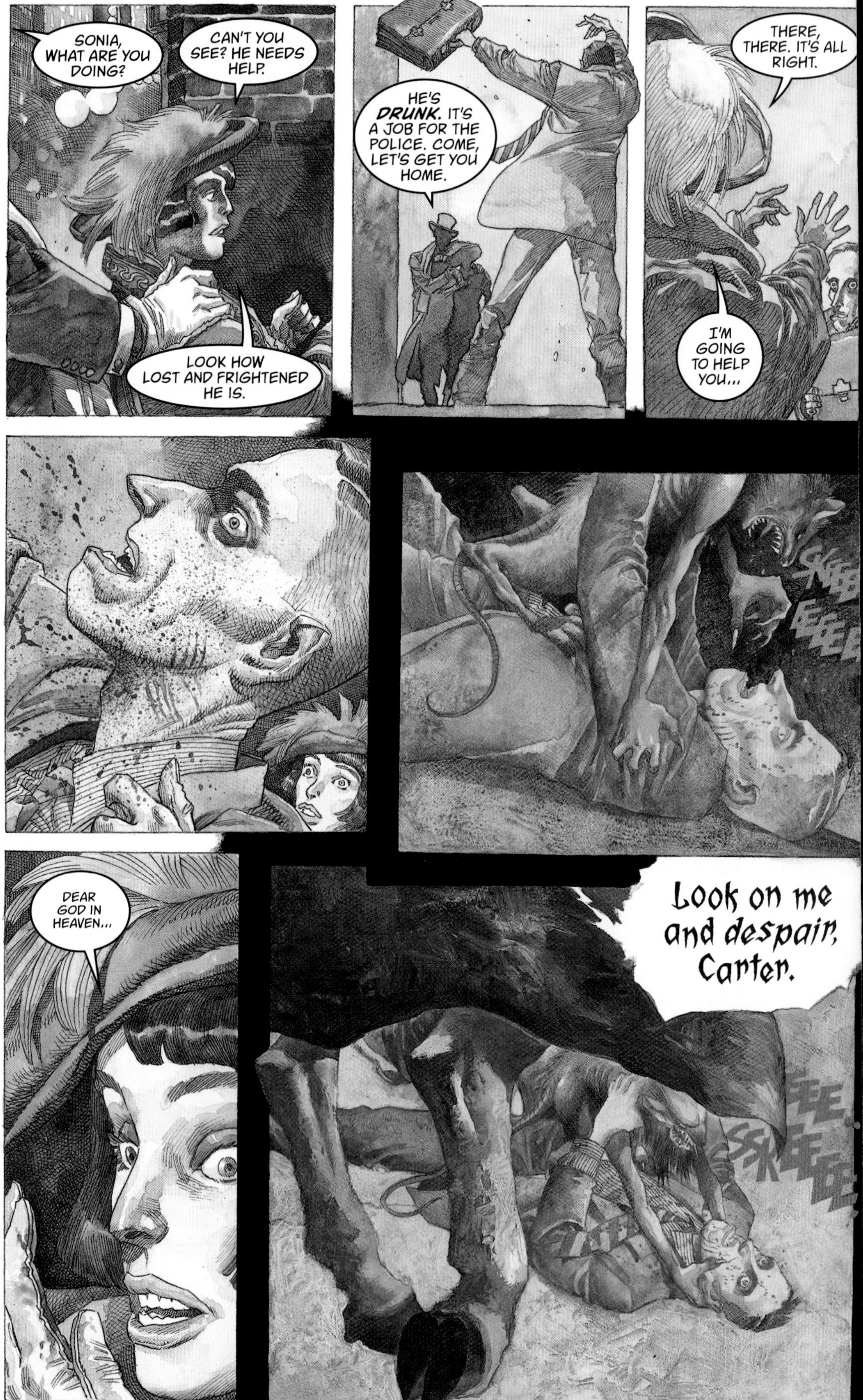
SONIA, WHAT ARE YOU DOING?
CAN'T YOU SEE? HE NEEDS HELP.
LOOK HOW LOST AND FRIGHTENED HE IS.
HE'S DRUNK. IT'S A JOB FOR THE POLICE. COME, LET'S GET YOU HOME.
THERE, THERE. IT'S ALL RIGHT.
I'M GOING TO HELP YOU...
SKREEEEE
DEAR GOD IN HEAVEN...
Look on me and despair, Carter.
EEE. SSKREEEEE

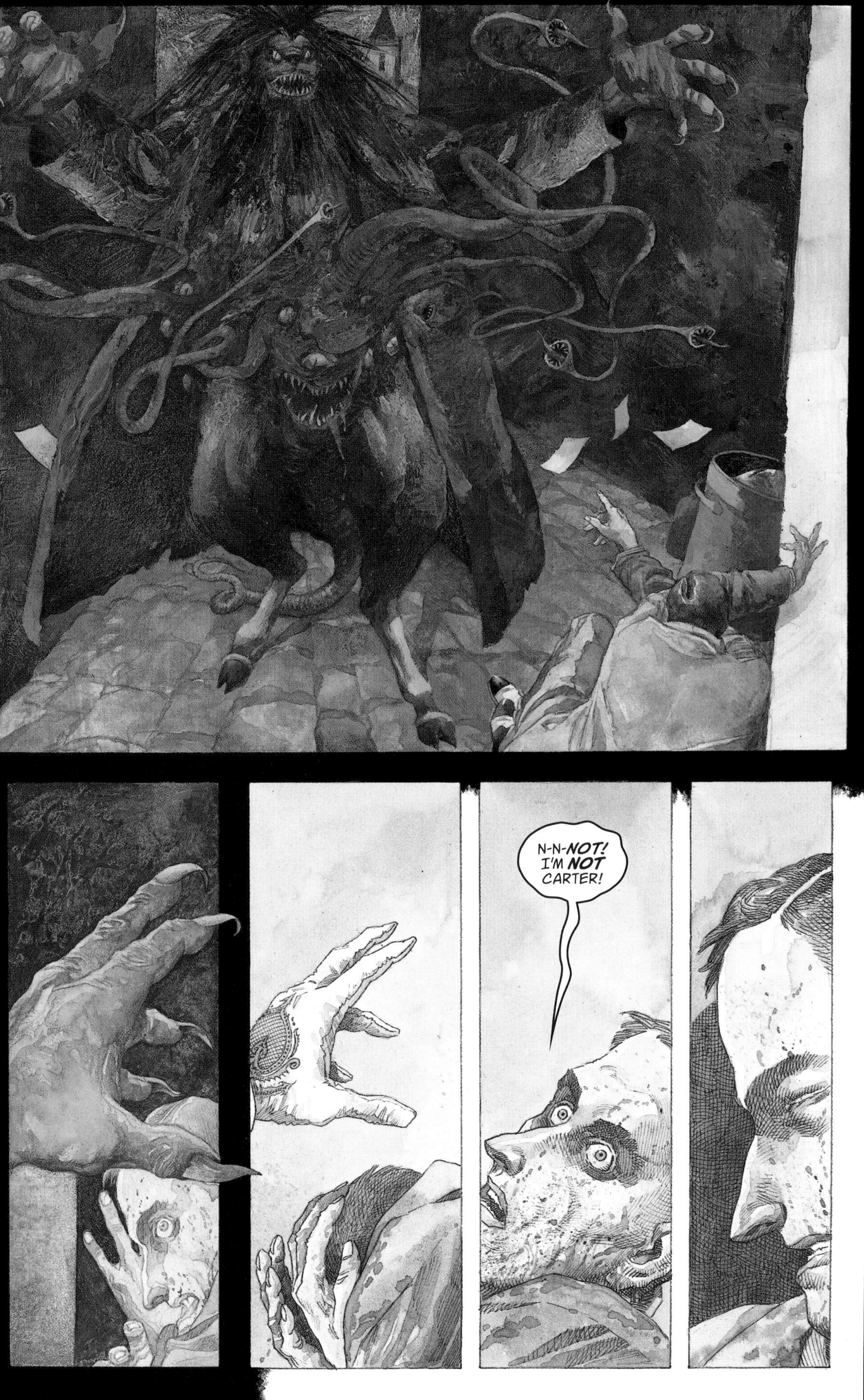
N-N-*NOT!* I'M *NOT* CARTER!

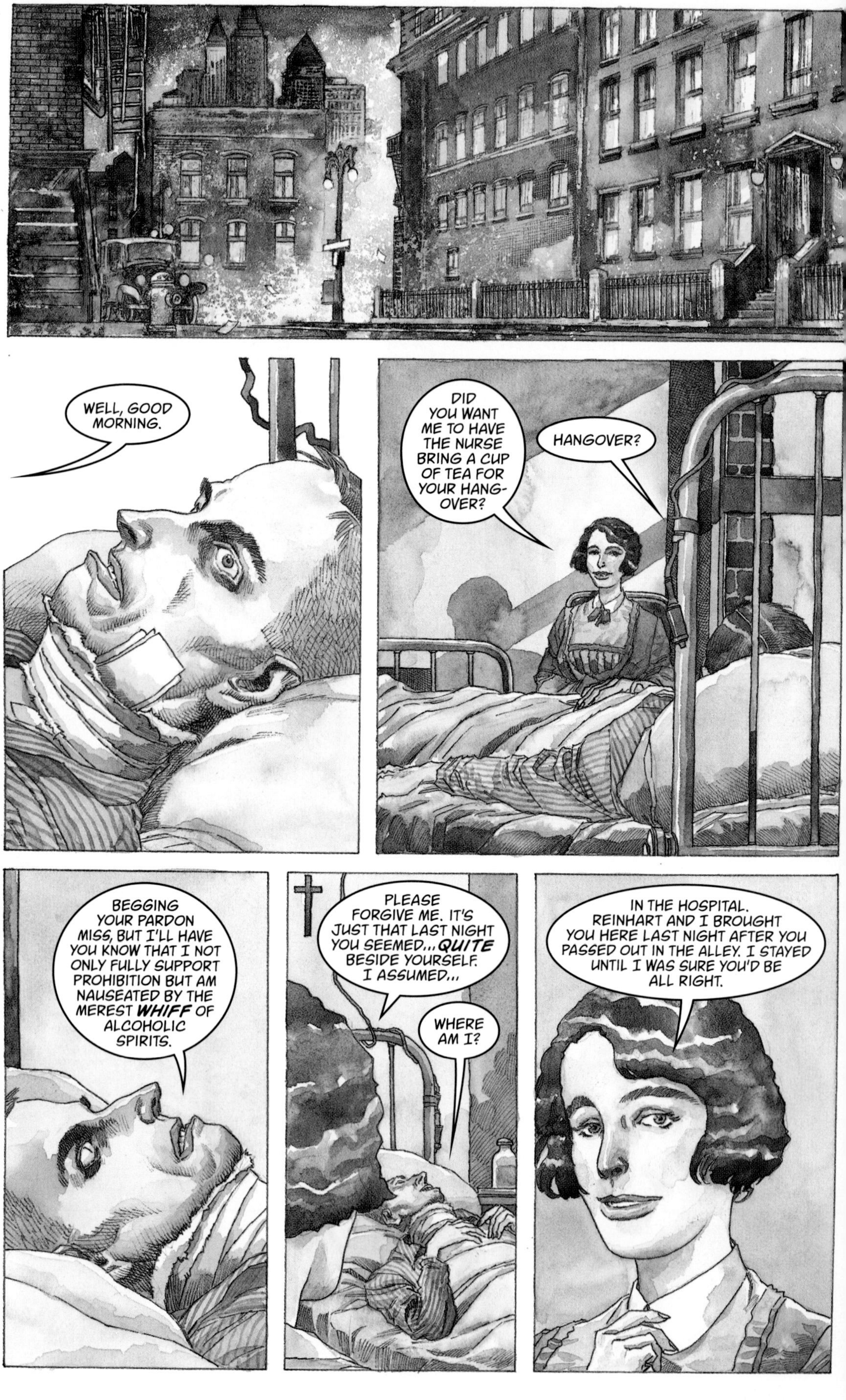
WELL, GOOD MORNING.
DID YOU WANT ME TO HAVE THE NURSE BRING A CUP OF TEA FOR YOUR HANG-OVER?
HANGOVER?
BEGGING YOUR PARDON MISS, BUT I'LL HAVE YOU KNOW THAT I NOT ONLY FULLY SUPPORT PROHIBITION BUT AM NAUSEATED BY THE MEREST WHIFF OF ALCOHOLIC SPIRITS.
PLEASE FORGIVE ME. IT'S JUST THAT LAST NIGHT YOU SEEMED... QUITE BESIDE YOURSELF. I ASSUMED...
WHERE AM I?
IN THE HOSPITAL. REINHART AND I BROUGHT YOU HERE LAST NIGHT AFTER YOU PASSED OUT IN THE ALLEY. I STAYED UNTIL I WAS SURE YOU'D BE ALL RIGHT.

THEN CLEARLY IT IS *I* WHO SHOULD APOLOGIZE FOR BEING SUCH A BURDEN.

SONIA. SONIA GREEN.

A PLEASURE... SONIA. MY NAME IS HOWARD. I WONDER IF YOU'D BE WILLING TO LET ME REPAY YOU BY TAKING YOU OUT TO BREAKFAST.

I'D LIKE THAT VERY MUCH.

BUT I IMAGINE THE DOCTOR WILL WANT TO TALK TO YOU ABOUT THAT CUT ON YOUR NECK FIRST.

OH. YES. TELL ME, DID YOU HAPPEN TO SEE HOW I...*SUSTAINED* THIS INJURY?

WELL, THAT'S AN ODD STORY. I'D THOUGHT *YOU'D* DONE IT. IT LOOKED TO ME AS IF YOU'D SCRATCHED YOURSELF SOMEHOW.

BUT THE DOCTOR IS CONVINCED THAT YOU WERE *BITTEN* BY SOMETHING.

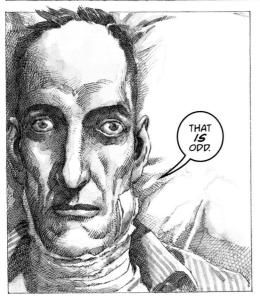

THAT *IS* ODD.

WELL, SONIA, I HAVE ENJOYED MEETING YOU *TREMENDOUSLY*. I'M ONLY SORRY THE CIRCUMSTANCES HAD TO BE SO PECULIAR.

THE FEELING IS MUTUAL, HOWARD.

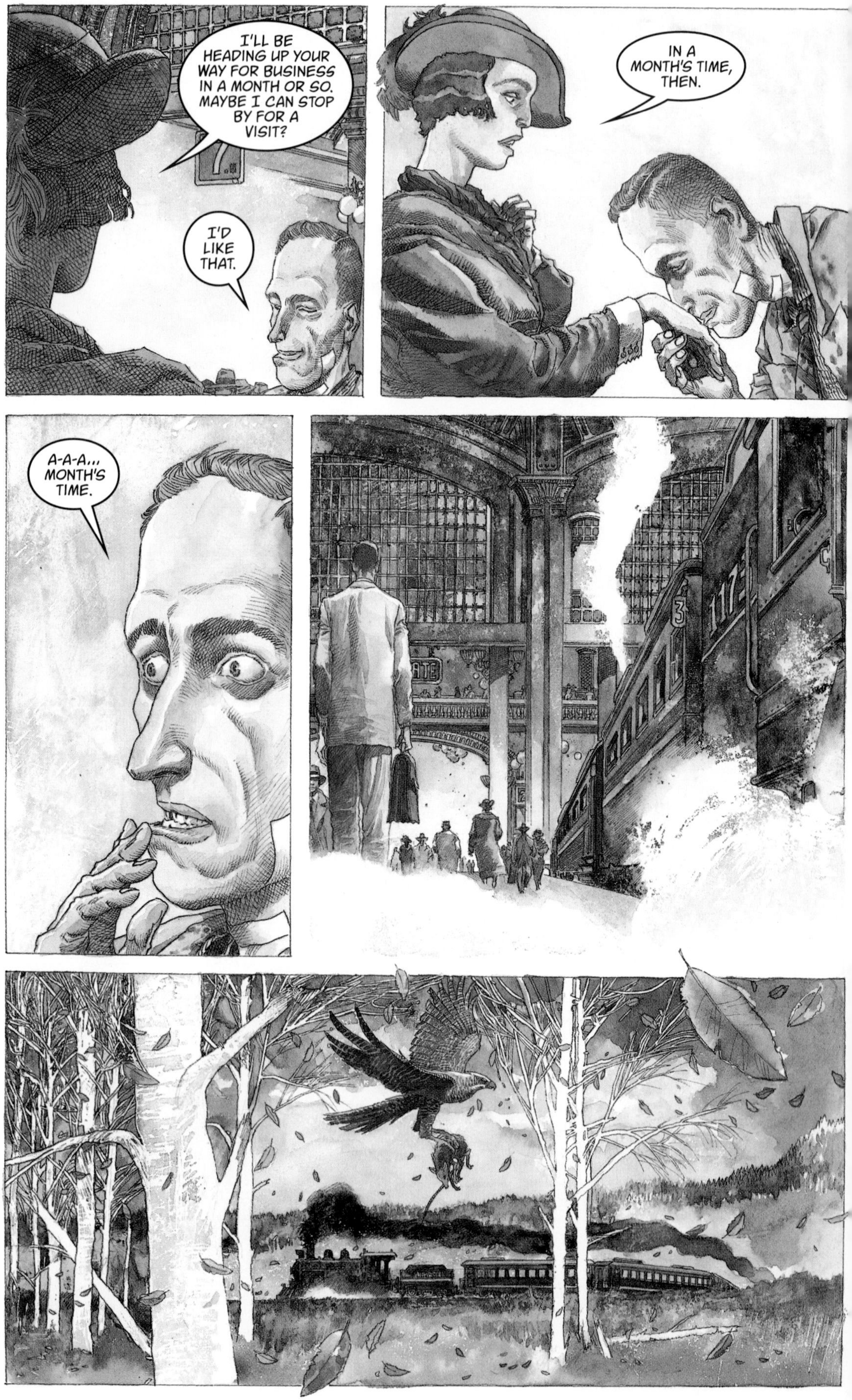
I'LL BE HEADING UP YOUR WAY FOR BUSINESS IN A MONTH OR SO. MAYBE I CAN STOP BY FOR A VISIT?
I'D LIKE THAT.
IN A MONTH'S TIME, THEN.
A-A-A... MONTH'S TIME.

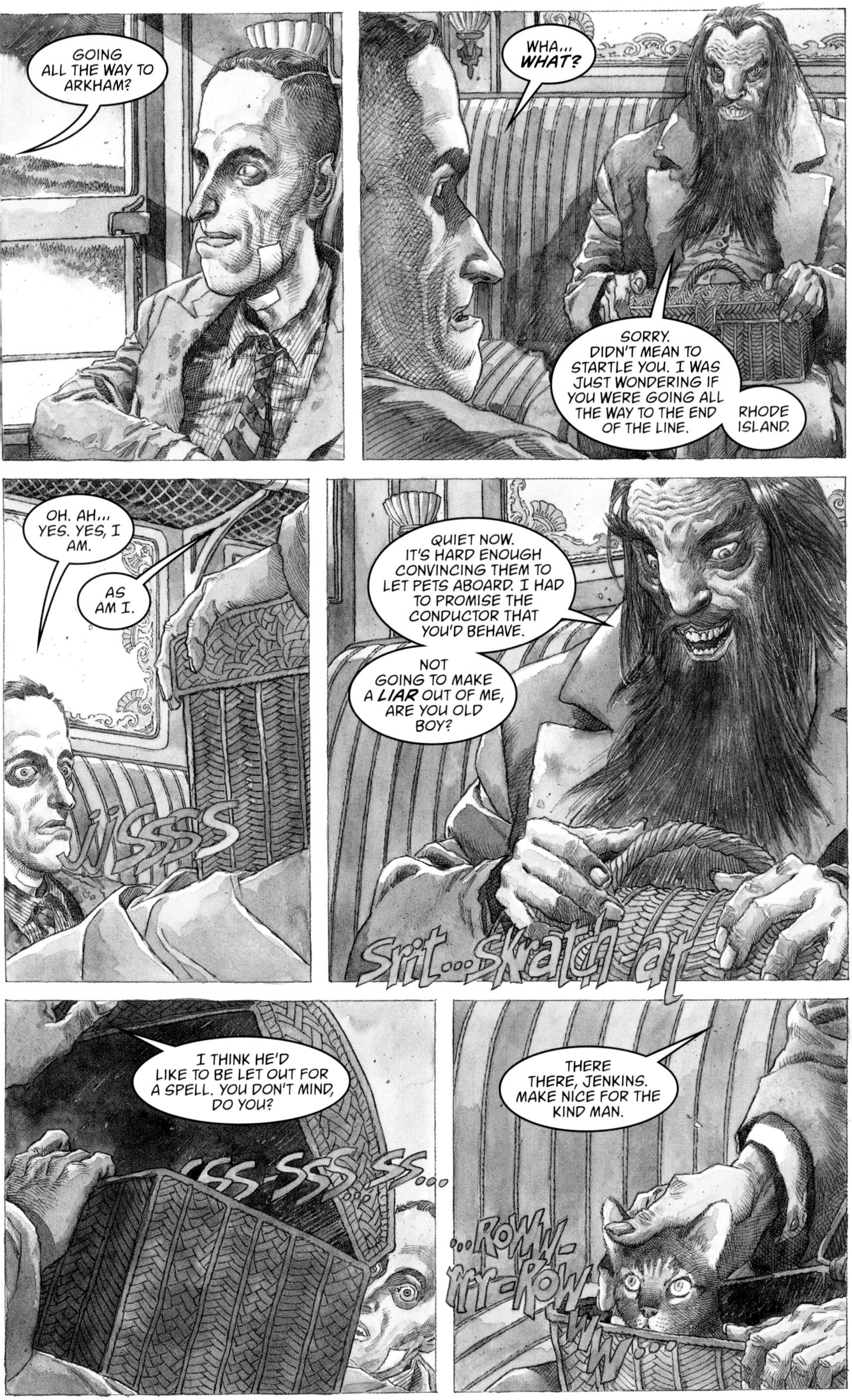
GOING ALL THE WAY TO ARKHAM?
WHA... WHAT?
SORRY. DIDN'T MEAN TO STARTLE YOU. I WAS JUST WONDERING IF YOU WERE GOING ALL THE WAY TO THE END OF THE LINE.
RHODE ISLAND.
OH. AH... YES. YES, I AM.
AS AM I.
JISSSS
QUIET NOW. IT'S HARD ENOUGH CONVINCING THEM TO LET PETS ABOARD. I HAD TO PROMISE THE CONDUCTOR THAT YOU'D BEHAVE.
NOT GOING TO MAKE A LIAR OUT OF ME, ARE YOU OLD BOY?
SRIT... SKRATCH AT
I THINK HE'D LIKE TO BE LET OUT FOR A SPELL. YOU DON'T MIND, DO YOU?
SSS-SSS SS...
THERE THERE, JENKINS. MAKE NICE FOR THE KIND MAN.
...ROWW-RR-ROWWW...

COME.

HOWARD?

MMM?

YOU... YOU HAVE A CALLER. SHE'S WAITING FOR YOU DOWNSTAIRS.

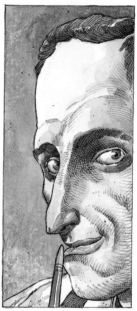

SONIA!

HELLO, HOWARD.

SONIA; MY MOTHER. SARAH LOVECRAFT.

YES, WE'VE MET ALREADY.

RIGHT. OF COURSE...WELL THEN...WELCOME TO PROVIDENCE!

THANK YOU. I'D LOVE TO SEE MORE OF IT.

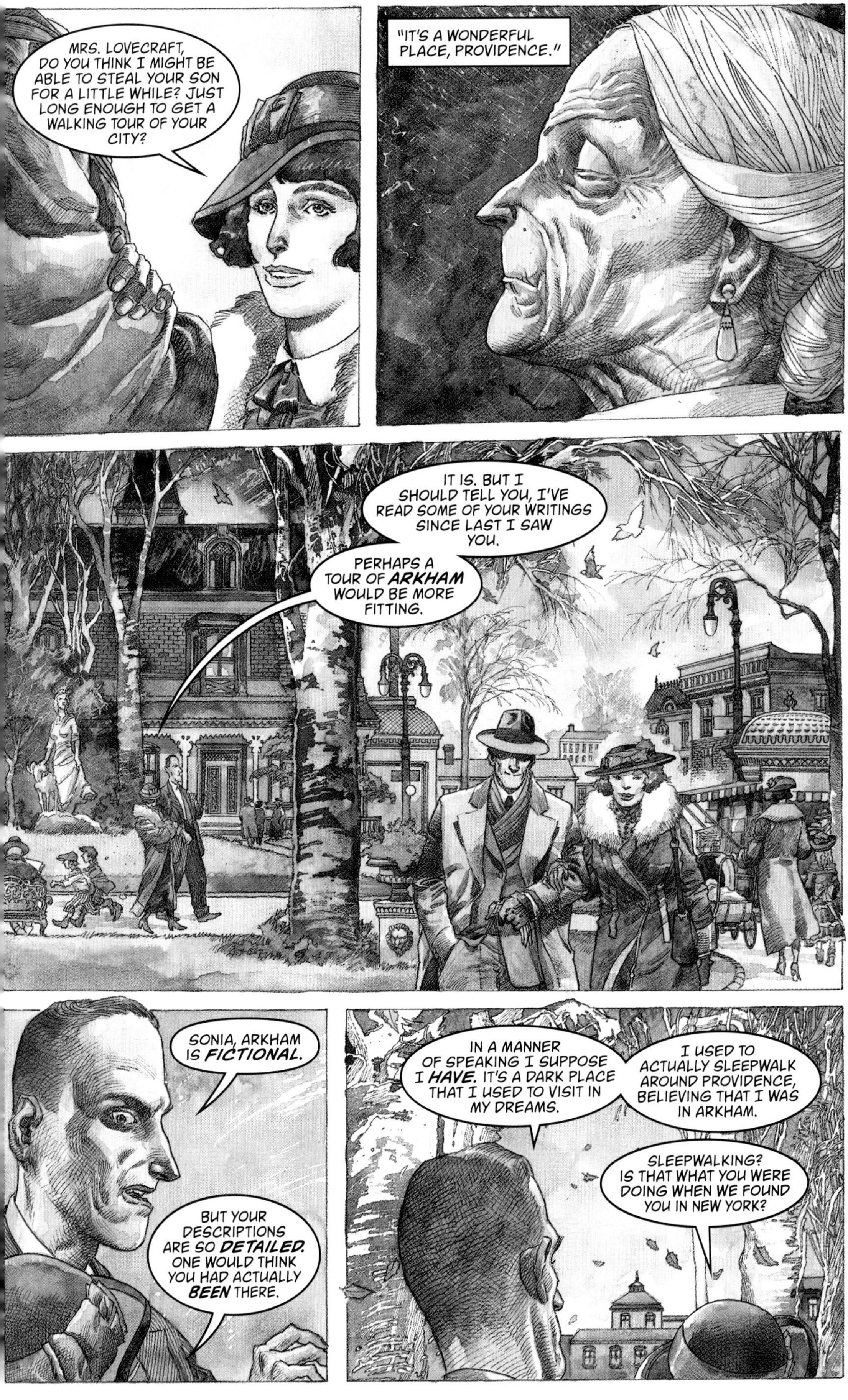
MRS. LOVECRAFT, DO YOU THINK I MIGHT BE ABLE TO STEAL YOUR SON FOR A LITTLE WHILE? JUST LONG ENOUGH TO GET A WALKING TOUR OF YOUR CITY?
"IT'S A WONDERFUL PLACE, PROVIDENCE."
IT IS. BUT I SHOULD TELL YOU, I'VE READ SOME OF YOUR WRITINGS SINCE LAST I SAW YOU.
PERHAPS A TOUR OF ARKHAM WOULD BE MORE FITTING.
SONIA, ARKHAM IS FICTIONAL.
BUT YOUR DESCRIPTIONS ARE SO DETAILED. ONE WOULD THINK YOU HAD ACTUALLY BEEN THERE.
IN A MANNER OF SPEAKING I SUPPOSE I HAVE. IT'S A DARK PLACE THAT I USED TO VISIT IN MY DREAMS.
I USED TO ACTUALLY SLEEPWALK AROUND PROVIDENCE, BELIEVING THAT I WAS IN ARKHAM.
SLEEPWALKING? IS THAT WHAT YOU WERE DOING WHEN WE FOUND YOU IN NEW YORK?

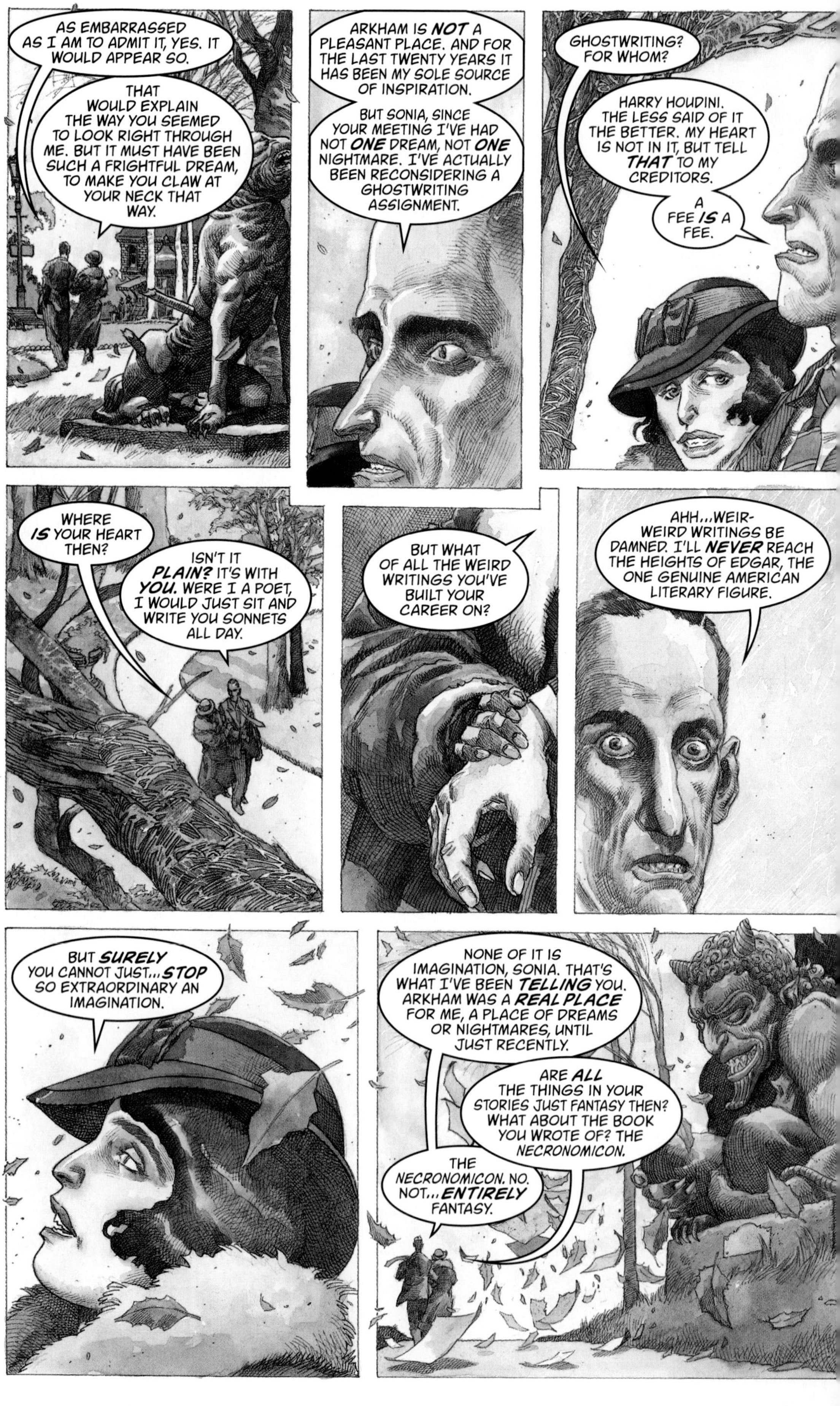
AS EMBARRASSED AS I AM TO ADMIT IT, YES. IT WOULD APPEAR SO.
THAT WOULD EXPLAIN THE WAY YOU SEEMED TO LOOK RIGHT THROUGH ME. BUT IT MUST HAVE BEEN SUCH A FRIGHTFUL DREAM, TO MAKE YOU CLAW AT YOUR NECK THAT WAY.
ARKHAM IS **NOT** A PLEASANT PLACE. AND FOR THE LAST TWENTY YEARS IT HAS BEEN MY SOLE SOURCE OF INSPIRATION.
BUT SONIA, SINCE YOUR MEETING I'VE HAD NOT **ONE** DREAM, NOT **ONE** NIGHTMARE. I'VE ACTUALLY BEEN RECONSIDERING A GHOSTWRITING ASSIGNMENT.
GHOSTWRITING? FOR WHOM?
HARRY HOUDINI. THE LESS SAID OF IT THE BETTER. MY HEART IS NOT IN IT, BUT TELL **THAT** TO MY CREDITORS.
A FEE **IS** A FEE.
WHERE **IS** YOUR HEART THEN?
ISN'T IT **PLAIN?** IT'S WITH **YOU.** WERE I A POET, I WOULD JUST SIT AND WRITE YOU SONNETS ALL DAY.
BUT WHAT OF ALL THE WEIRD WRITINGS YOU'VE BUILT YOUR CAREER ON?
AHH...WEIR-WEIRD WRITINGS BE DAMNED. I'LL **NEVER** REACH THE HEIGHTS OF EDGAR, THE ONE GENUINE AMERICAN LITERARY FIGURE.
BUT **SURELY** YOU CANNOT JUST...**STOP** SO EXTRAORDINARY AN IMAGINATION.
NONE OF IT IS IMAGINATION, SONIA. THAT'S WHAT I'VE BEEN **TELLING** YOU. ARKHAM WAS A **REAL PLACE** FOR ME, A PLACE OF DREAMS OR NIGHTMARES, UNTIL JUST RECENTLY.
ARE **ALL** THE THINGS IN YOUR STORIES JUST FANTASY THEN? WHAT ABOUT THE BOOK YOU WROTE OF? THE *NECRONOMICON.*
THE *NECRONOMICON.* NO. NOT...**ENTIRELY** FANTASY.

"IT'S A REAL BOOK LEFT TO ME BY MY FATHER.

"FULL OF HOKUM AND MYSTICAL DRIVEL.

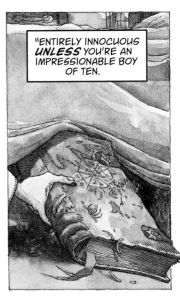

"ENTIRELY INNOCUOUS *UNLESS* YOU'RE AN IMPRESSIONABLE BOY OF TEN.

"I'M AFRAID READING IT HAD A DIS-AGREEABLE EFFECT ON MY YOUNG MIND."

WHIPPLE LOVECRAFT

• 1828 •

HE WAS THE ONE WHO GAVE ME MY TASTE FOR THE MACABRE, I THINK. HE WOULD TELL ME STORIES LATE AT NIGHT OF THE MOST *FEARFUL* SORT, *FILLED* WITH HIDEOUS APPARITIONS.

AND YOUR FATHER LET THIS GO ON?

MY *FATHER...* DIED WHEN I WAS EIGHT YEARS OLD.

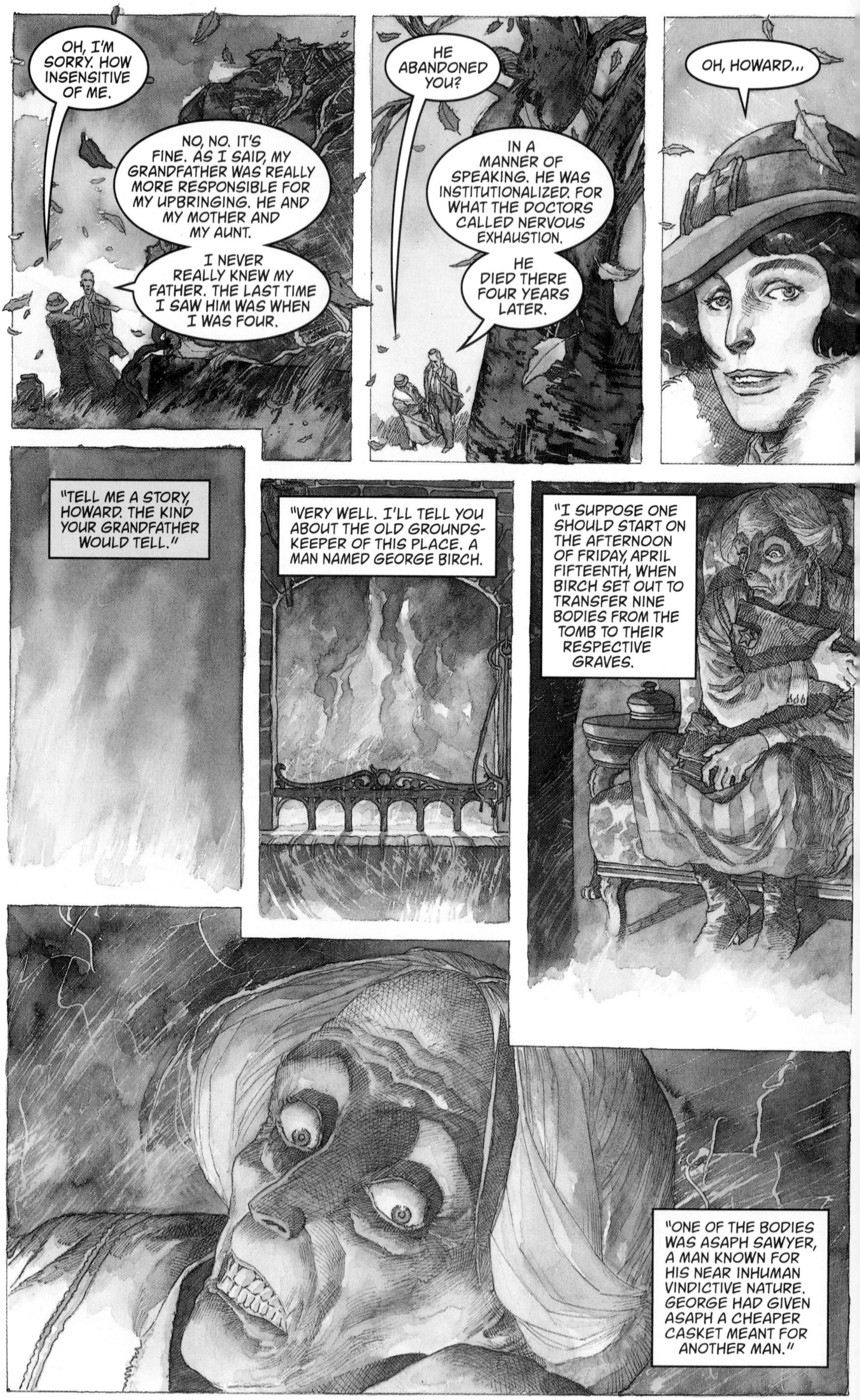

OH, I'M SORRY. HOW INSENSITIVE OF ME.
NO, NO. IT'S FINE. AS I SAID, MY GRANDFATHER WAS REALLY MORE RESPONSIBLE FOR MY UPBRINGING. HE AND MY MOTHER AND MY AUNT.
I NEVER REALLY KNEW MY FATHER. THE LAST TIME I SAW HIM WAS WHEN I WAS FOUR.
HE ABANDONED YOU?
IN A MANNER OF SPEAKING. HE WAS INSTITUTIONALIZED. FOR WHAT THE DOCTORS CALLED NERVOUS EXHAUSTION.
HE DIED THERE FOUR YEARS LATER.
OH, HOWARD...
"TELL ME A STORY, HOWARD. THE KIND YOUR GRANDFATHER WOULD TELL."
"VERY WELL. I'LL TELL YOU ABOUT THE OLD GROUNDS-KEEPER OF THIS PLACE. A MAN NAMED GEORGE BIRCH.
"I SUPPOSE ONE SHOULD START ON THE AFTERNOON OF FRIDAY, APRIL FIFTEENTH, WHEN BIRCH SET OUT TO TRANSFER NINE BODIES FROM THE TOMB TO THEIR RESPECTIVE GRAVES.
"ONE OF THE BODIES WAS ASAPH SAWYER, A MAN KNOWN FOR HIS NEAR INHUMAN VINDICTIVE NATURE. GEORGE HAD GIVEN ASAPH A CHEAPER CASKET MEANT FOR ANOTHER MAN."

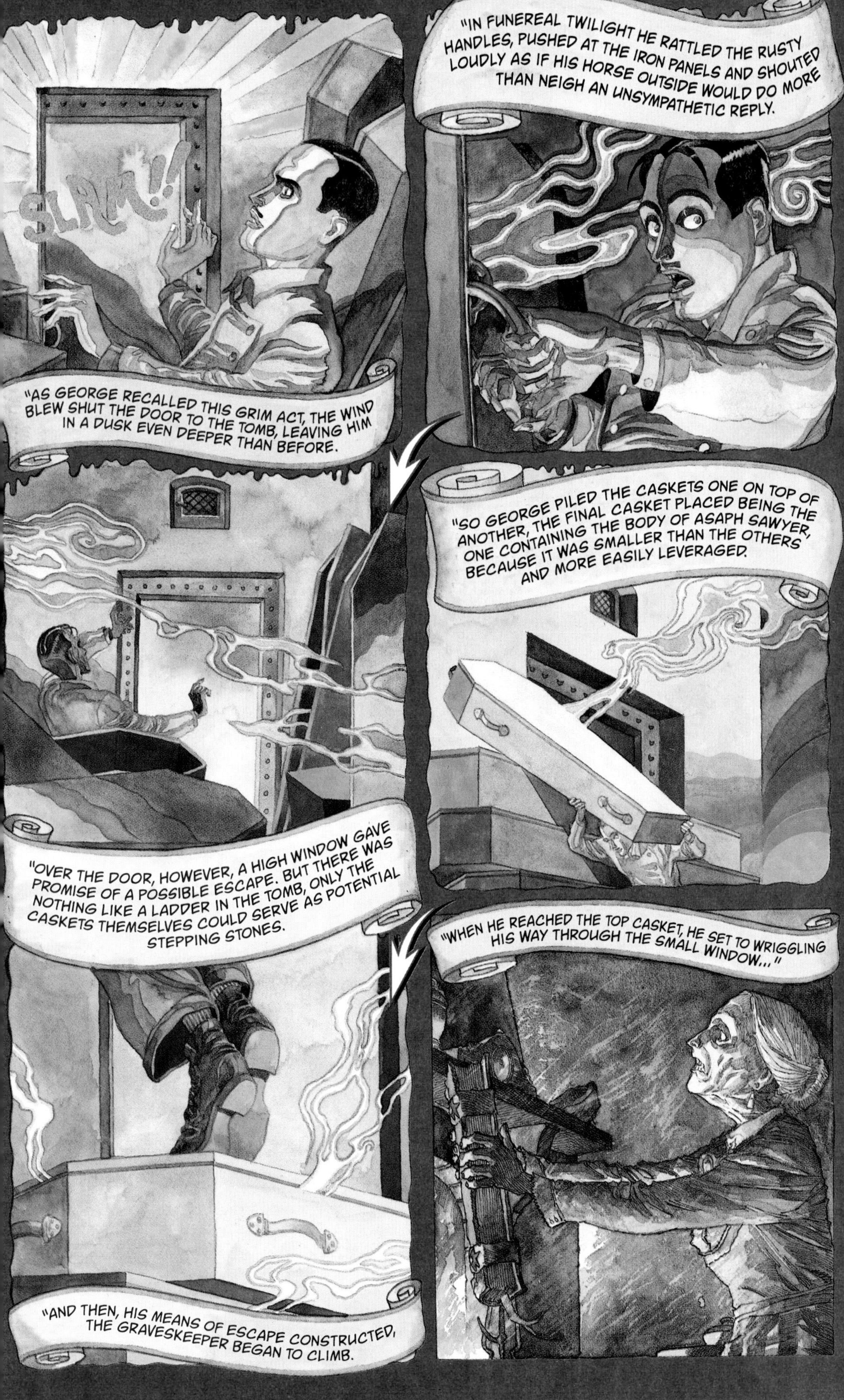
SLAM!!
"AS GEORGE RECALLED THIS GRIM ACT, THE WIND BLEW SHUT THE DOOR TO THE TOMB, LEAVING HIM IN A DUSK EVEN DEEPER THAN BEFORE.
"IN FUNEREAL TWILIGHT HE RATTLED THE RUSTY HANDLES, PUSHED AT THE IRON PANELS AND SHOUTED LOUDLY AS IF HIS HORSE OUTSIDE WOULD DO MORE THAN NEIGH AN UNSYMPATHETIC REPLY.
"OVER THE DOOR, HOWEVER, A HIGH WINDOW GAVE PROMISE OF A POSSIBLE ESCAPE. BUT THERE WAS NOTHING LIKE A LADDER IN THE TOMB, ONLY THE CASKETS THEMSELVES COULD SERVE AS POTENTIAL STEPPING STONES.
"SO GEORGE PILED THE CASKETS ONE ON TOP OF ANOTHER, THE FINAL CASKET PLACED BEING THE ONE CONTAINING THE BODY OF ASAPH SAWYER, BECAUSE IT WAS SMALLER THAN THE OTHERS AND MORE EASILY LEVERAGED.
"AND THEN, HIS MEANS OF ESCAPE CONSTRUCTED, THE GRAVESKEEPER BEGAN TO CLIMB.
"WHEN HE REACHED THE TOP CASKET, HE SET TO WRIGGLING HIS WAY THROUGH THE SMALL WINDOW..."

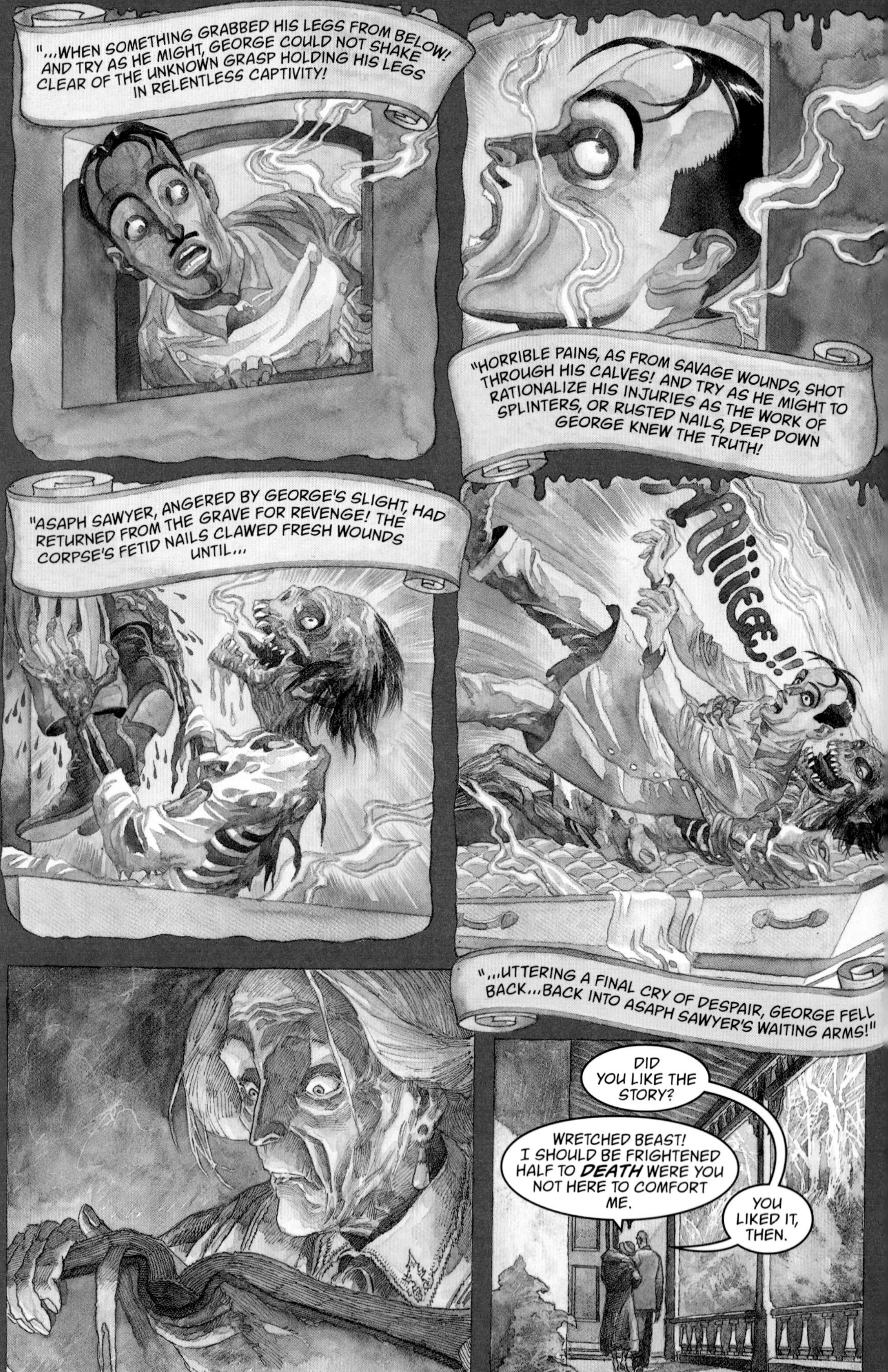
"...WHEN SOMETHING GRABBED HIS LEGS FROM BELOW! AND TRY AS HE MIGHT, GEORGE COULD NOT SHAKE CLEAR OF THE UNKNOWN GRASP HOLDING HIS LEGS IN RELENTLESS CAPTIVITY!
"HORRIBLE PAINS, AS FROM SAVAGE WOUNDS, SHOT THROUGH HIS CALVES! AND TRY AS HE MIGHT TO RATIONALIZE HIS INJURIES AS THE WORK OF SPLINTERS, OR RUSTED NAILS, DEEP DOWN GEORGE KNEW THE TRUTH!
"ASAPH SAWYER, ANGERED BY GEORGE'S SLIGHT, HAD RETURNED FROM THE GRAVE FOR REVENGE! THE CORPSE'S FETID NAILS CLAWED FRESH WOUNDS UNTIL...
AIIIEEE!!!
"...UTTERING A FINAL CRY OF DESPAIR, GEORGE FELL BACK...BACK INTO ASAPH SAWYER'S WAITING ARMS!"
DID YOU LIKE THE STORY?
WRETCHED BEAST! I SHOULD BE FRIGHTENED HALF TO ***DEATH*** WERE YOU NOT HERE TO COMFORT ME.
YOU LIKED IT, THEN.

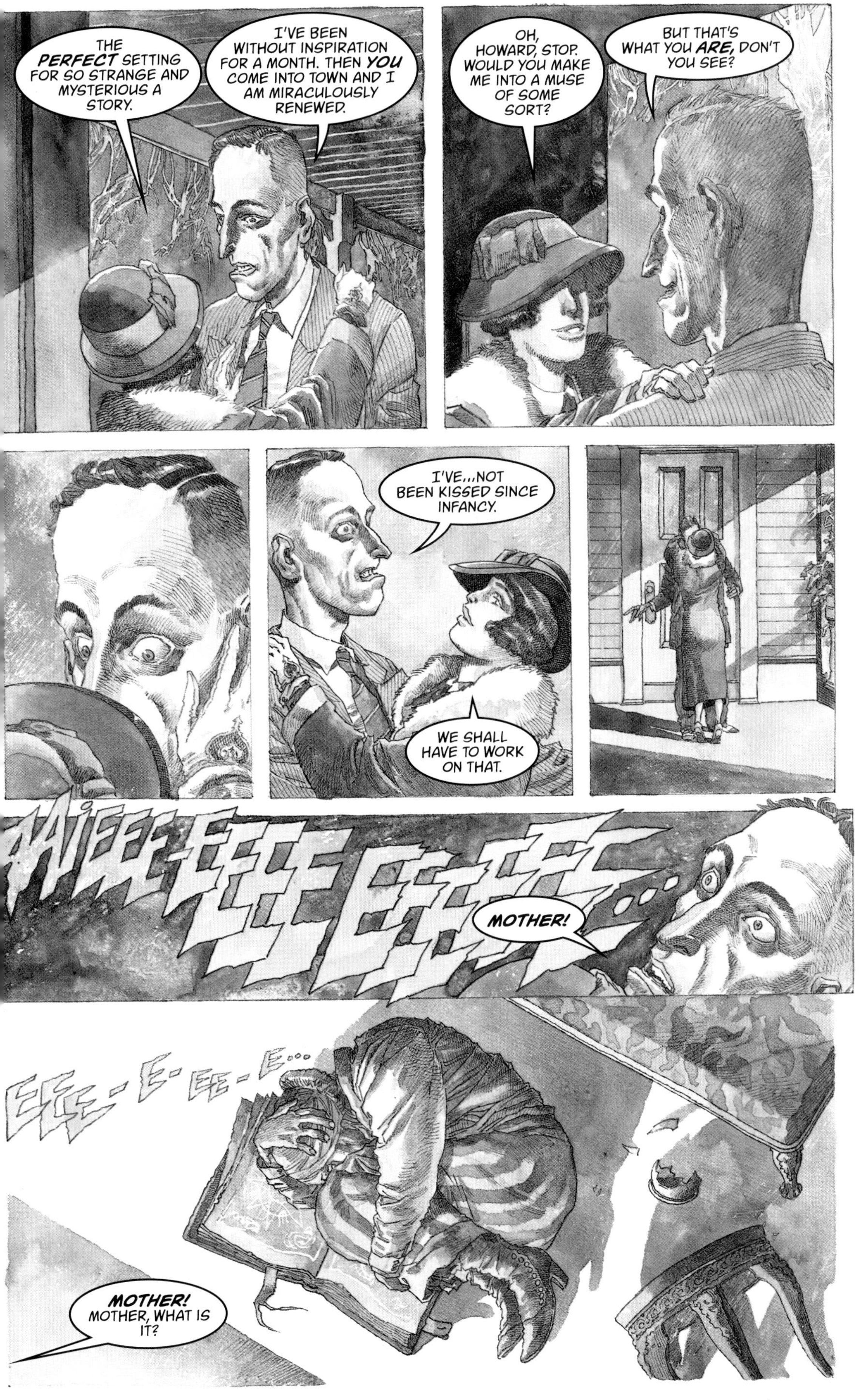

THE PERFECT SETTING FOR SO STRANGE AND MYSTERIOUS A STORY.
I'VE BEEN WITHOUT INSPIRATION FOR A MONTH. THEN YOU COME INTO TOWN AND I AM MIRACULOUSLY RENEWED.
OH, HOWARD, STOP. WOULD YOU MAKE ME INTO A MUSE OF SOME SORT?
BUT THAT'S WHAT YOU ARE, DON'T YOU SEE?
I'VE...NOT BEEN KISSED SINCE INFANCY.
WE SHALL HAVE TO WORK ON THAT.
MOTHER!
MOTHER! MOTHER, WHAT IS IT?

MOTHER!

GET HER UP.

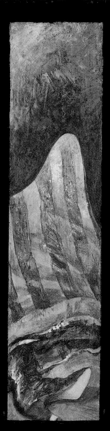

HOWARD! PAY ATTENTION!

HOWARD!

YES...YES, OF COURSE...

MRS. LOVECRAFT?

IT'S NOT REAL. IT'S NOT REAL, MOTHER. MOTHER... PLEASE.

IT HAD YOUR FACE!

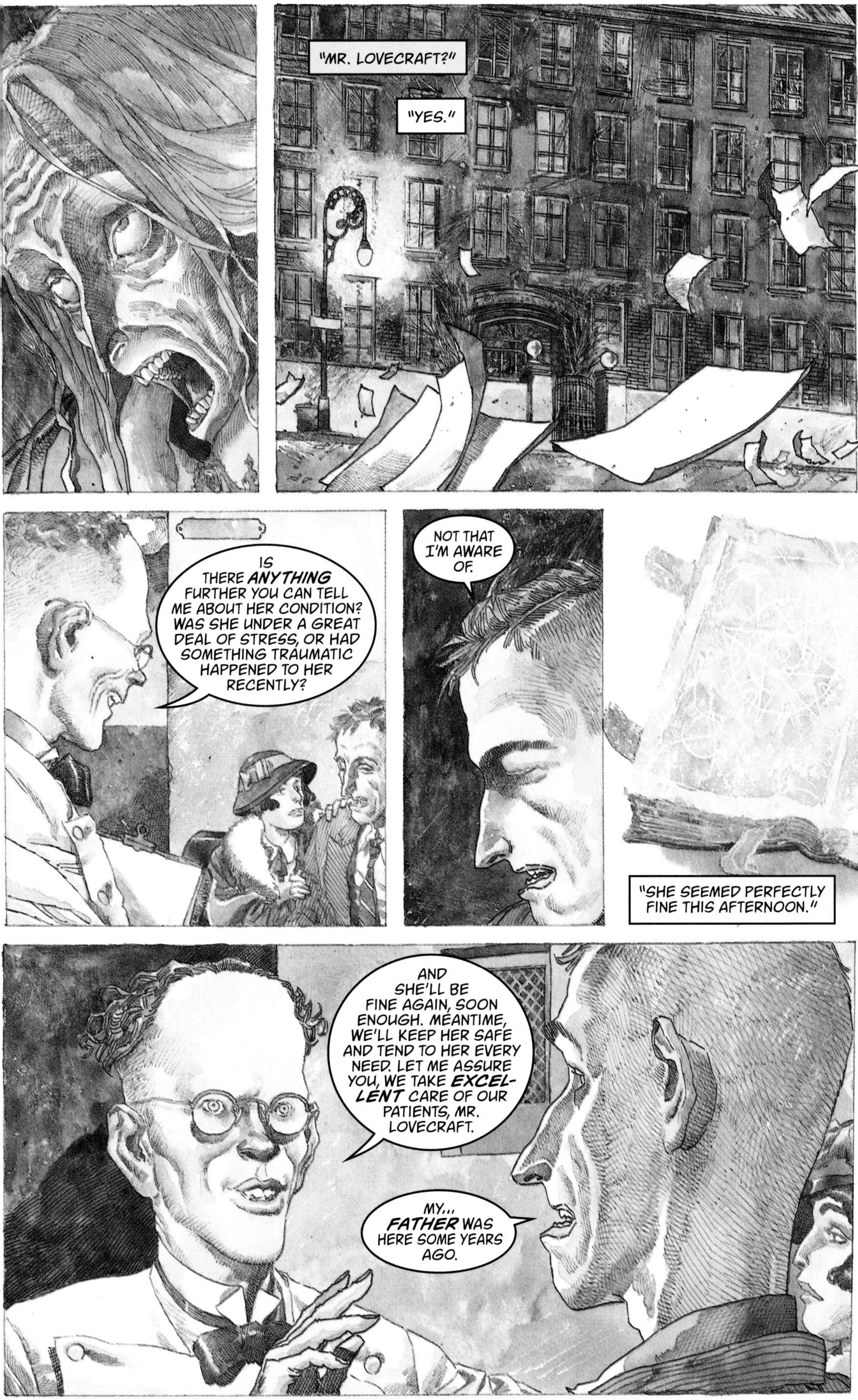
"MR. LOVECRAFT?"
"YES."
IS THERE ANYTHING FURTHER YOU CAN TELL ME ABOUT HER CONDITION? WAS SHE UNDER A GREAT DEAL OF STRESS, OR HAD SOMETHING TRAUMATIC HAPPENED TO HER RECENTLY?
NOT THAT I'M AWARE OF.
"SHE SEEMED PERFECTLY FINE THIS AFTERNOON."
AND SHE'LL BE FINE AGAIN, SOON ENOUGH. MEANTIME, WE'LL KEEP HER SAFE AND TEND TO HER EVERY NEED. LET ME ASSURE YOU, WE TAKE EXCEL-LENT CARE OF OUR PATIENTS, MR. LOVECRAFT.
MY... FATHER WAS HERE SOME YEARS AGO.

AH. WE HAVE ALL OF YOUR INFORMATION ON FILE THEN, I IMAGINE.

YOU SHOULD.

WE'LL KEEP YOU POSTED OF ANY CHANGES.

THANK YOU, DOCTOR.

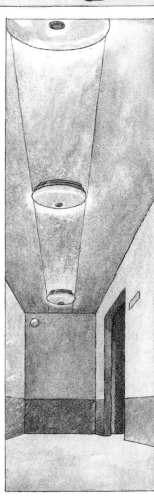

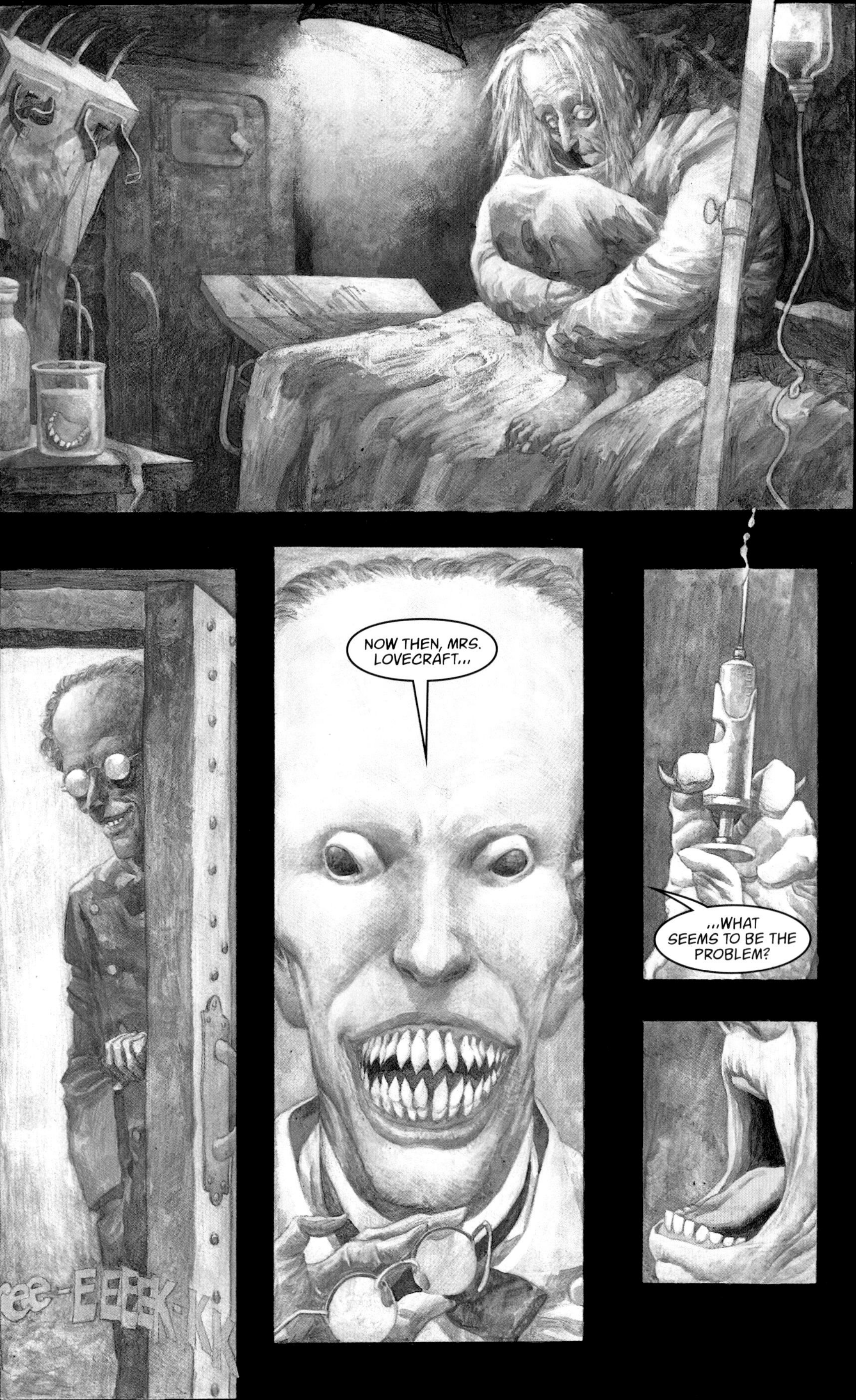
ee-EEEEK-KK
NOW THEN, MRS. LOVECRAFT...
...WHAT SEEMS TO BE THE PROBLEM?

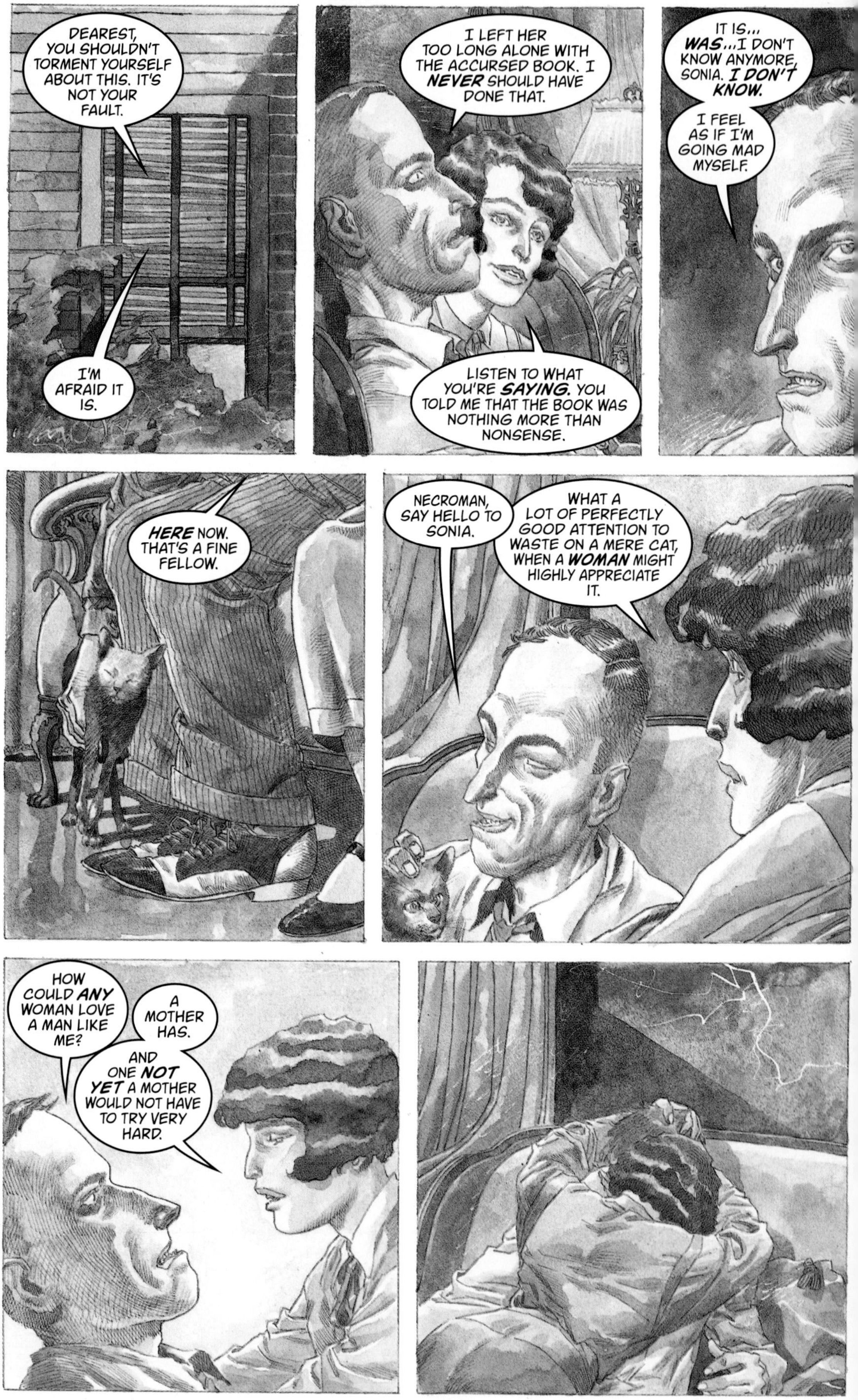
DEAREST, YOU SHOULDN'T TORMENT YOURSELF ABOUT THIS. IT'S NOT YOUR FAULT.
I'M AFRAID IT IS.
I LEFT HER TOO LONG ALONE WITH THE ACCURSED BOOK. I NEVER SHOULD HAVE DONE THAT.
LISTEN TO WHAT YOU'RE SAYING. YOU TOLD ME THAT THE BOOK WAS NOTHING MORE THAN NONSENSE.
IT IS... WAS...I DON'T KNOW ANYMORE, SONIA. I DON'T KNOW.
I FEEL AS IF I'M GOING MAD MYSELF.
HERE NOW. THAT'S A FINE FELLOW.
NECROMAN, SAY HELLO TO SONIA.
WHAT A LOT OF PERFECTLY GOOD ATTENTION TO WASTE ON A MERE CAT, WHEN A WOMAN MIGHT HIGHLY APPRECIATE IT.
HOW COULD ANY WOMAN LOVE A MAN LIKE ME?
A MOTHER HAS.
AND ONE NOT YET A MOTHER WOULD NOT HAVE TO TRY VERY HARD.

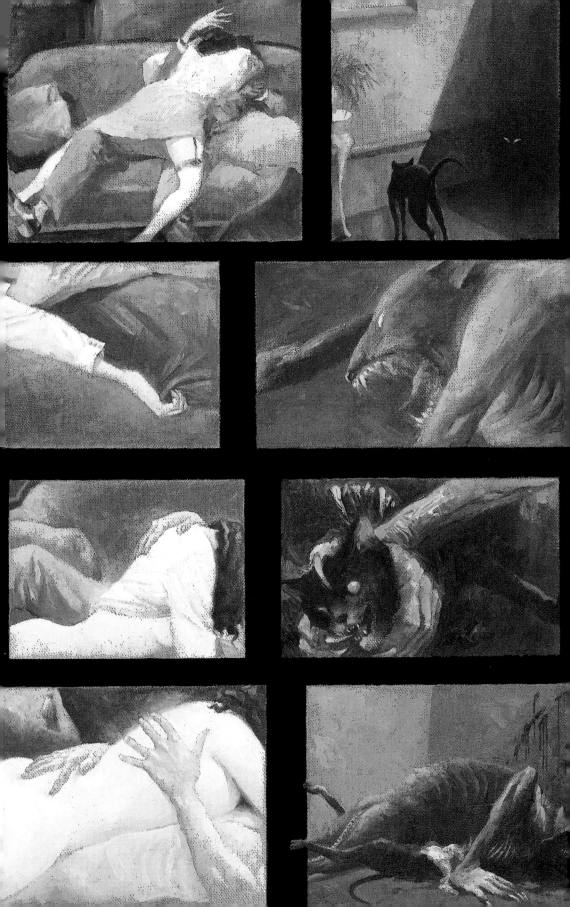

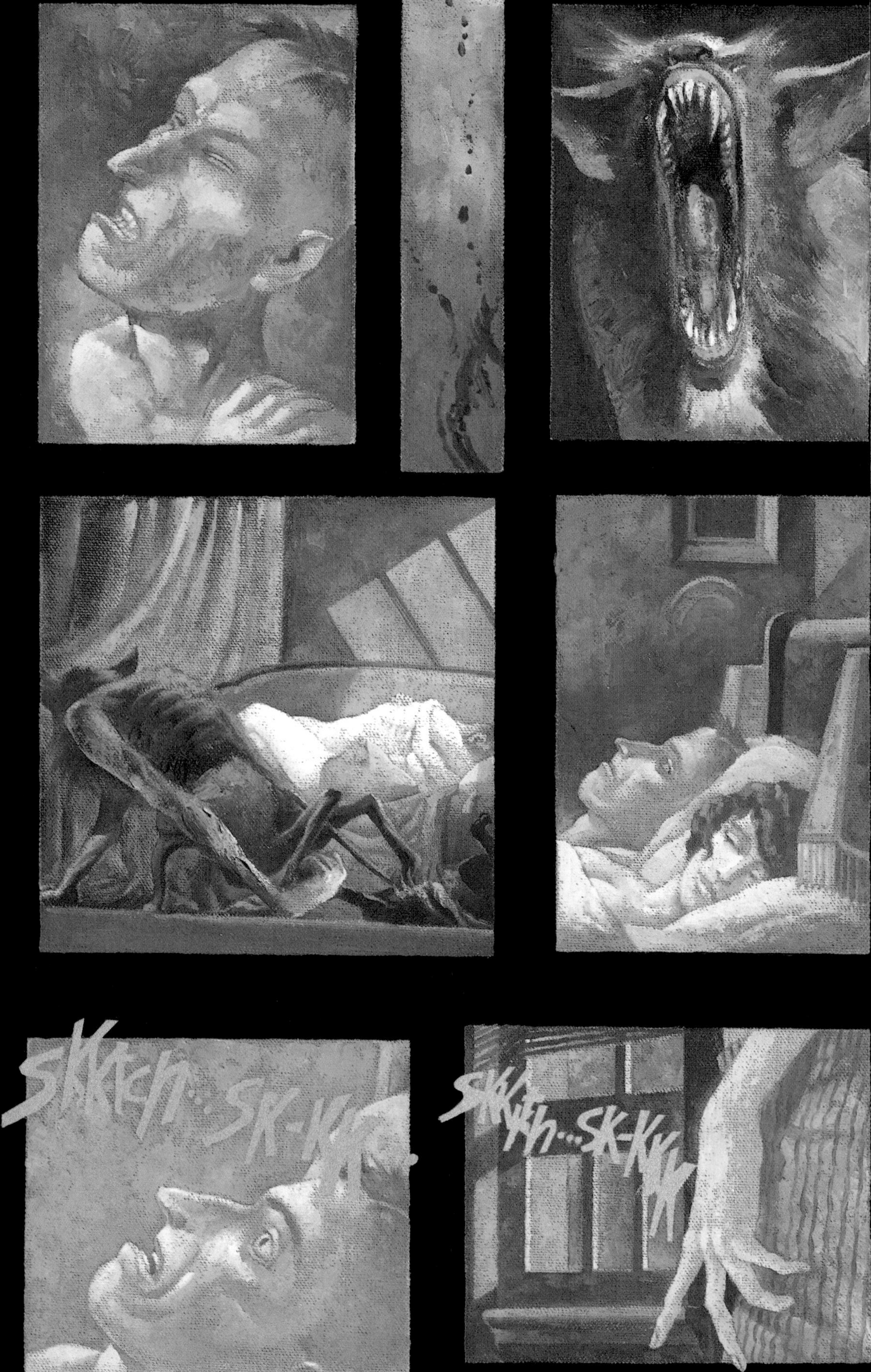
SKKTCH...SK-KKK...
SKKTCH...SK-KKK

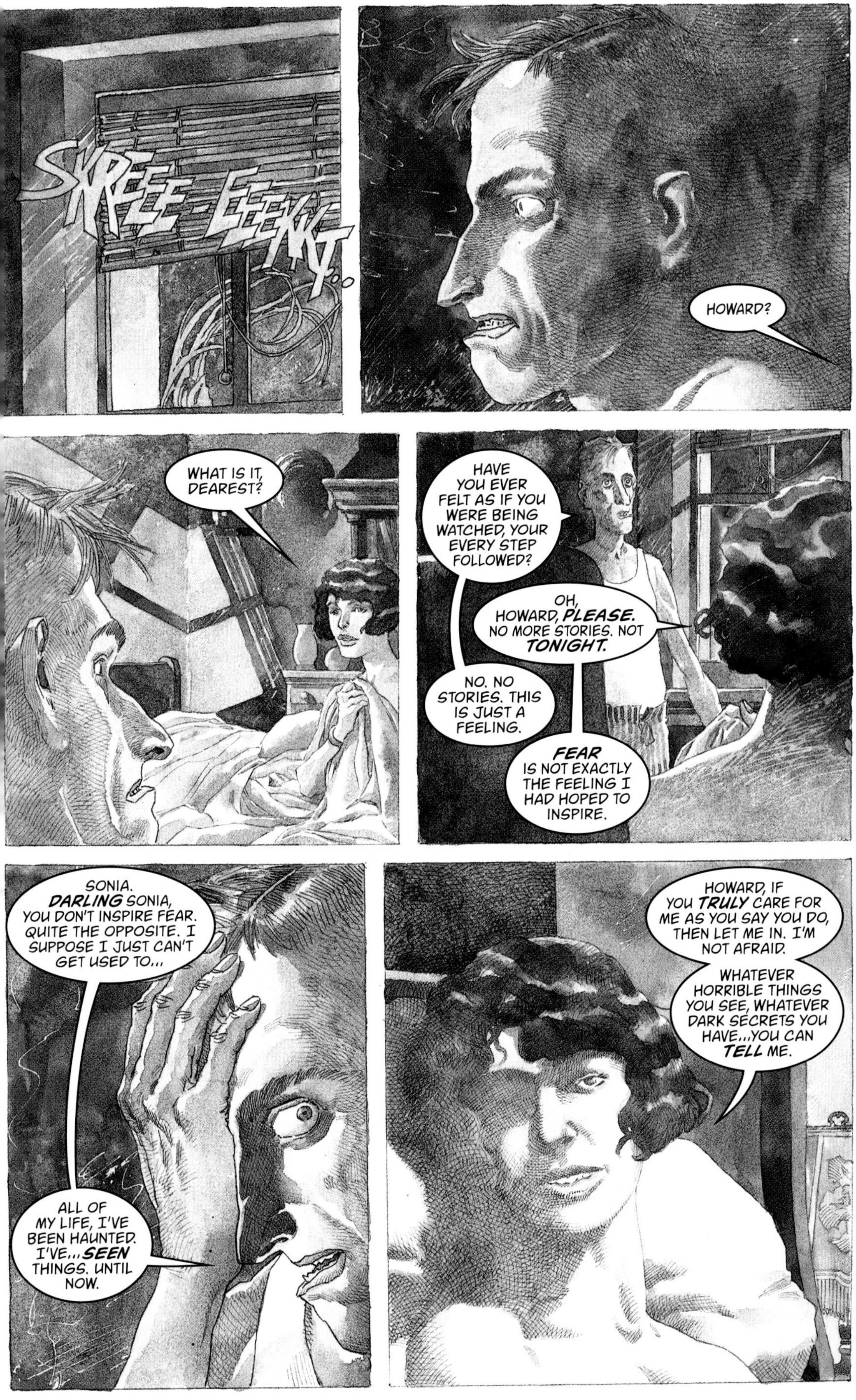
SKREEE-EEEKKT..
HOWARD?
WHAT IS IT, DEAREST?
HAVE YOU EVER FELT AS IF YOU WERE BEING WATCHED, YOUR EVERY STEP FOLLOWED?
OH, HOWARD, PLEASE. NO MORE STORIES. NOT TONIGHT.
NO. NO STORIES. THIS IS JUST A FEELING.
FEAR IS NOT EXACTLY THE FEELING I HAD HOPED TO INSPIRE.
SONIA. DARLING SONIA, YOU DON'T INSPIRE FEAR. QUITE THE OPPOSITE. I SUPPOSE I JUST CAN'T GET USED TO...
ALL OF MY LIFE, I'VE BEEN HAUNTED. I'VE... SEEN THINGS. UNTIL NOW.
HOWARD, IF YOU TRULY CARE FOR ME AS YOU SAY YOU DO, THEN LET ME IN. I'M NOT AFRAID.
WHATEVER HORRIBLE THINGS YOU SEE, WHATEVER DARK SECRETS YOU HAVE... YOU CAN TELL ME.

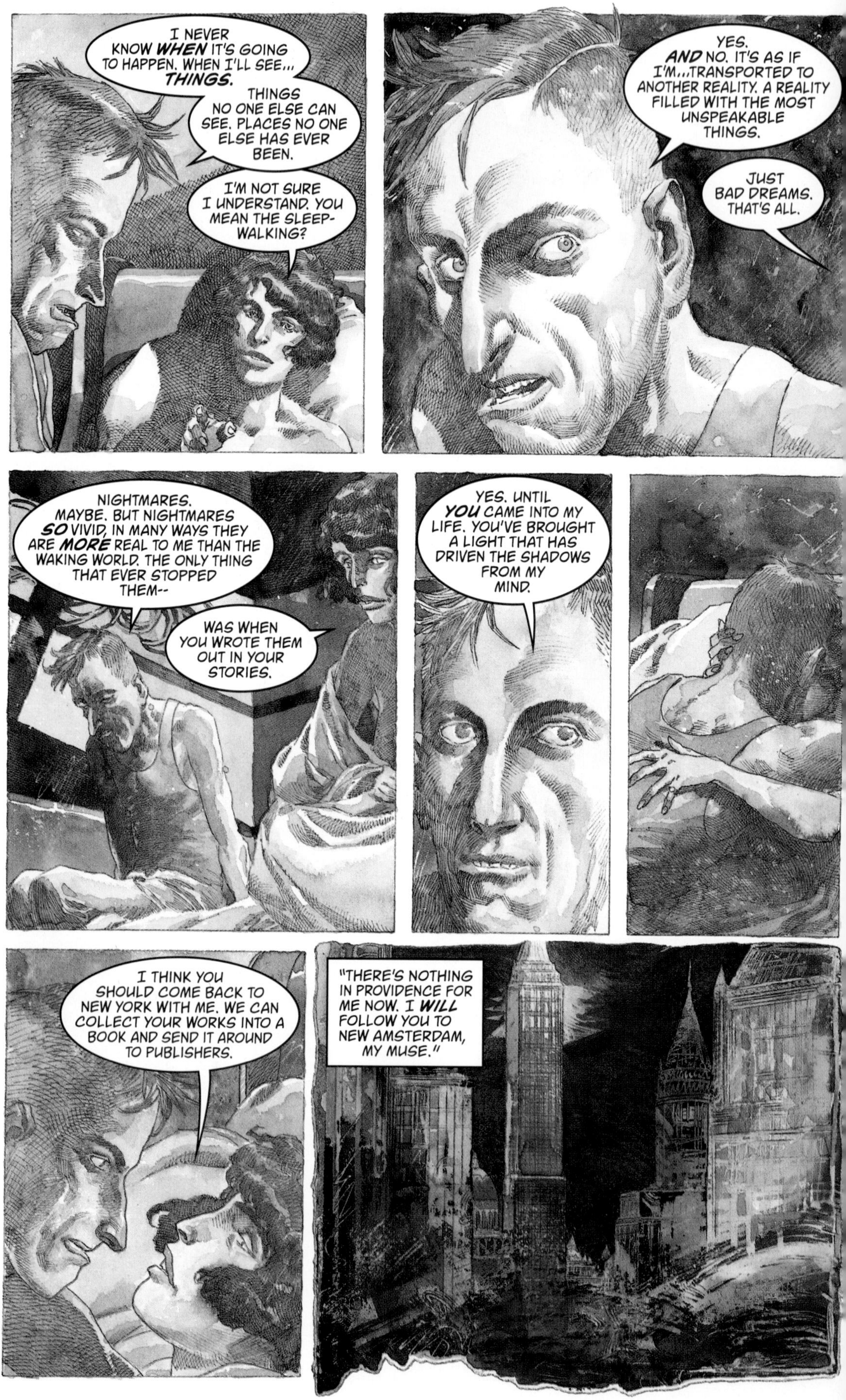
I NEVER KNOW **WHEN** IT'S GOING TO HAPPEN. WHEN I'LL SEE... **THINGS.**
THINGS NO ONE ELSE CAN SEE. PLACES NO ONE ELSE HAS EVER BEEN.
I'M NOT SURE I UNDERSTAND. YOU MEAN THE SLEEP-WALKING?
YES. **AND** NO. IT'S AS IF I'M...TRANSPORTED TO ANOTHER REALITY. A REALITY FILLED WITH THE MOST UNSPEAKABLE THINGS.
JUST BAD DREAMS. THAT'S ALL.
NIGHTMARES. MAYBE. BUT NIGHTMARES **SO** VIVID, IN MANY WAYS THEY ARE **MORE** REAL TO ME THAN THE WAKING WORLD. THE ONLY THING THAT EVER STOPPED THEM--
WAS WHEN YOU WROTE THEM OUT IN YOUR STORIES.
YES. UNTIL **YOU** CAME INTO MY LIFE. YOU'VE BROUGHT A LIGHT THAT HAS DRIVEN THE SHADOWS FROM MY MIND.
I THINK YOU SHOULD COME BACK TO NEW YORK WITH ME. WE CAN COLLECT YOUR WORKS INTO A BOOK AND SEND IT AROUND TO PUBLISHERS.
"THERE'S NOTHING IN PROVIDENCE FOR ME NOW. I **WILL** FOLLOW YOU TO NEW AMSTERDAM, MY MUSE."

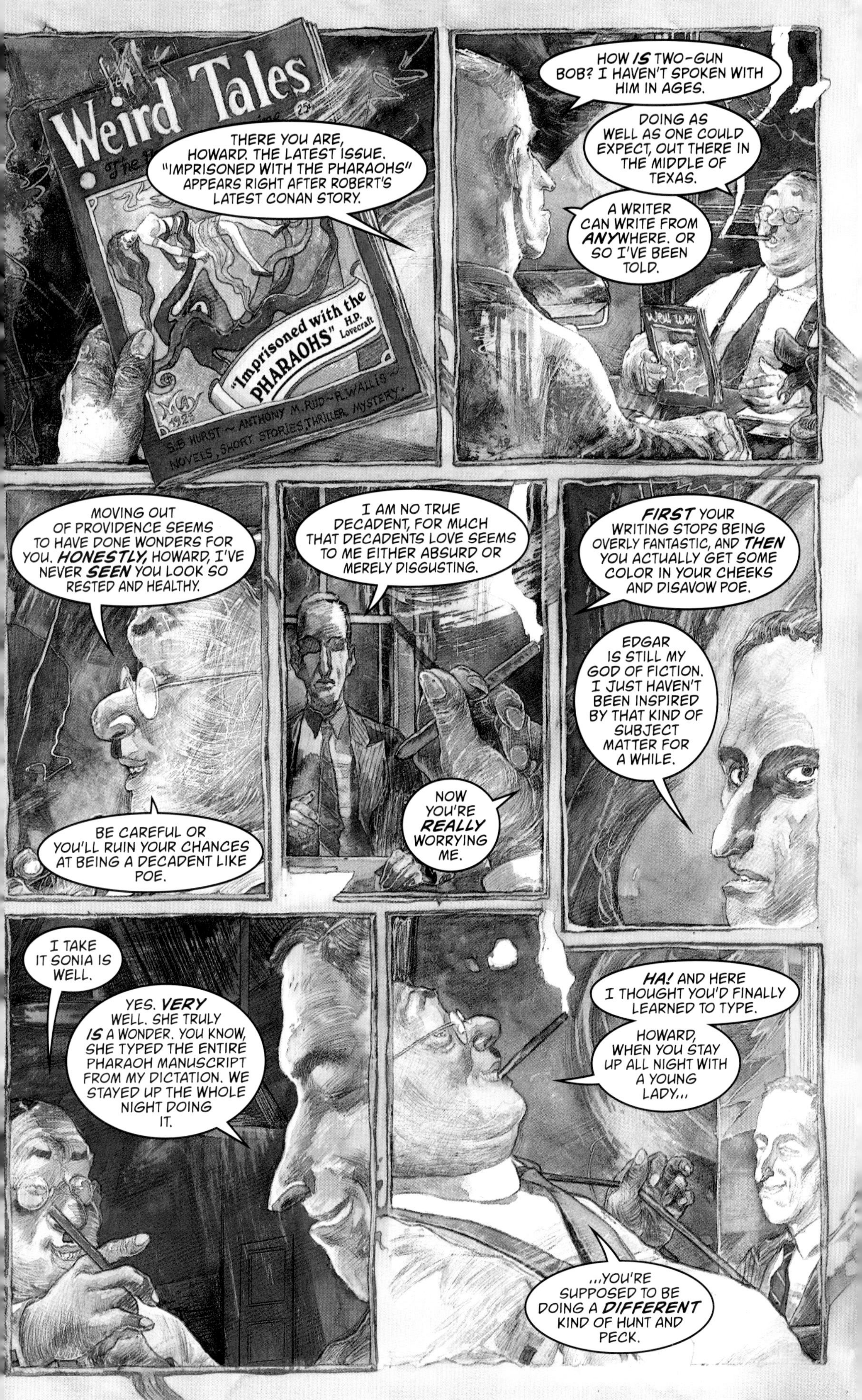

Weird Tales
"Imprisoned with the PHARAOHS" H.P. Lovecraft
S.B. HURST ~ ANTHONY M. RUD ~ R. WALLIS ~
NOVELS, SHORT STORIES, THRILLER, MYSTERY.
THERE YOU ARE, HOWARD. THE LATEST ISSUE. "IMPRISONED WITH THE PHARAOHS" APPEARS RIGHT AFTER ROBERT'S LATEST CONAN STORY.
HOW *IS* TWO-GUN BOB? I HAVEN'T SPOKEN WITH HIM IN AGES.
DOING AS WELL AS ONE COULD EXPECT, OUT THERE IN THE MIDDLE OF TEXAS.
A WRITER CAN WRITE FROM *ANY*WHERE. OR SO I'VE BEEN TOLD.
MOVING OUT OF PROVIDENCE SEEMS TO HAVE DONE WONDERS FOR YOU. *HONESTLY,* HOWARD, I'VE NEVER *SEEN* YOU LOOK SO RESTED AND HEALTHY.
BE CAREFUL OR YOU'LL RUIN YOUR CHANCES AT BEING A DECADENT LIKE POE.
I AM NO TRUE DECADENT, FOR MUCH THAT DECADENTS LOVE SEEMS TO ME EITHER ABSURD OR MERELY DISGUSTING.
NOW YOU'RE *REALLY* WORRYING ME.
FIRST YOUR WRITING STOPS BEING OVERLY FANTASTIC, AND *THEN* YOU ACTUALLY GET SOME COLOR IN YOUR CHEEKS AND DISAVOW POE.
EDGAR IS STILL MY GOD OF FICTION. I JUST HAVEN'T BEEN INSPIRED BY THAT KIND OF SUBJECT MATTER FOR A WHILE.
I TAKE IT SONIA IS WELL.
YES. *VERY* WELL. SHE TRULY *IS* A WONDER. YOU KNOW, SHE TYPED THE ENTIRE PHARAOH MANUSCRIPT FROM MY DICTATION. WE STAYED UP THE WHOLE NIGHT DOING IT.
HA! AND HERE I THOUGHT YOU'D FINALLY LEARNED TO TYPE.
HOWARD, WHEN YOU STAY UP ALL NIGHT WITH A YOUNG LADY...
...YOU'RE SUPPOSED TO BE DOING A *DIFFERENT* KIND OF HUNT AND PECK.

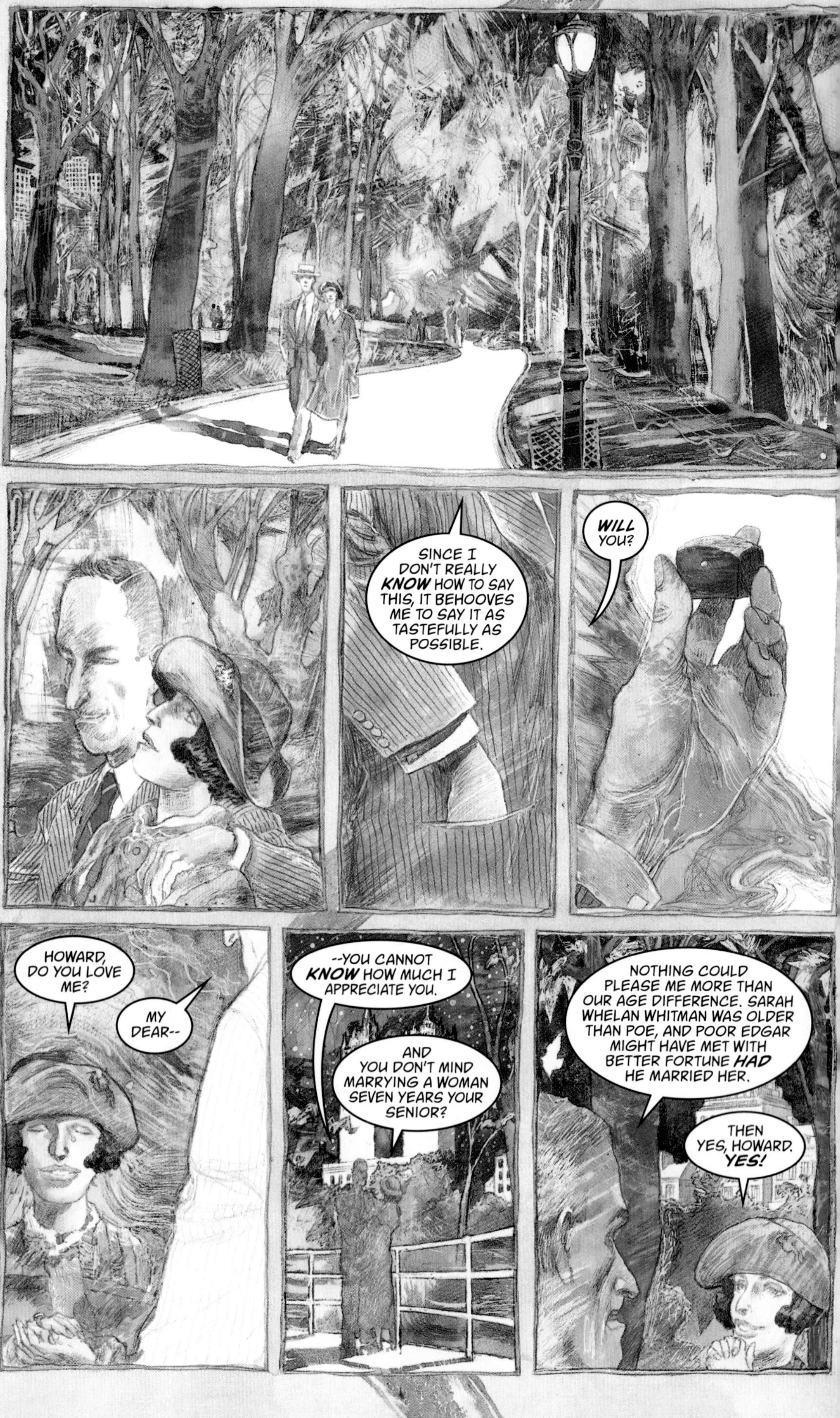
SINCE I DON'T REALLY KNOW HOW TO SAY THIS, IT BEHOOVES ME TO SAY IT AS TASTEFULLY AS POSSIBLE.
WILL YOU?
HOWARD, DO YOU LOVE ME?
MY DEAR--
--YOU CANNOT KNOW HOW MUCH I APPRECIATE YOU.
AND YOU DON'T MIND MARRYING A WOMAN SEVEN YEARS YOUR SENIOR?
NOTHING COULD PLEASE ME MORE THAN OUR AGE DIFFERENCE. SARAH WHELAN WHITMAN WAS OLDER THAN POE, AND POOR EDGAR MIGHT HAVE MET WITH BETTER FORTUNE HAD HE MARRIED HER.
THEN YES, HOWARD. YES!

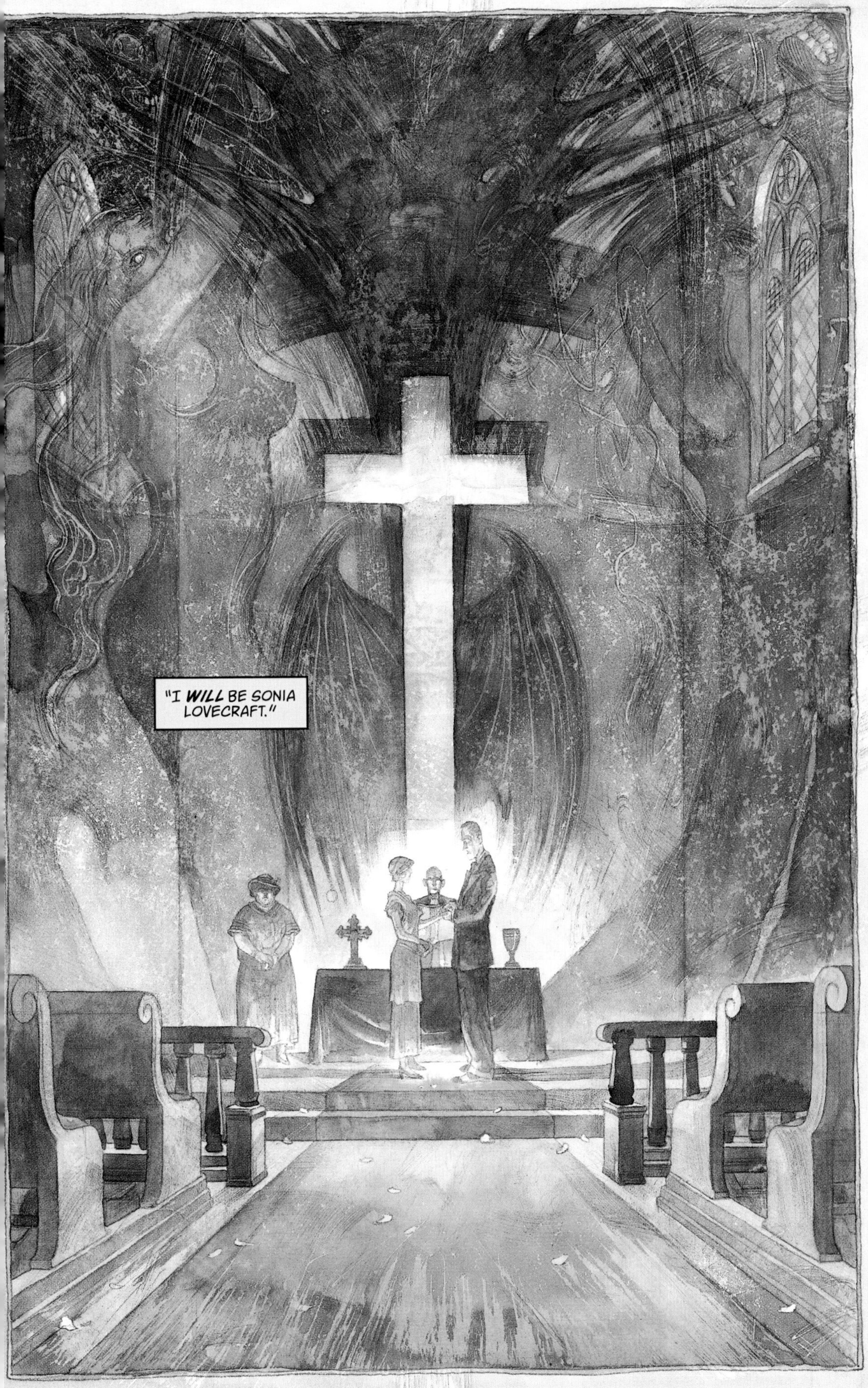
"I **WILL** BE SONIA LOVECRAFT."

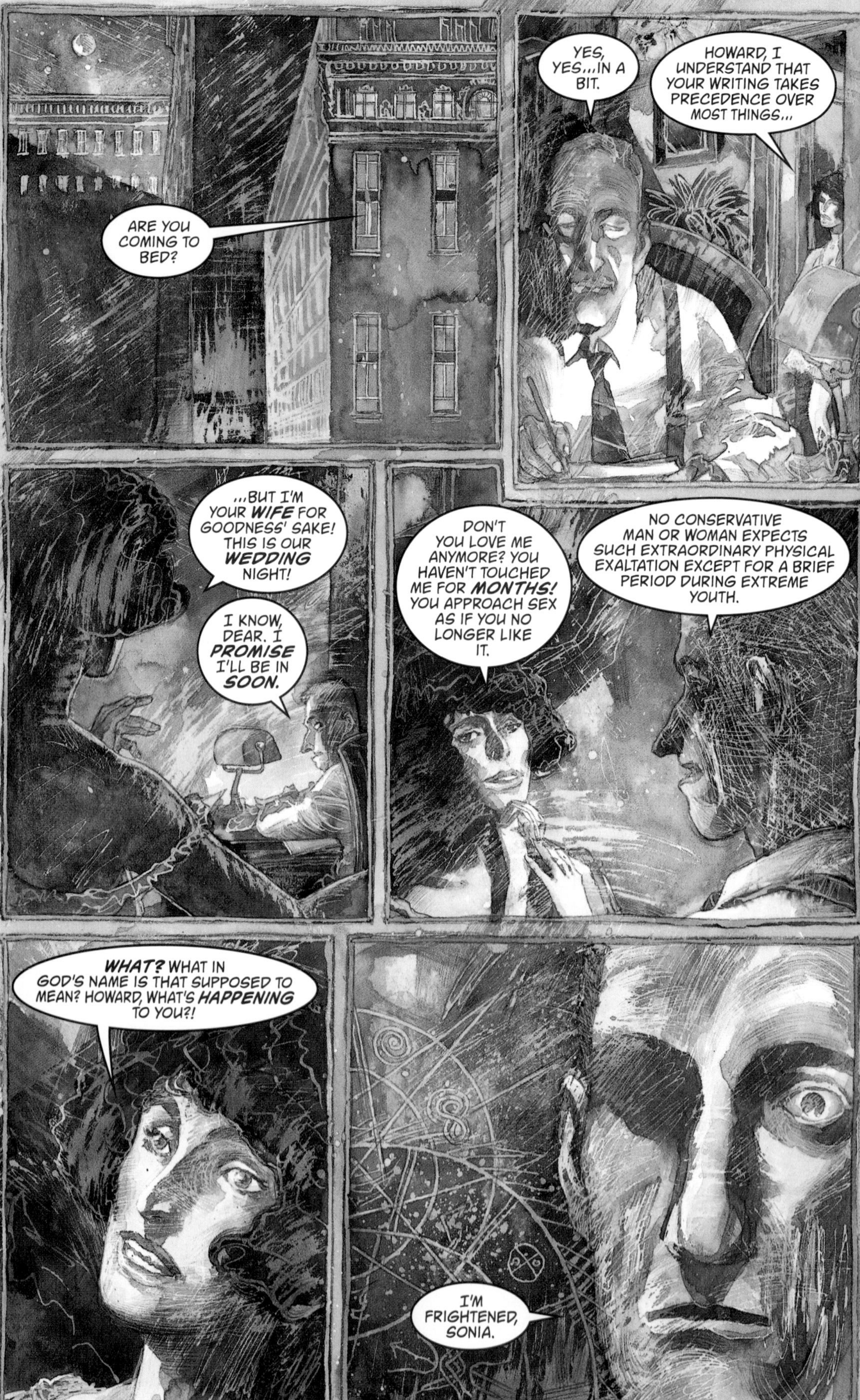

ARE YOU COMING TO BED?
HOWARD, I UNDERSTAND THAT YOUR WRITING TAKES PRECEDENCE OVER MOST THINGS...
YES, YES...IN A BIT.
...BUT I'M YOUR **WIFE** FOR GOODNESS' SAKE! THIS IS OUR **WEDDING** NIGHT!
I KNOW, DEAR. I **PROMISE** I'LL BE IN **SOON.**
DON'T YOU LOVE ME ANYMORE? YOU HAVEN'T TOUCHED ME FOR **MONTHS!** YOU APPROACH SEX AS IF YOU NO LONGER LIKE IT.
NO CONSERVATIVE MAN OR WOMAN EXPECTS SUCH EXTRAORDINARY PHYSICAL EXALTATION EXCEPT FOR A BRIEF PERIOD DURING EXTREME YOUTH.
WHAT? WHAT IN GOD'S NAME IS THAT SUPPOSED TO MEAN? HOWARD, WHAT'S **HAPPENING** TO YOU?!
I'M FRIGHTENED, SONIA.

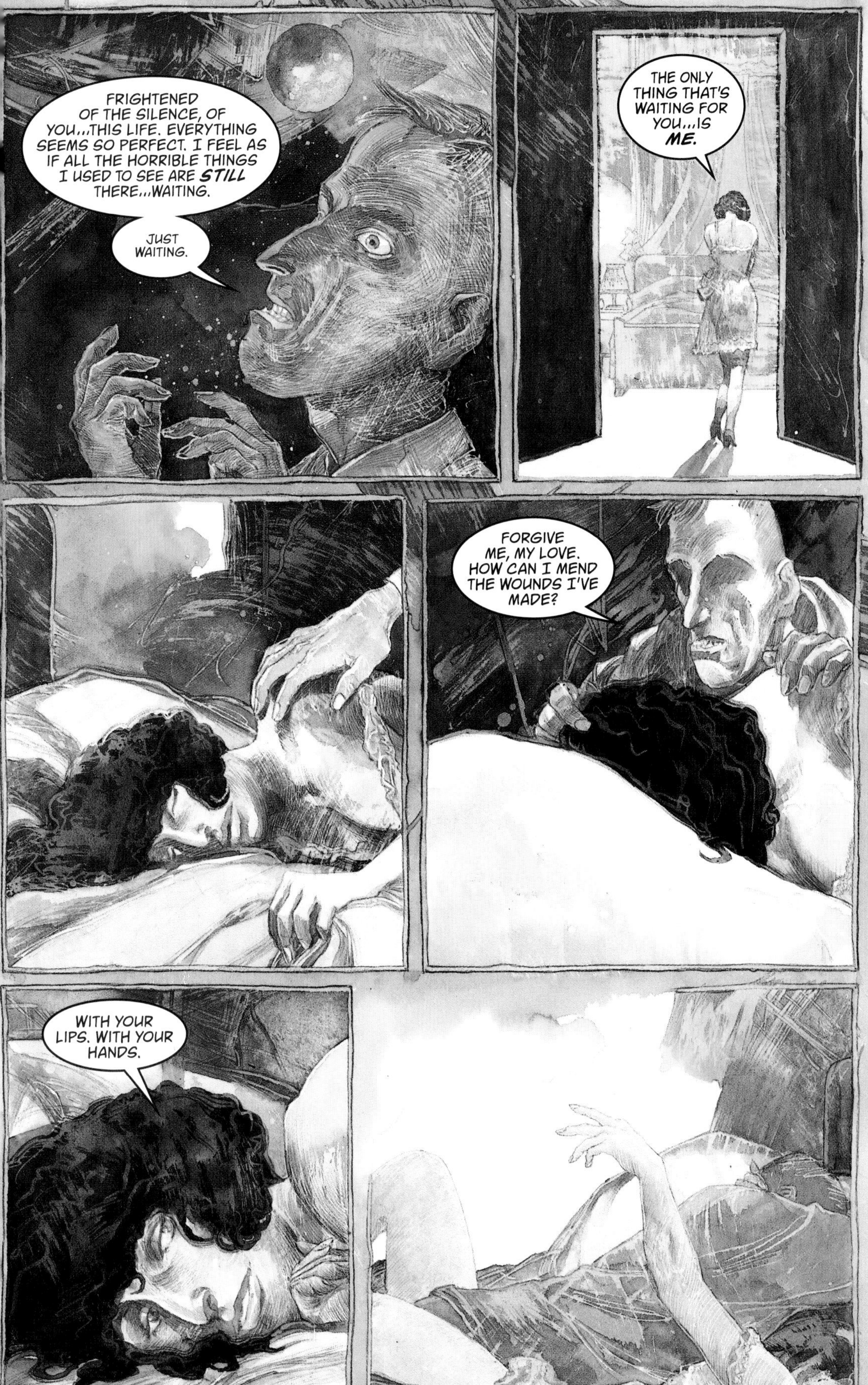
FRIGHTENED OF THE SILENCE, OF YOU...THIS LIFE. EVERYTHING SEEMS SO PERFECT. I FEEL AS IF ALL THE HORRIBLE THINGS I USED TO SEE ARE STILL THERE...WAITING.
JUST WAITING.
THE ONLY THING THAT'S WAITING FOR YOU...IS ME.
FORGIVE ME, MY LOVE. HOW CAN I MEND THE WOUNDS I'VE MADE?
WITH YOUR LIPS. WITH YOUR HANDS.

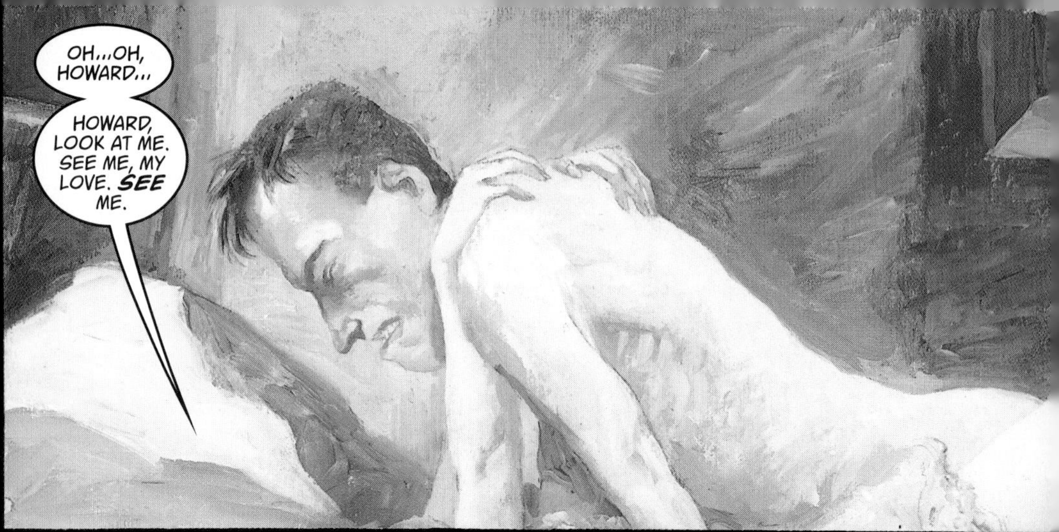
OH...OH, HOWARD...
HOWARD, LOOK AT ME. SEE ME, MY LOVE. *SEE* ME.

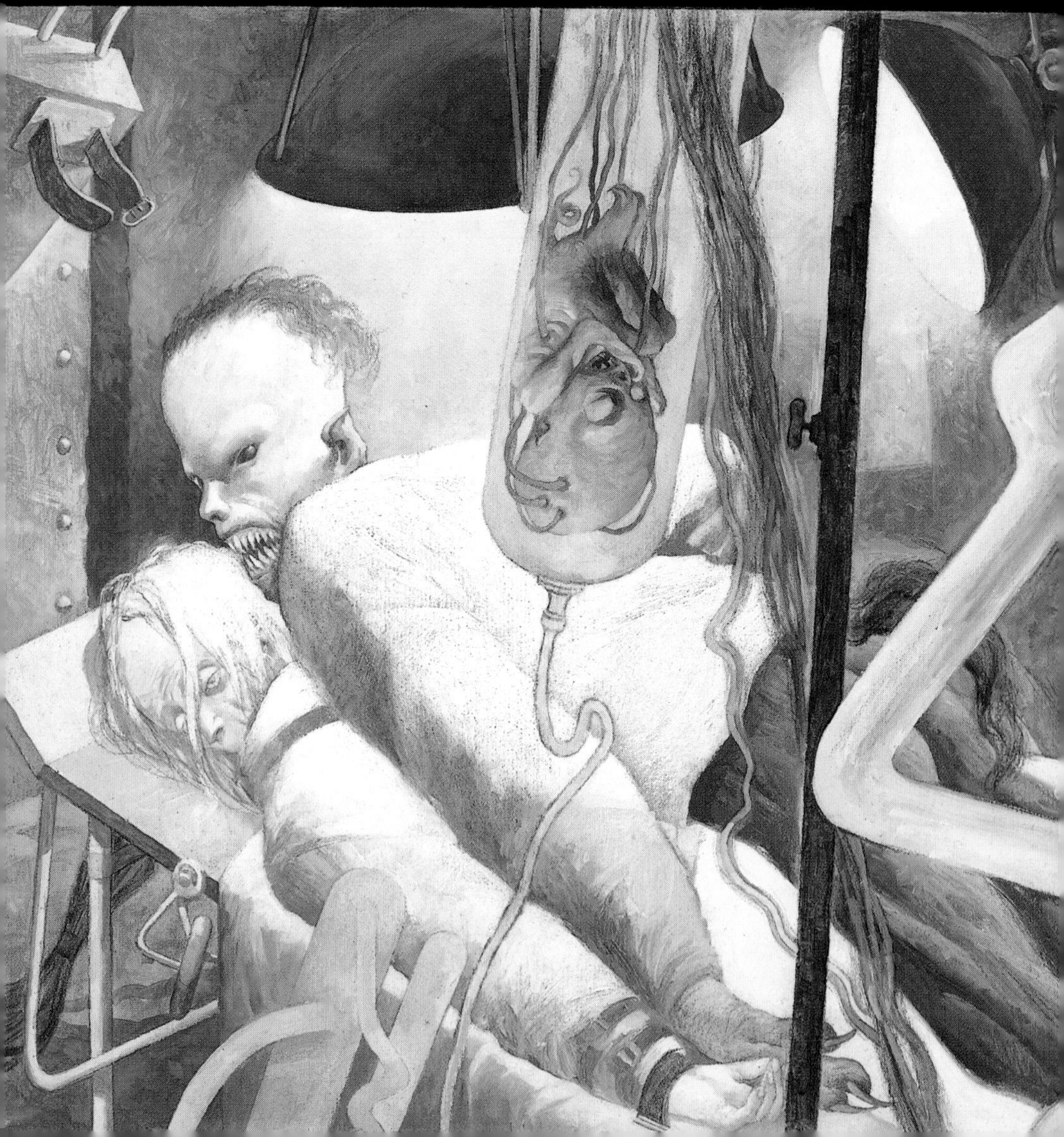

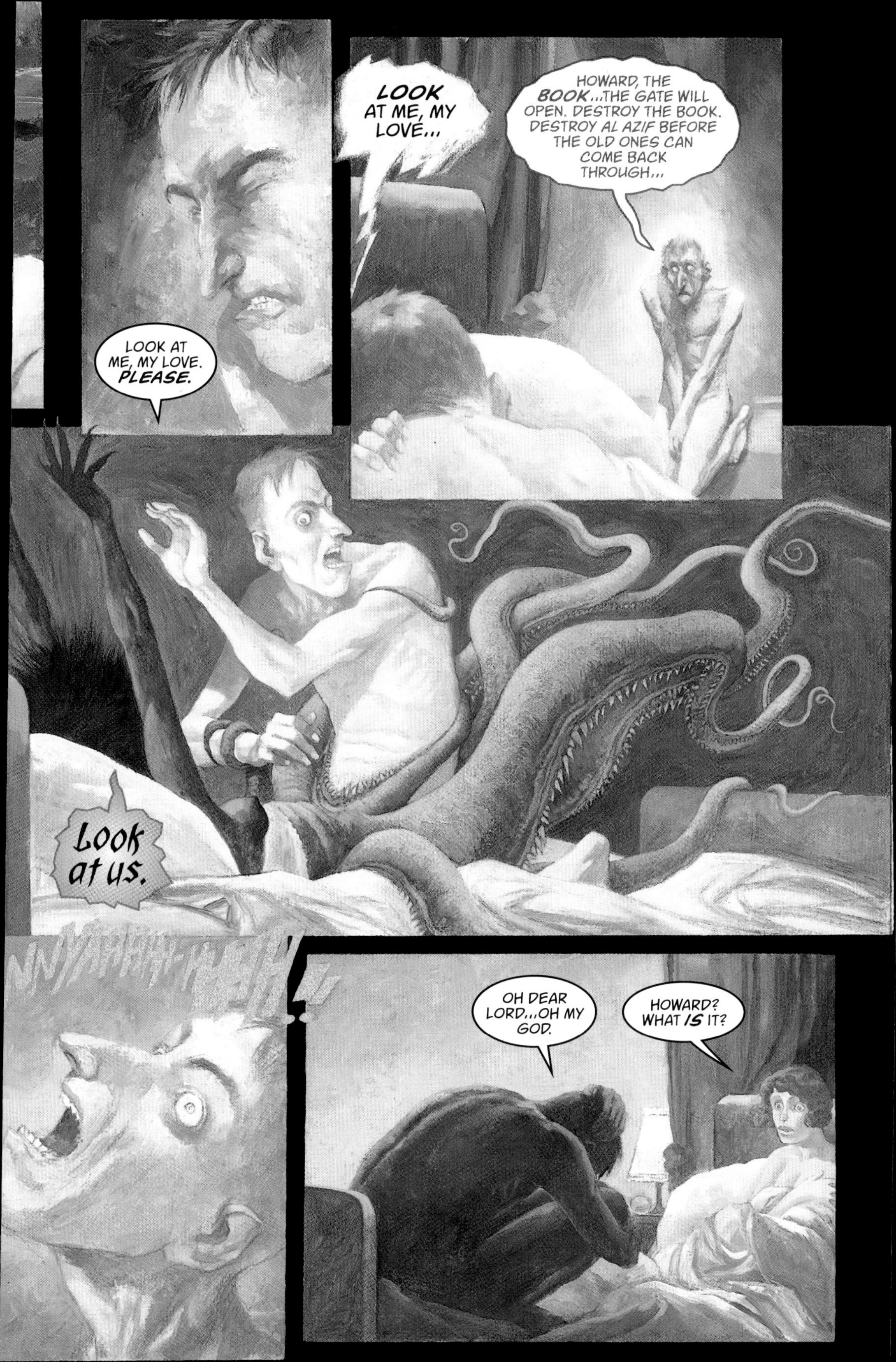
LOOK AT ME, MY LOVE. PLEASE.
LOOK AT ME, MY LOVE...
HOWARD, THE BOOK...THE GATE WILL OPEN. DESTROY THE BOOK. DESTROY AL AZIF BEFORE THE OLD ONES CAN COME BACK THROUGH...
Look at us.
OH DEAR LORD...OH MY GOD.
HOWARD? WHAT IS IT?

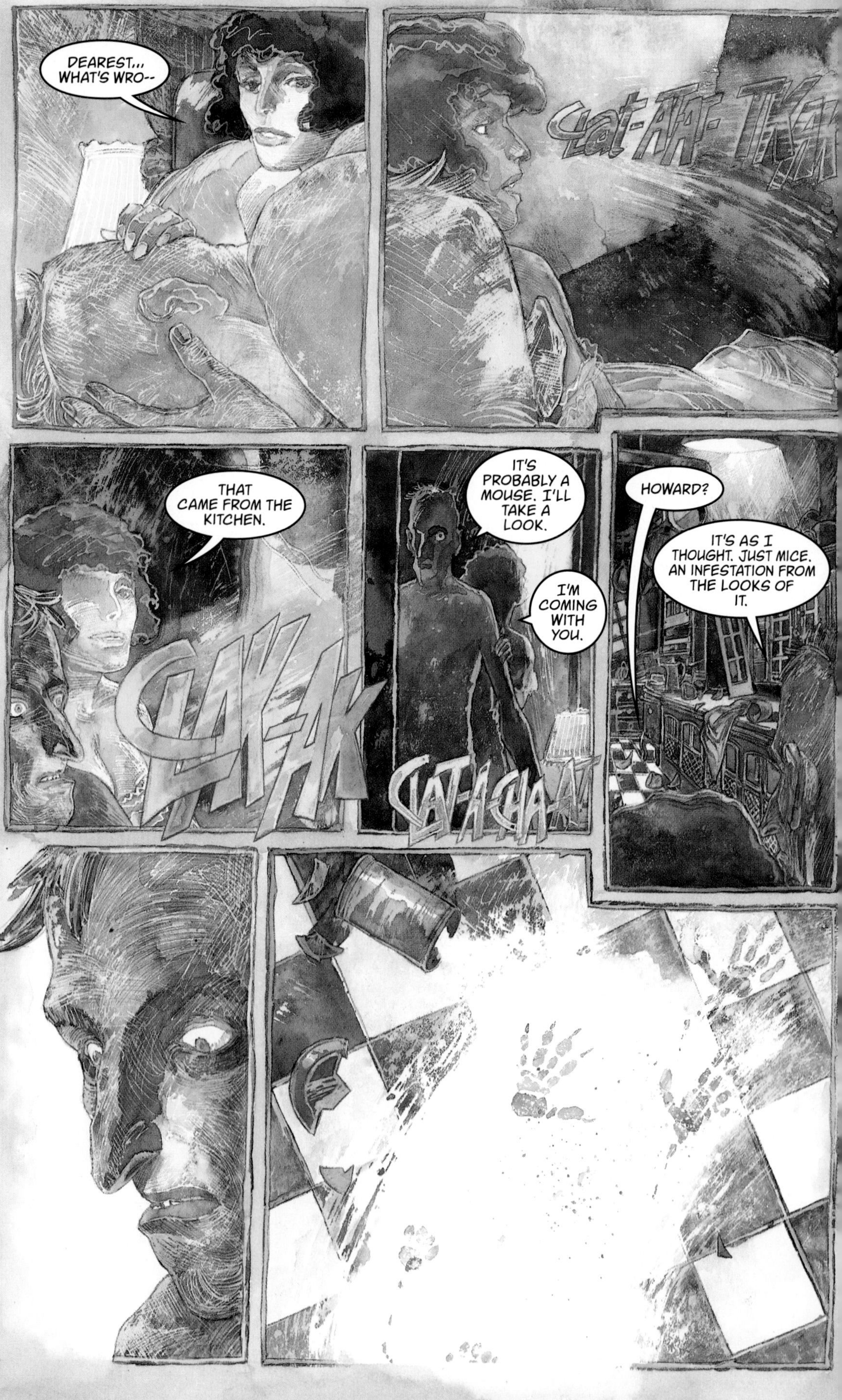
DEAREST... WHAT'S WRO--
CLAT-AAA-TKA
THAT CAME FROM THE KITCHEN.
CLAK-AK
IT'S PROBABLY A MOUSE. I'LL TAKE A LOOK.
I'M COMING WITH YOU.
CLAT-A-CHA-AT
HOWARD?
IT'S AS I THOUGHT. JUST MICE. AN INFESTATION FROM THE LOOKS OF IT.

I'LL... I'LL HAVE THE EXTERMINATOR COME AROUND TOMORROW.

TOMORROW WILL KEEP. *TONIGHT'S* WORK IS SET BEFORE US.

I'M OFF TO THE SHOP, DEAREST. I'VE LEFT SOME MONEY ON THE DRESSER. COME BY AND VISIT IF YOU HAVE THE CHANCE.

YES. YES, I WILL.

ONLY IF YOU GET THE CHANCE AND YOU *WANT* TO TAKE A BREAK FROM YOUR WRITING.

I....*DO* HAVE SOME WRITING TO DO...

THEN LET THAT BE TODAY'S PRIORITY. TA.

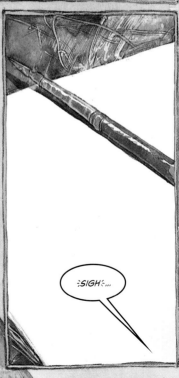

{SIGH}...

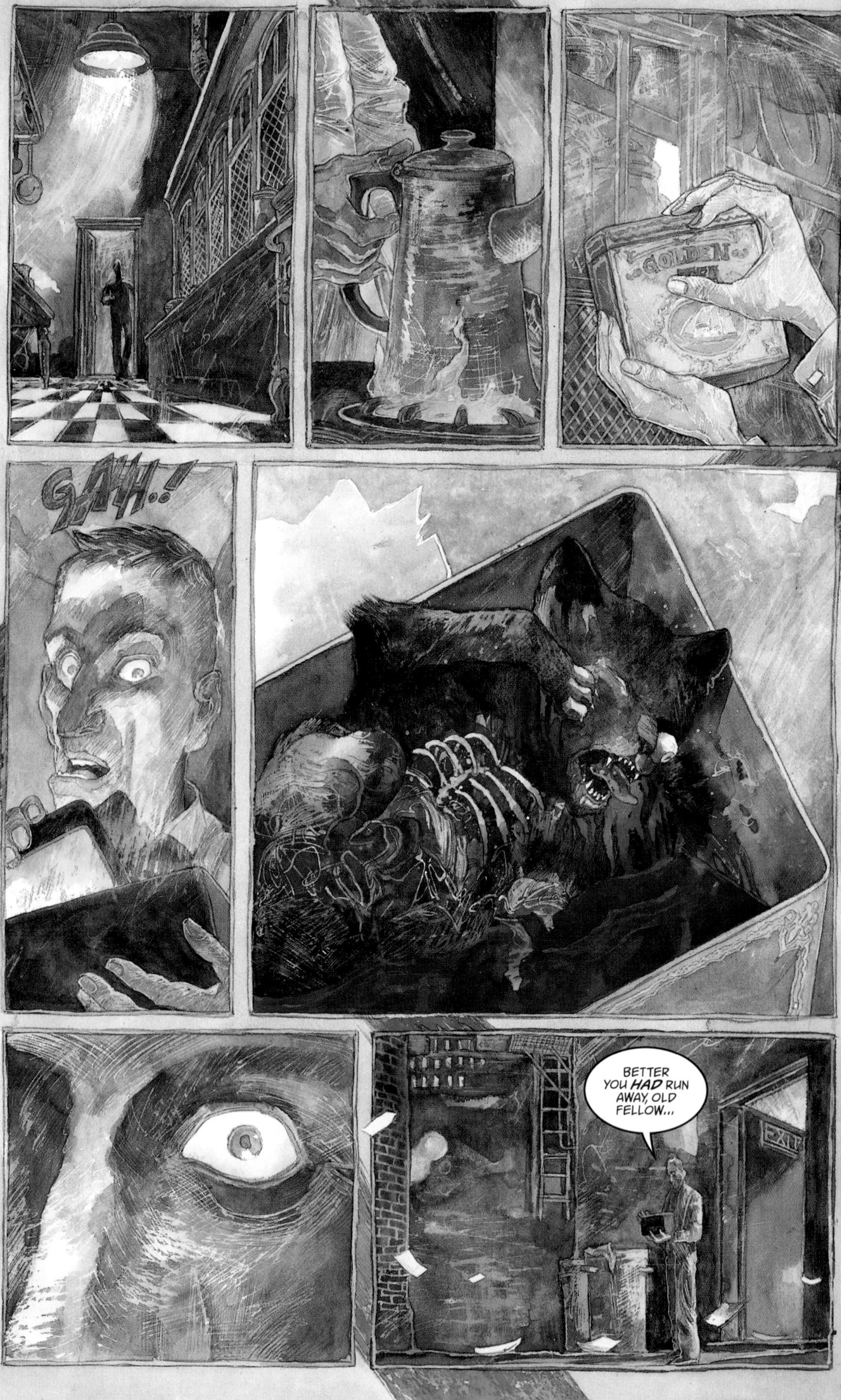
GAAH..!
BETTER YOU HAD RUN AWAY, OLD FELLOW...
EXIT

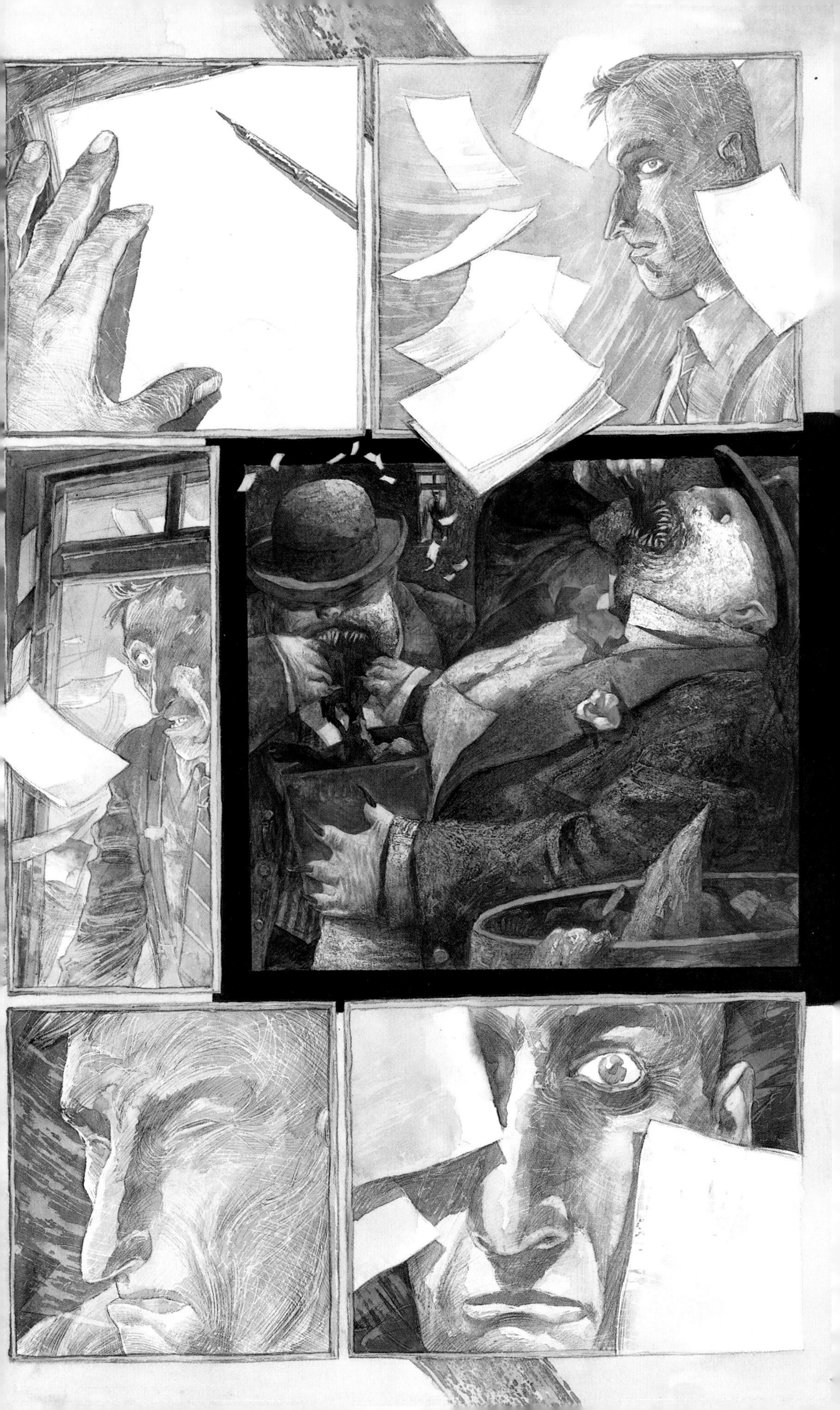

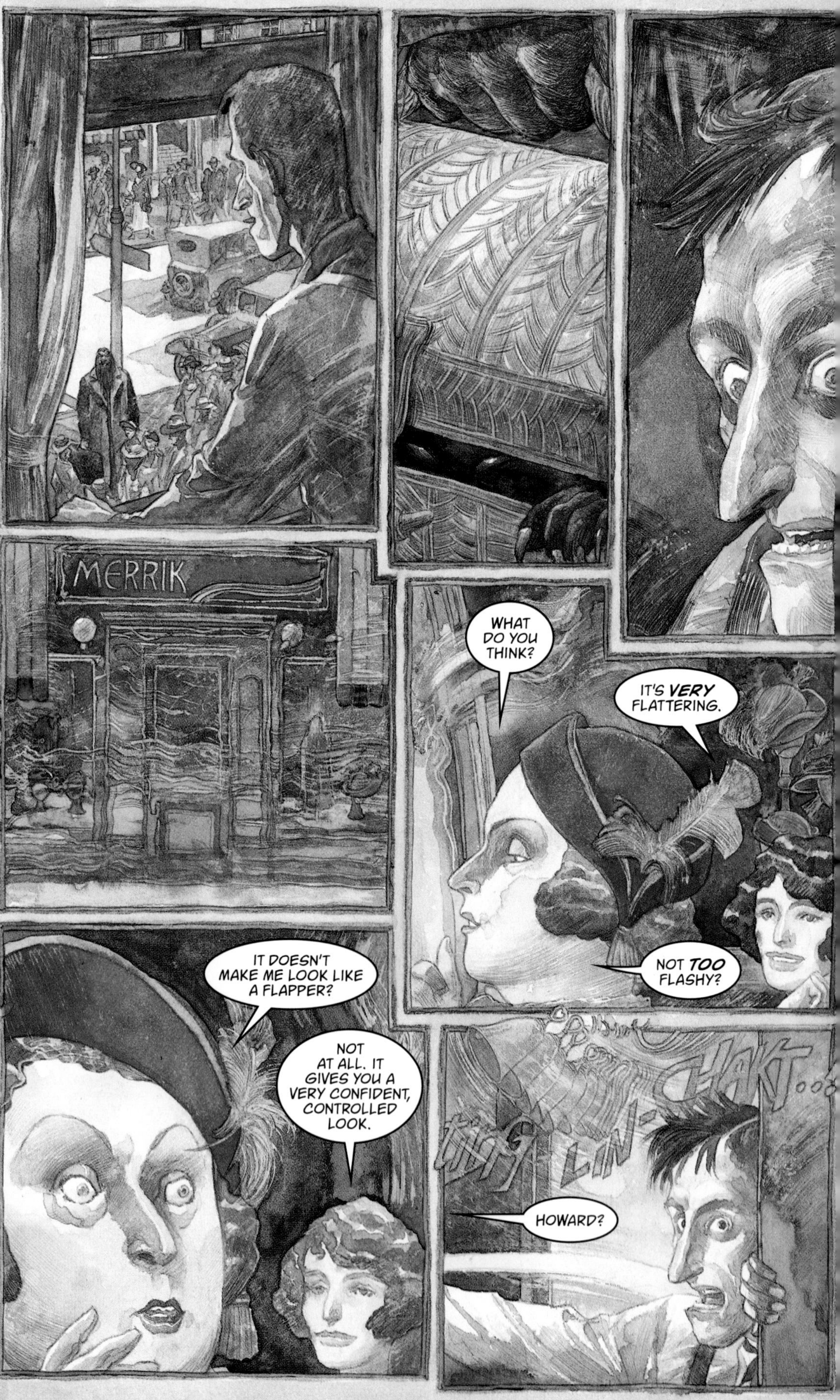
MERRIK
WHAT DO YOU THINK?
IT'S VERY FLATTERING.
NOT TOO FLASHY?
IT DOESN'T MAKE ME LOOK LIKE A FLAPPER?
NOT AT ALL. IT GIVES YOU A VERY CONFIDENT, CONTROLLED LOOK.
LIN-CHAKT...
HOWARD?

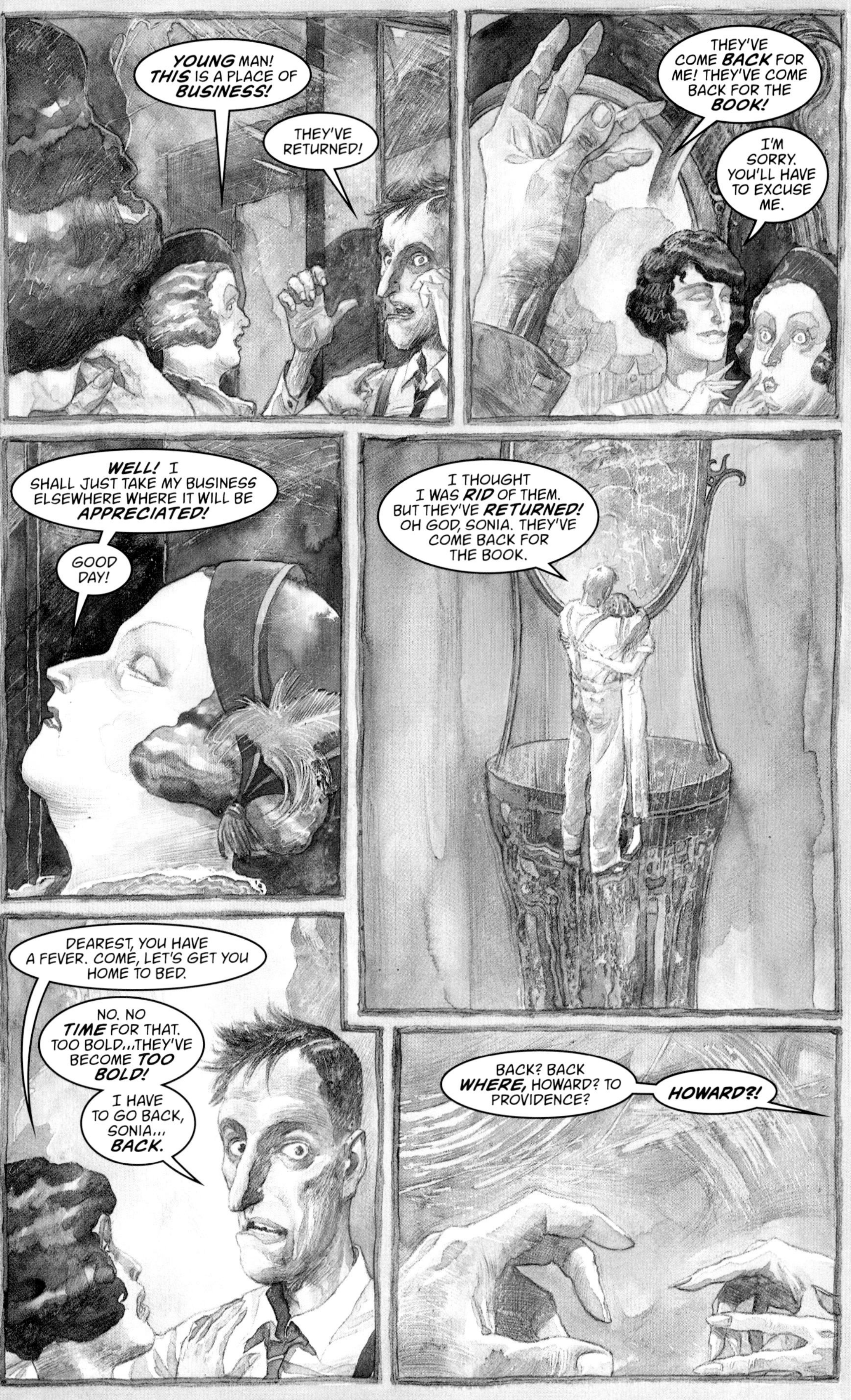
YOUNG MAN! THIS IS A PLACE OF BUSINESS!
THEY'VE RETURNED!
THEY'VE COME BACK FOR ME! THEY'VE COME BACK FOR THE BOOK!
I'M SORRY. YOU'LL HAVE TO EXCUSE ME.
WELL! I SHALL JUST TAKE MY BUSINESS ELSEWHERE WHERE IT WILL BE APPRECIATED!
GOOD DAY!
I THOUGHT I WAS RID OF THEM. BUT THEY'VE RETURNED! OH GOD, SONIA. THEY'VE COME BACK FOR THE BOOK.
DEAREST, YOU HAVE A FEVER. COME, LET'S GET YOU HOME TO BED.
NO. NO TIME FOR THAT. TOO BOLD...THEY'VE BECOME TOO BOLD!
I HAVE TO GO BACK, SONIA... BACK.
BACK? BACK WHERE, HOWARD? TO PROVIDENCE?
HOWARD?!

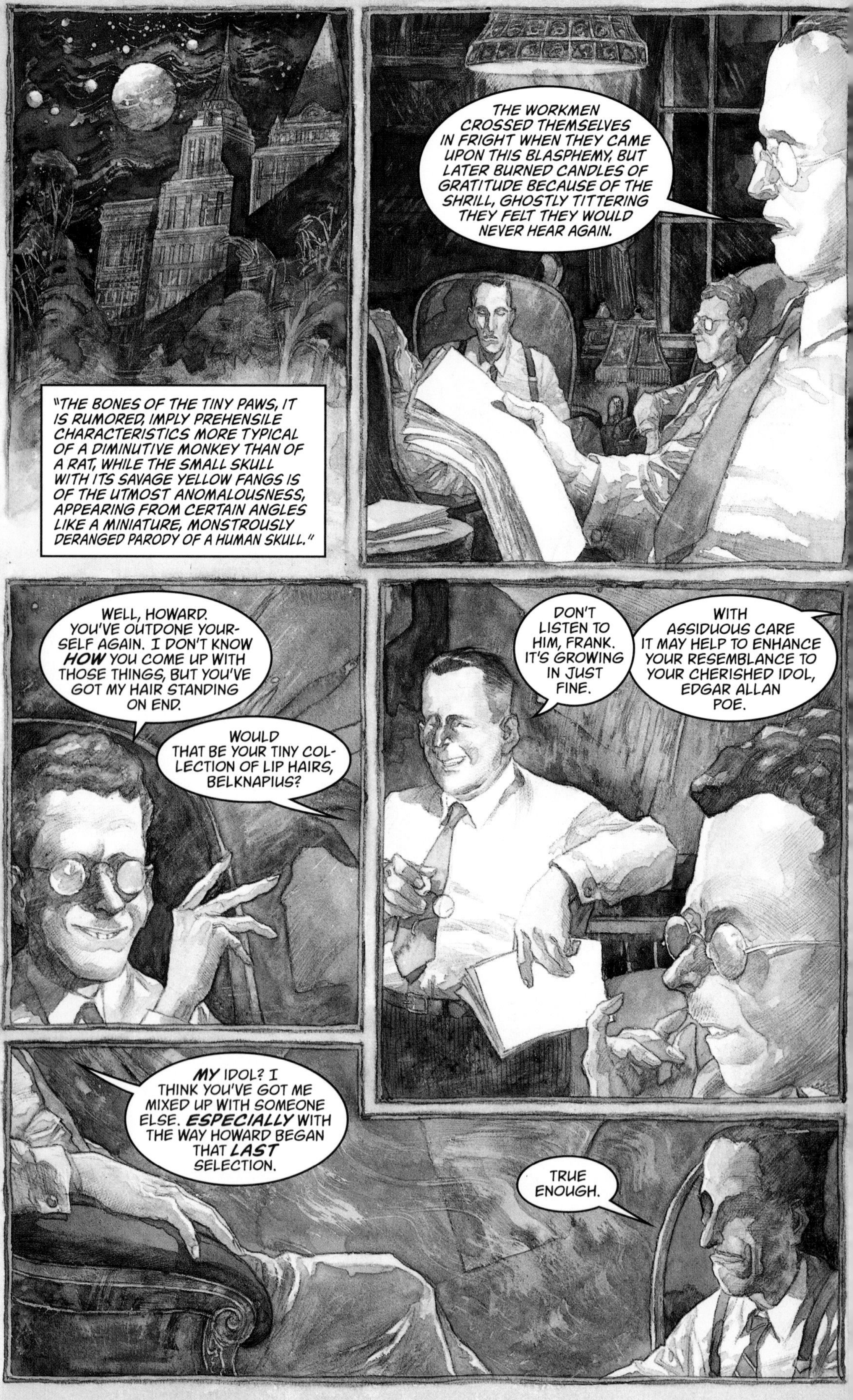
"THE BONES OF THE TINY PAWS, IT IS RUMORED, IMPLY PREHENSILE CHARACTERISTICS MORE TYPICAL OF A DIMINUTIVE MONKEY THAN OF A RAT, WHILE THE SMALL SKULL WITH ITS SAVAGE YELLOW FANGS IS OF THE UTMOST ANOMALOUSNESS, APPEARING FROM CERTAIN ANGLES LIKE A MINIATURE, MONSTROUSLY DERANGED PARODY OF A HUMAN SKULL."
THE WORKMEN CROSSED THEMSELVES IN FRIGHT WHEN THEY CAME UPON THIS BLASPHEMY, BUT LATER BURNED CANDLES OF GRATITUDE BECAUSE OF THE SHRILL, GHOSTLY TITTERING THEY FELT THEY WOULD NEVER HEAR AGAIN.
WELL, HOWARD. YOU'VE OUTDONE YOURSELF AGAIN. I DON'T KNOW **HOW** YOU COME UP WITH THOSE THINGS, BUT YOU'VE GOT MY HAIR STANDING ON END.
WOULD THAT BE YOUR TINY COLLECTION OF LIP HAIRS, BELKNAPIUS?
DON'T LISTEN TO HIM, FRANK. IT'S GROWING IN JUST FINE.
WITH ASSIDUOUS CARE IT MAY HELP TO ENHANCE YOUR RESEMBLANCE TO YOUR CHERISHED IDOL, EDGAR ALLAN POE.
MY IDOL? I THINK YOU'VE GOT ME MIXED UP WITH SOMEONE ELSE. **ESPECIALLY** WITH THE WAY HOWARD BEGAN THAT **LAST** SELECTION.
TRUE ENOUGH.

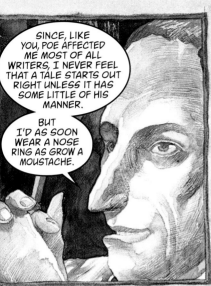

SINCE, LIKE YOU, POE AFFECTED ME MOST OF ALL WRITERS, I NEVER FEEL THAT A TALE STARTS OUT RIGHT UNLESS IT HAS SOME LITTLE OF HIS MANNER.

BUT I'D AS SOON WEAR A NOSE RING AS GROW A MOUSTACHE.

YOU MIGHT LOOK *GOOD* WITH A NOSE RING.

WELL, THE TALE DID ITS JOB. IF FEAR WAS YOUR INTENDED RESPONSE, IT WORKED.

THE *INTENDED* RESPONSE...IS CAUTION, MY FRIENDS. I INTEND THESE STORIES TO BE A WARNING.

AGAINST WHAT? SMALL RAT CREATURES WITH HUMAN FACES?

A WARNING OF WHAT IS TO COME...SHOULD I FAIL.

HOWARD, WE ALL ENJOY YOUR FLAIR FOR THE DRAMATIC, BUT *WHAT* IN HEAVEN'S NAME ARE YOU *TALKING* ABOUT?

I AM GOING AWAY. I DON'T KNOW WHEN I'LL RETURN, IF EVER.

WHAT DO YOU MEAN, GOING AWAY? GOING AWAY TO *WHERE?*

ARKHAM.

ARKHAM?! YOU MEAN YOUR FICTIONAL TOWN? AND WHAT WILL YOU BE DOING THERE, HOWIE, STUDYING THE *NECRONOMICON* AT GOOD OLD MISKATONIC UNIVERSITY?

WHAT DOES SONIA SAY ABOUT THIS?

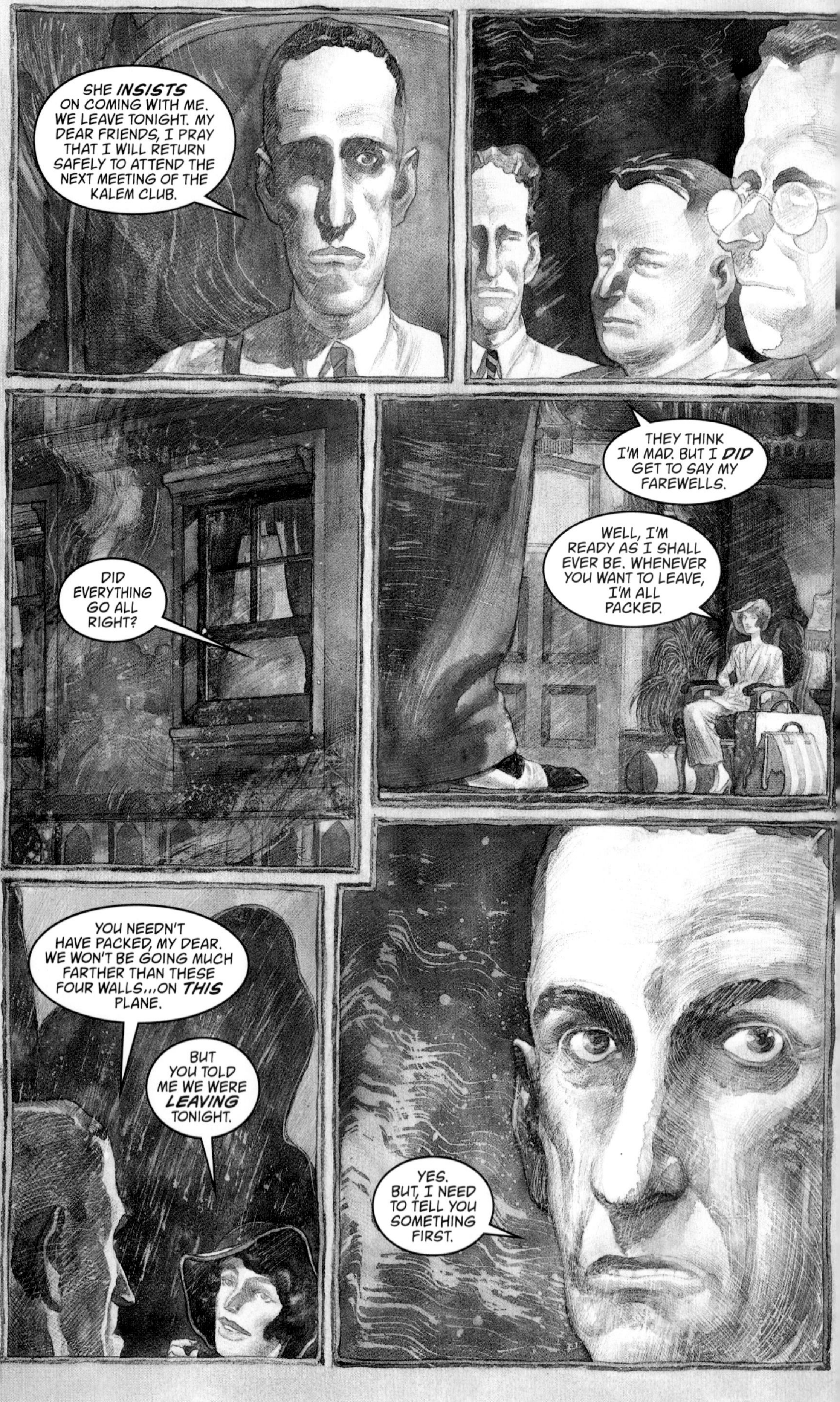
SHE *INSISTS* ON COMING WITH ME. WE LEAVE TONIGHT. MY DEAR FRIENDS, I PRAY THAT I WILL RETURN SAFELY TO ATTEND THE NEXT MEETING OF THE KALEM CLUB.
DID EVERYTHING GO ALL RIGHT?
THEY THINK I'M MAD. BUT I *DID* GET TO SAY MY FAREWELLS.
WELL, I'M READY AS I SHALL EVER BE. WHENEVER YOU WANT TO LEAVE, I'M ALL PACKED.
YOU NEEDN'T HAVE PACKED, MY DEAR. WE WON'T BE GOING MUCH FARTHER THAN THESE FOUR WALLS...ON *THIS* PLANE.
BUT YOU TOLD ME WE WERE *LEAVING* TONIGHT.
YES. BUT, I NEED TO TELL YOU SOMETHING FIRST.

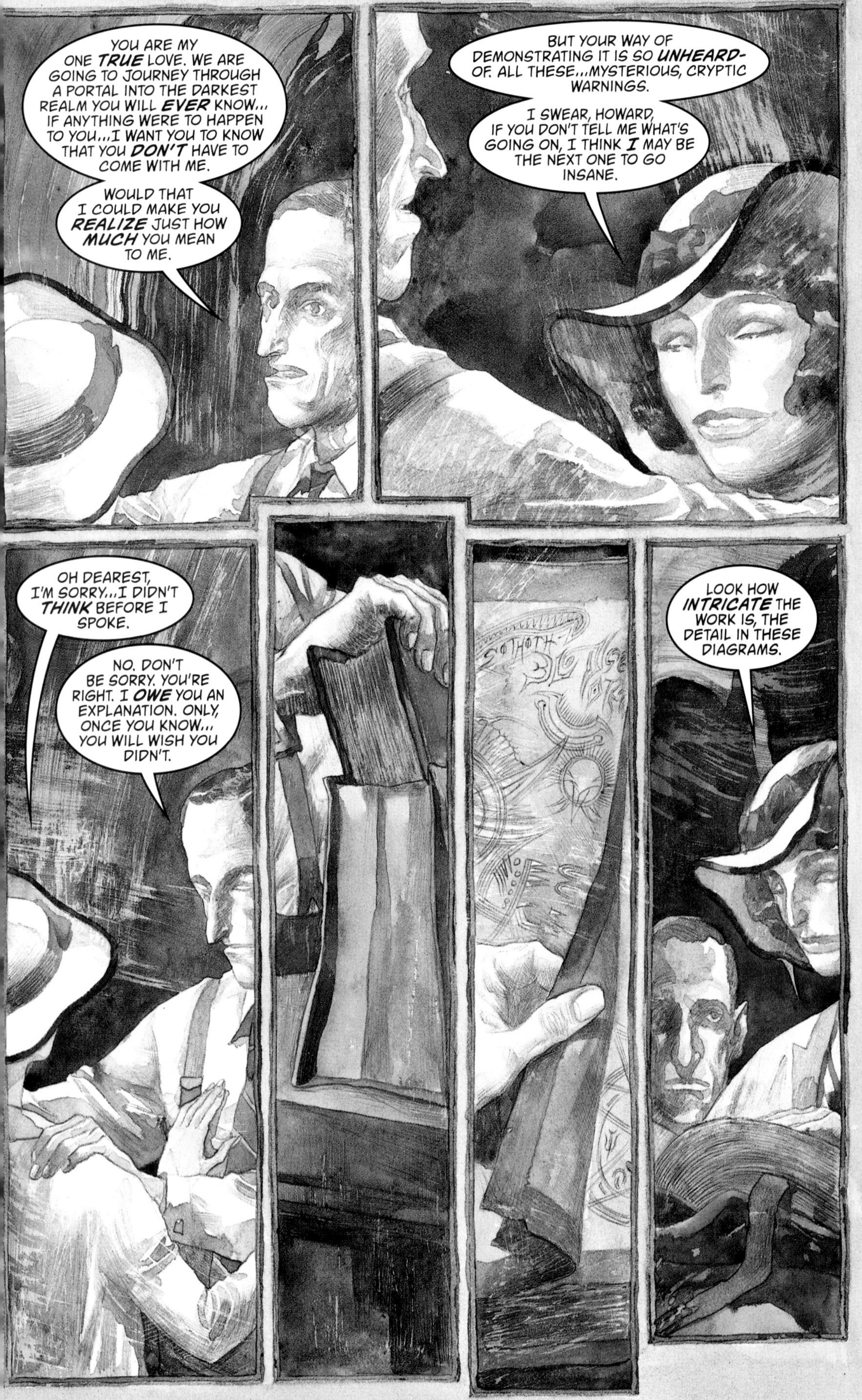
YOU ARE MY ONE TRUE LOVE. WE ARE GOING TO JOURNEY THROUGH A PORTAL INTO THE DARKEST REALM YOU WILL EVER KNOW... IF ANYTHING WERE TO HAPPEN TO YOU...I WANT YOU TO KNOW THAT YOU DON'T HAVE TO COME WITH ME.
WOULD THAT I COULD MAKE YOU REALIZE JUST HOW MUCH YOU MEAN TO ME.
BUT YOUR WAY OF DEMONSTRATING IT IS SO UNHEARD-OF. ALL THESE...MYSTERIOUS, CRYPTIC WARNINGS.
I SWEAR, HOWARD, IF YOU DON'T TELL ME WHAT'S GOING ON, I THINK I MAY BE THE NEXT ONE TO GO INSANE.
OH DEAREST, I'M SORRY...I DIDN'T THINK BEFORE I SPOKE.
NO. DON'T BE SORRY. YOU'RE RIGHT. I OWE YOU AN EXPLANATION. ONLY, ONCE YOU KNOW... YOU WILL WISH YOU DIDN'T.
LOOK HOW INTRICATE THE WORK IS, THE DETAIL IN THESE DIAGRAMS.

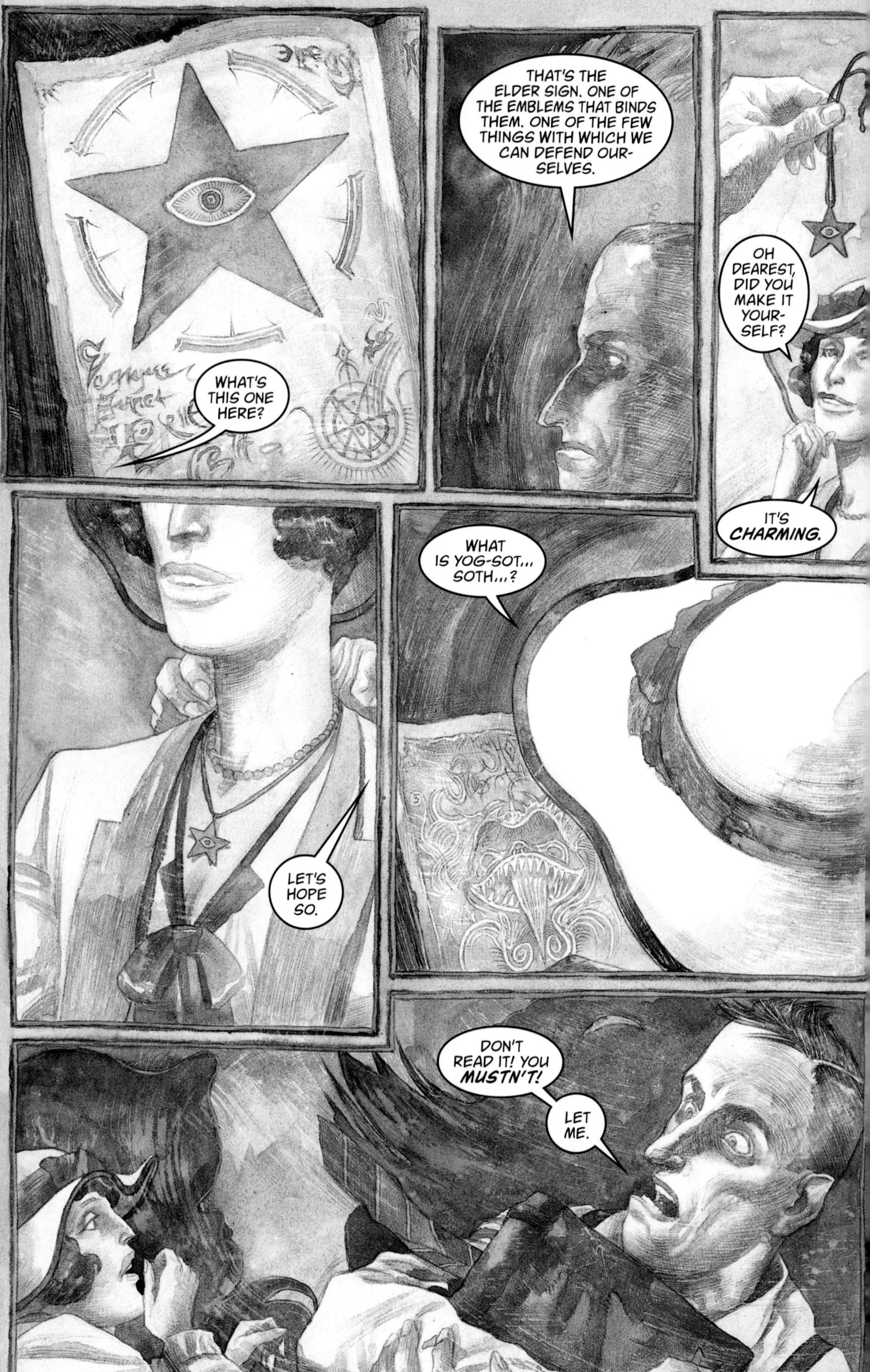
WHAT'S THIS ONE HERE?
THAT'S THE ELDER SIGN. ONE OF THE EMBLEMS THAT BINDS THEM. ONE OF THE FEW THINGS WITH WHICH WE CAN DEFEND OUR-SELVES.
OH DEAREST, DID YOU MAKE IT YOUR-SELF?
IT'S CHARMING.
LET'S HOPE SO.
WHAT IS YOG-SOT... SOTH...?
DON'T READ IT! YOU MUSTN'T!
LET ME.

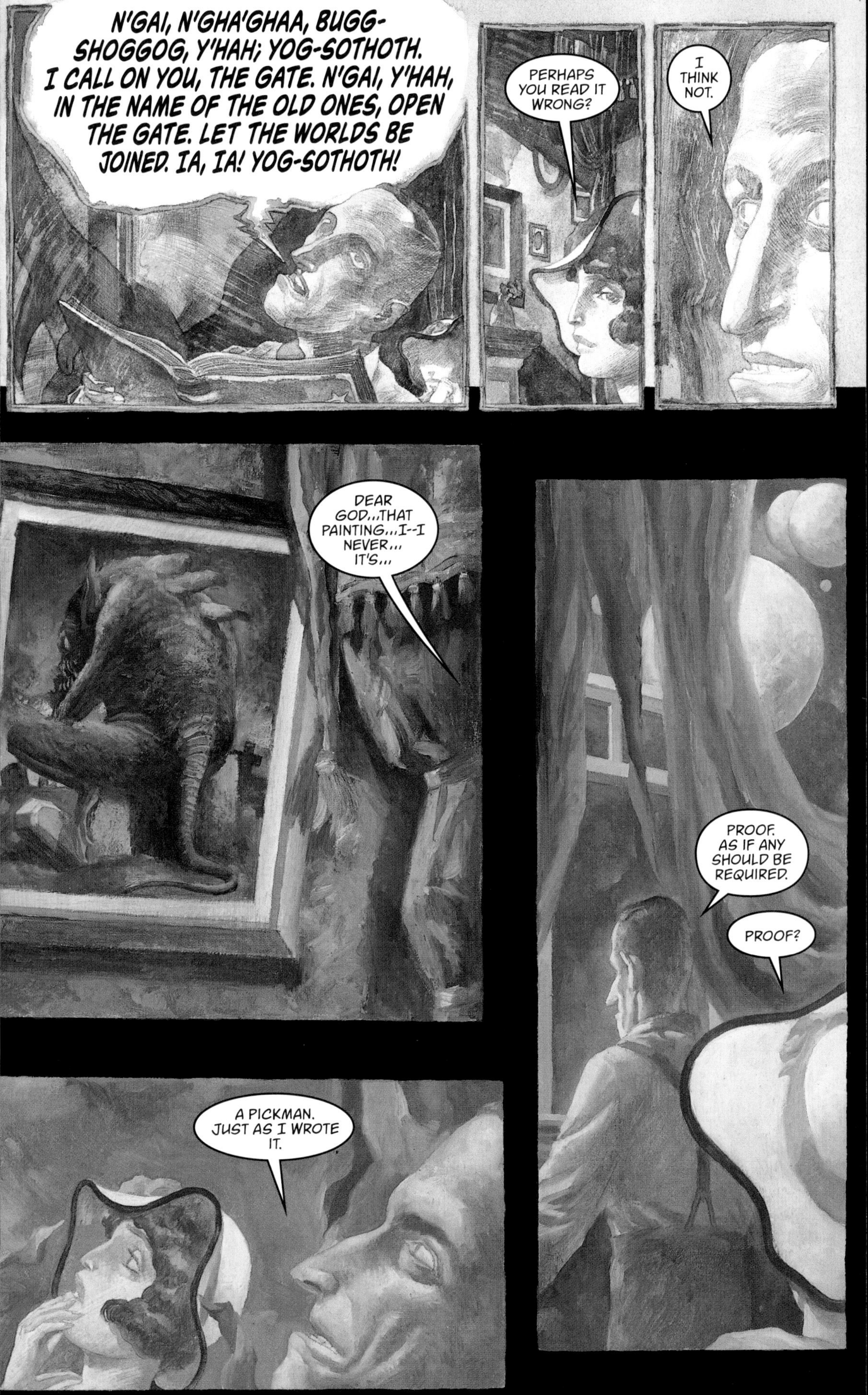
N'GAI, N'GHA'GHAA, BUGG-SHOGGOG, Y'HAH; YOG-SOTHOTH. I CALL ON YOU, THE GATE. N'GAI, Y'HAH, IN THE NAME OF THE OLD ONES, OPEN THE GATE. LET THE WORLDS BE JOINED. IA, IA! YOG-SOTHOTH!
PERHAPS YOU READ IT WRONG?
I THINK NOT.
DEAR GOD...THAT PAINTING...I--I NEVER... IT'S...
PROOF. AS IF ANY SHOULD BE REQUIRED.
PROOF?
A PICKMAN. JUST AS I WROTE IT.

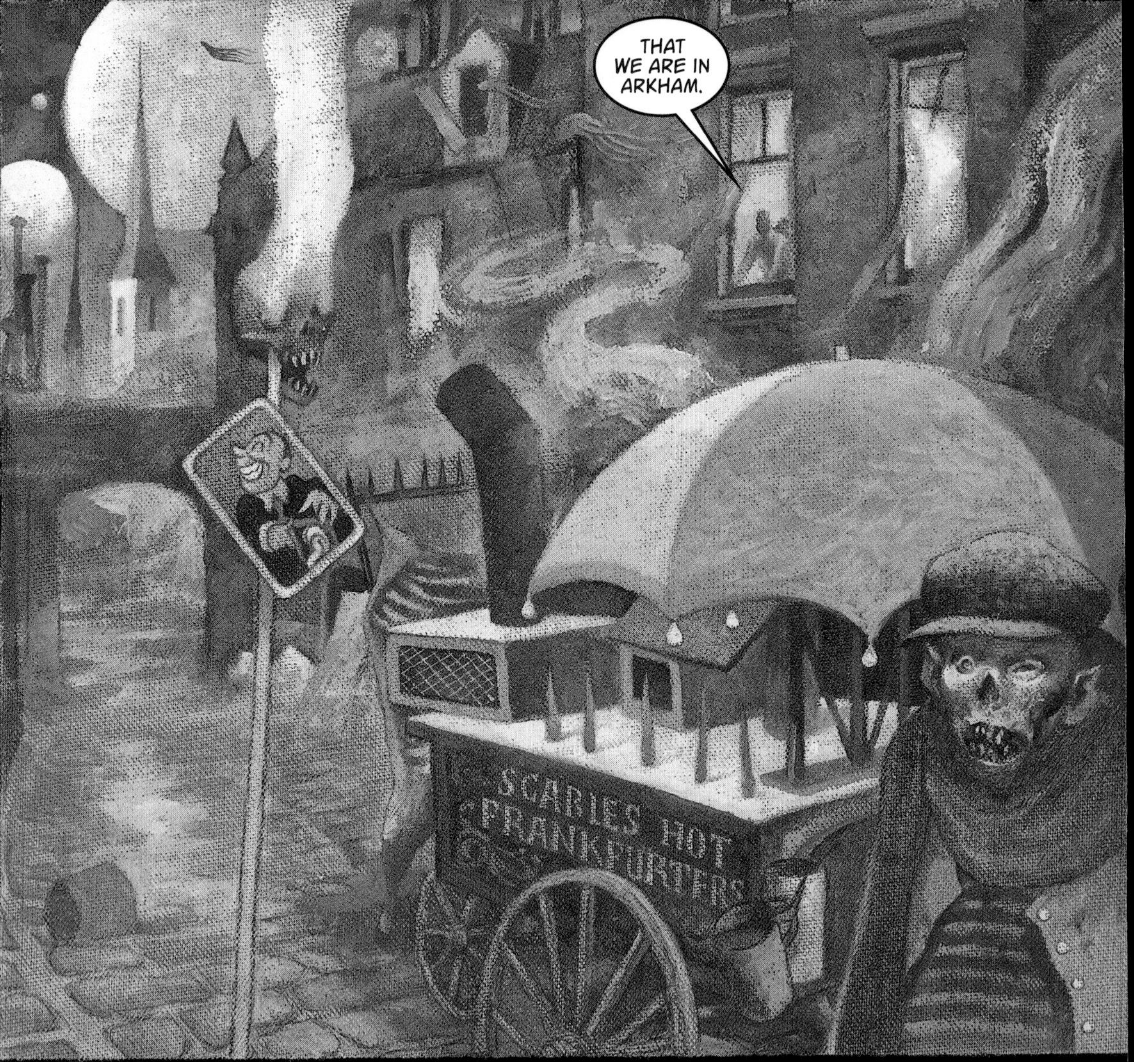
THAT WE ARE IN ARKHAM.
SCABIES HOT FRANKFURTERS

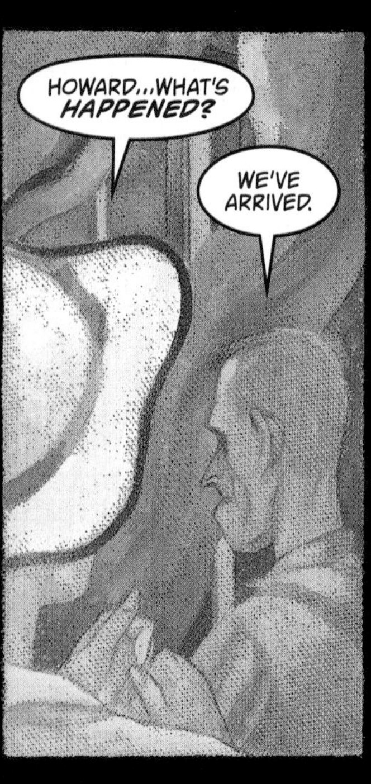
HOWARD...WHAT'S *HAPPENED?*
WE'VE ARRIVED.

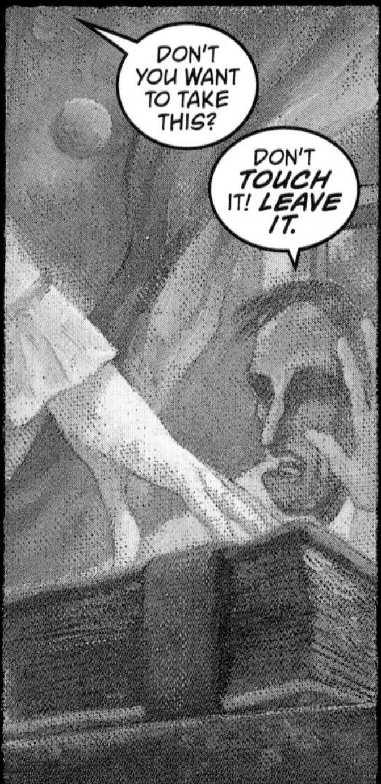
DON'T YOU WANT TO TAKE THIS?
DON'T *TOUCH* IT! *LEAVE IT.*

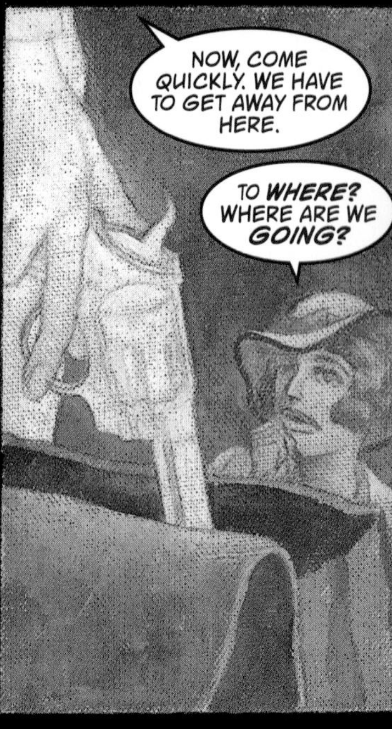
NOW, COME QUICKLY. WE HAVE TO GET AWAY FROM HERE.
TO *WHERE?* WHERE ARE WE *GOING?*

OUTSIDE.

I DON'T LIKE THIS. I DON'T LIKE THIS *AT ALL.*

THERE'S NOTHING TO LIKE ABOUT IT. *HURRY* NOW. WE *MUST* GET AWAY FROM HERE.

AS SOON AS THEY KNOW I'M HERE, THEY'LL BEGIN TO LOOK FOR THE GATE.

WHAT GATE? WHAT *THEY?* EXPLAIN THIS TO ME, *PLEASE!*

I'VE GOT TO MAKE SENSE OF THIS *SOME-* HOW.

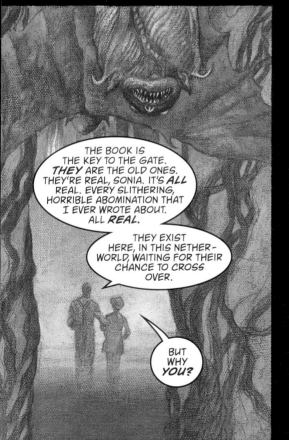

THE BOOK IS THE KEY TO THE GATE. *THEY* ARE THE OLD ONES. THEY'RE REAL, SONIA. IT'S *ALL* REAL. EVERY SLITHERING, HORRIBLE ABOMINATION THAT I EVER WROTE ABOUT. ALL *REAL.*

THEY EXIST HERE, IN THIS NETHER-WORLD, WAITING FOR THEIR CHANCE TO CROSS OVER.

BUT WHY *YOU?*

MY FATHER. HE FOUND THE BOOK, GOD KNOWS HOW. HE READ FROM THE ACCURSED THING AND OPENED THE GATE. HE WAS LUCKY ENOUGH TO CLOSE IT AGAIN BEFORE THEY COULD GET THROUGH, BUT THEY HAUNTED HIM HIS ENTIRE LIFE.

HE URGED MY MOTHER TO FIND THE BOOK AND BURN IT, BUT IT GOT TO ME BEFORE SHE COULD.

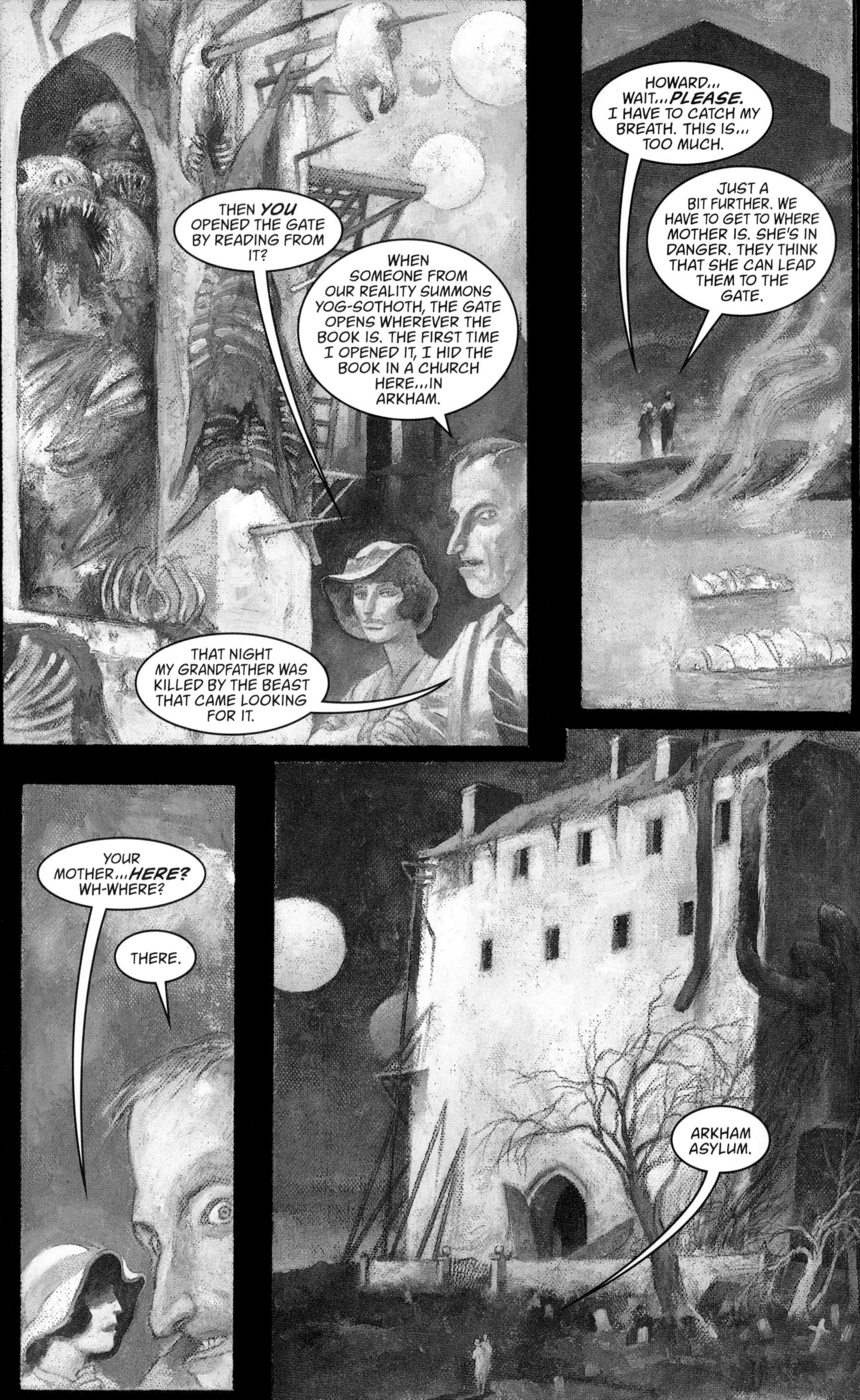
THEN *YOU* OPENED THE GATE BY READING FROM IT?
WHEN SOMEONE FROM OUR REALITY SUMMONS YOG-SOTHOTH, THE GATE OPENS WHEREVER THE BOOK IS. THE FIRST TIME I OPENED IT, I HID THE BOOK IN A CHURCH HERE...IN ARKHAM.
THAT NIGHT MY GRANDFATHER WAS KILLED BY THE BEAST THAT CAME LOOKING FOR IT.
HOWARD... WAIT...*PLEASE.* I HAVE TO CATCH MY BREATH. THIS IS... TOO MUCH.
JUST A BIT FURTHER. WE HAVE TO GET TO WHERE MOTHER IS. SHE'S IN DANGER. THEY THINK THAT SHE CAN LEAD THEM TO THE GATE.
YOUR MOTHER...*HERE?* WH-WHERE?
THERE.
ARKHAM ASYLUM.

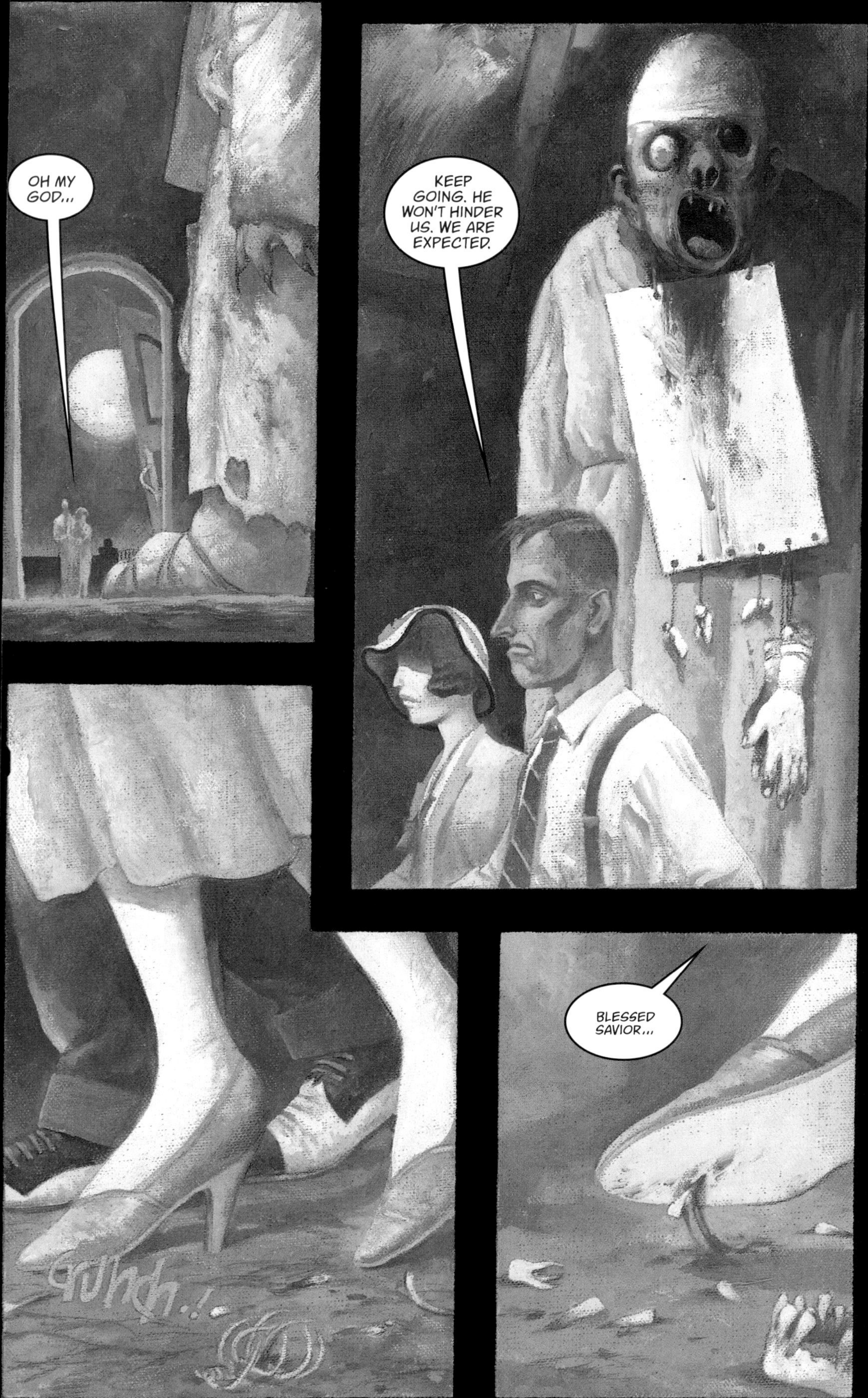
OH MY GOD...
KEEP GOING. HE WON'T HINDER US. WE ARE EXPECTED.
Crunch..!
BLESSED SAVIOR...

MOTHER!

ER

MOTHER. IT'S HOWARD.

I'VE COME TO TAKE YOU BACK THROUGH THE GATE. TO THE OTHER SIDE.

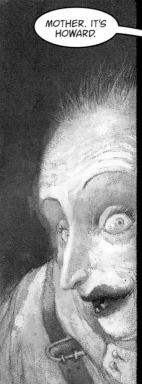

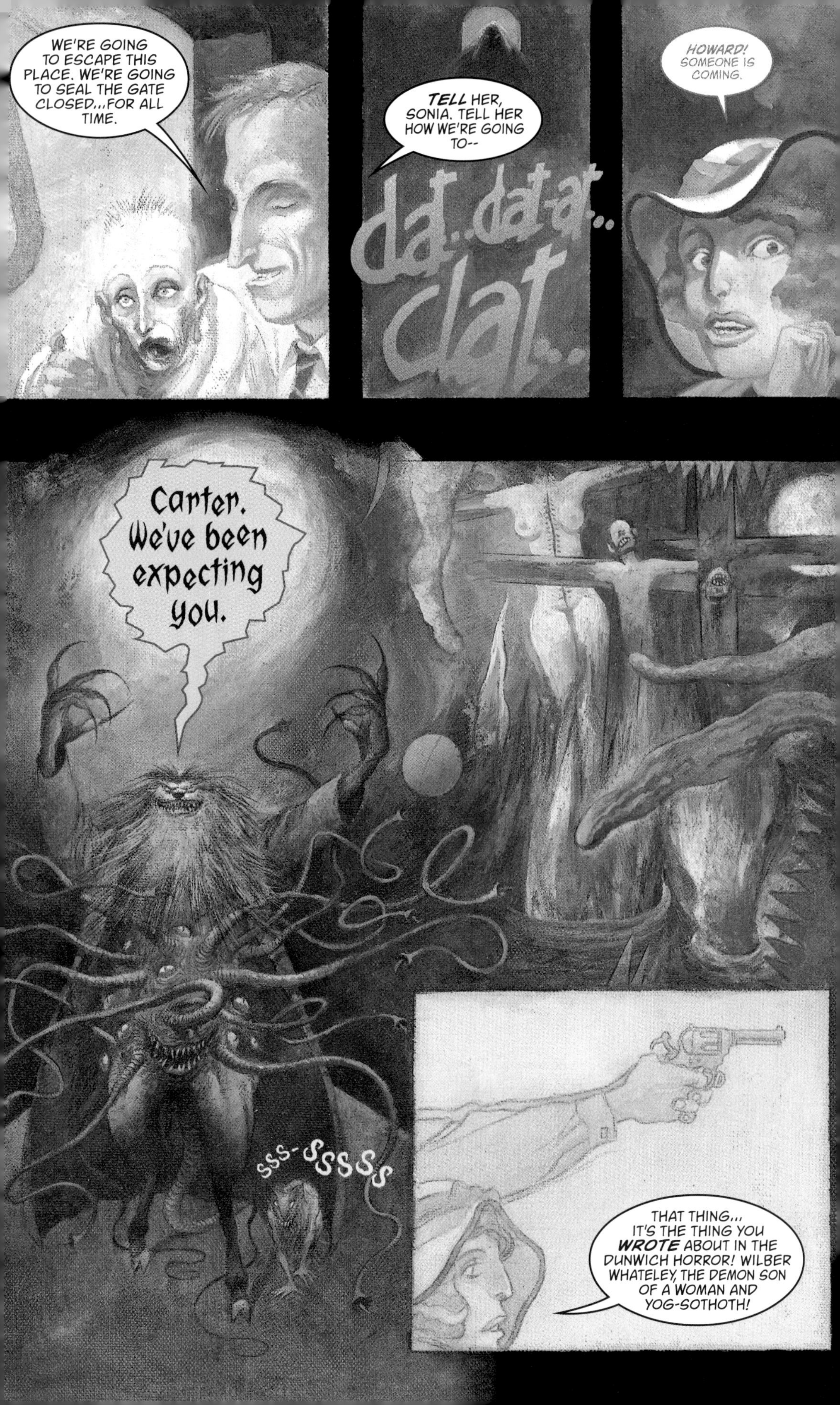
WE'RE GOING TO ESCAPE THIS PLACE. WE'RE GOING TO SEAL THE GATE CLOSED...FOR ALL TIME.
TELL HER, SONIA. TELL HER HOW WE'RE GOING TO--
dat..dat-at.. dat..
HOWARD! SOMEONE IS COMING.
Carter. We've been expecting you.
SSS-SSSSS
THAT THING... IT'S THE THING YOU WROTE ABOUT IN THE DUNWICH HORROR! WILBER WHATELEY, THE DEMON SON OF A WOMAN AND YOG-SOTHOTH!

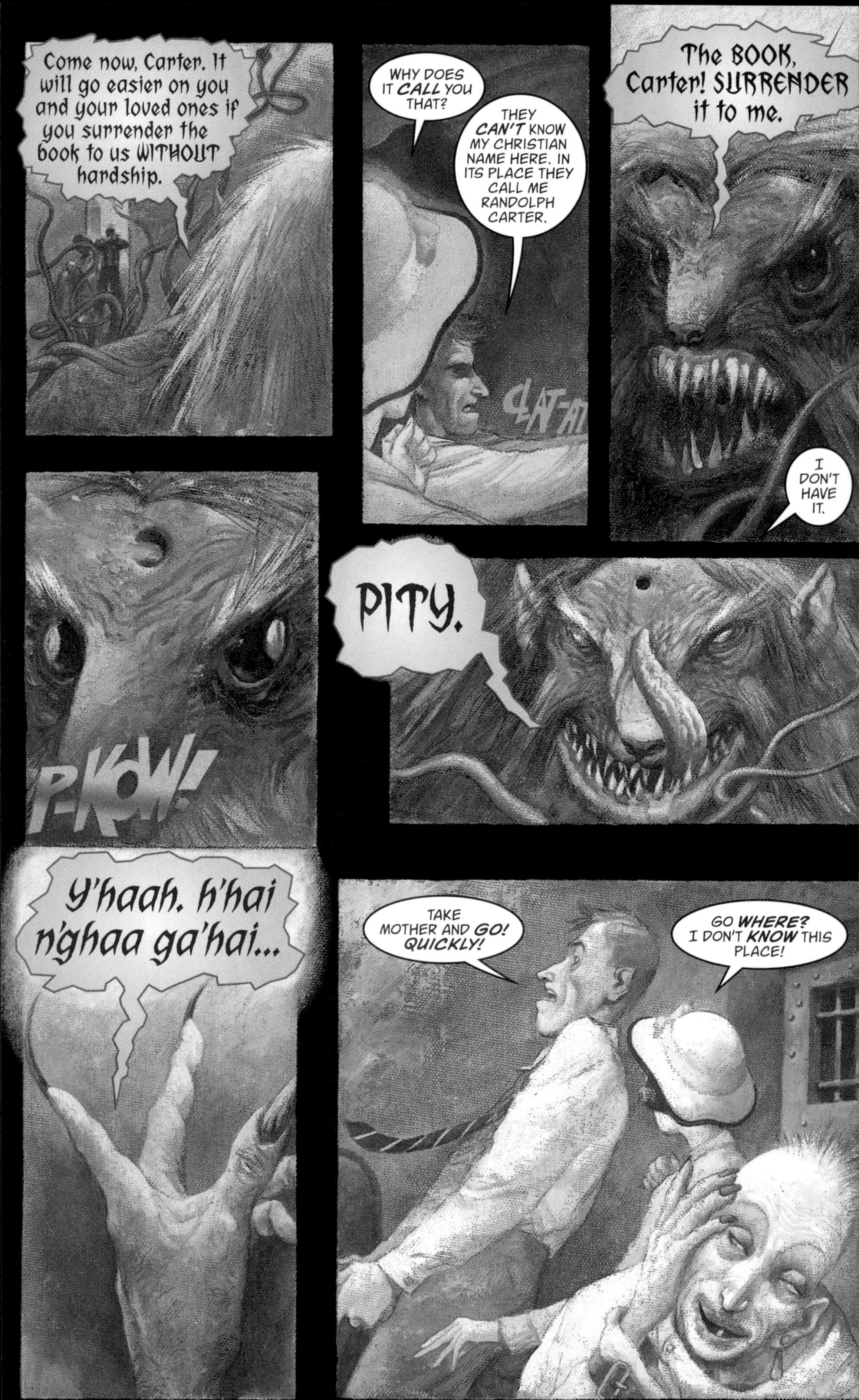
Come now, Carter. It will go easier on you and your loved ones if you surrender the book to us WITHOUT hardship.
WHY DOES IT CALL YOU THAT?
THEY CAN'T KNOW MY CHRISTIAN NAME HERE. IN ITS PLACE THEY CALL ME RANDOLPH CARTER.
CLAT-AT-AT
The BOOK, Carter! SURRENDER it to me.
I DON'T HAVE IT.
P-KOW!
PITY.
Y'haah. h'hai n'ghaa ga'hai...
TAKE MOTHER AND GO! QUICKLY!
GO WHERE? I DON'T KNOW THIS PLACE!

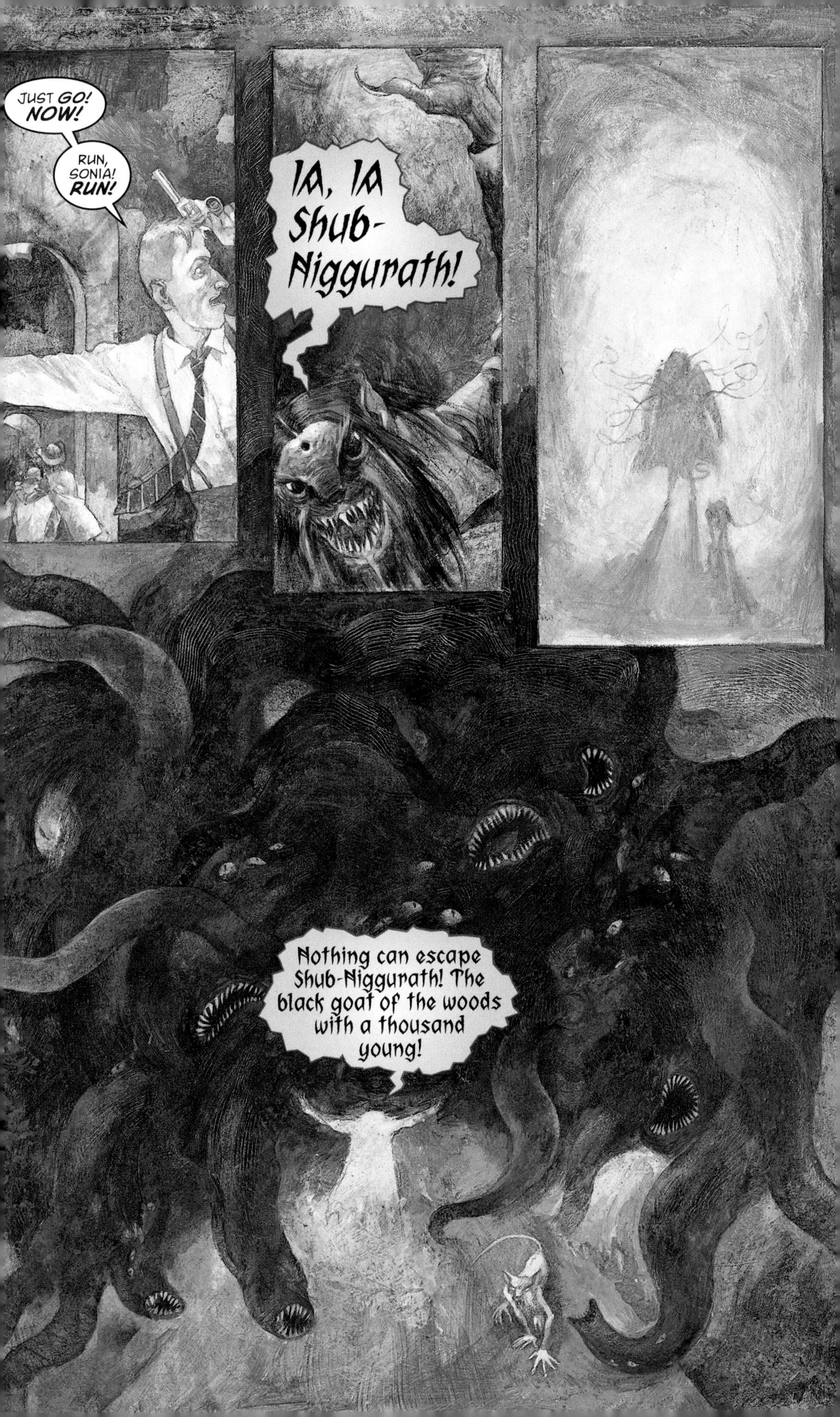
JUST GO! NOW!
RUN, SONIA! RUN!
IA, IA Shub-Niggurath!
Nothing can escape Shub-Niggurath! The black goat of the woods with a thousand young!

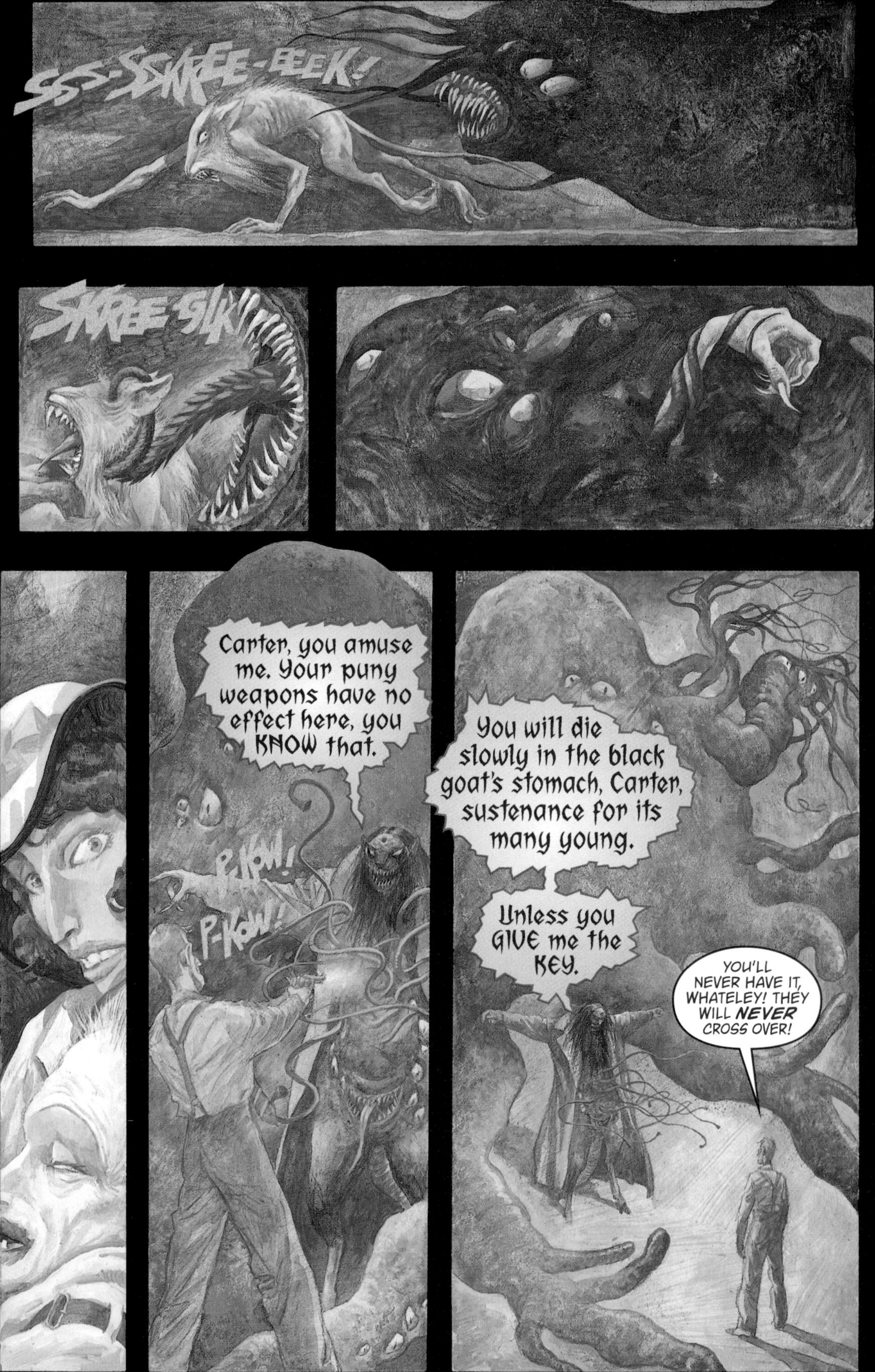
SSS-SSKREE-EEEK!
SKREE-SLK
Carter, you amuse me. Your puny weapons have no effect here, you KNOW that.
P-KOW!
P-KOW!
You will die slowly in the black goat's stomach, Carter, sustenance for its many young.
Unless you GIVE me the KEY.
YOU'LL NEVER HAVE IT, WHATELEY! THEY WILL NEVER CROSS OVER!

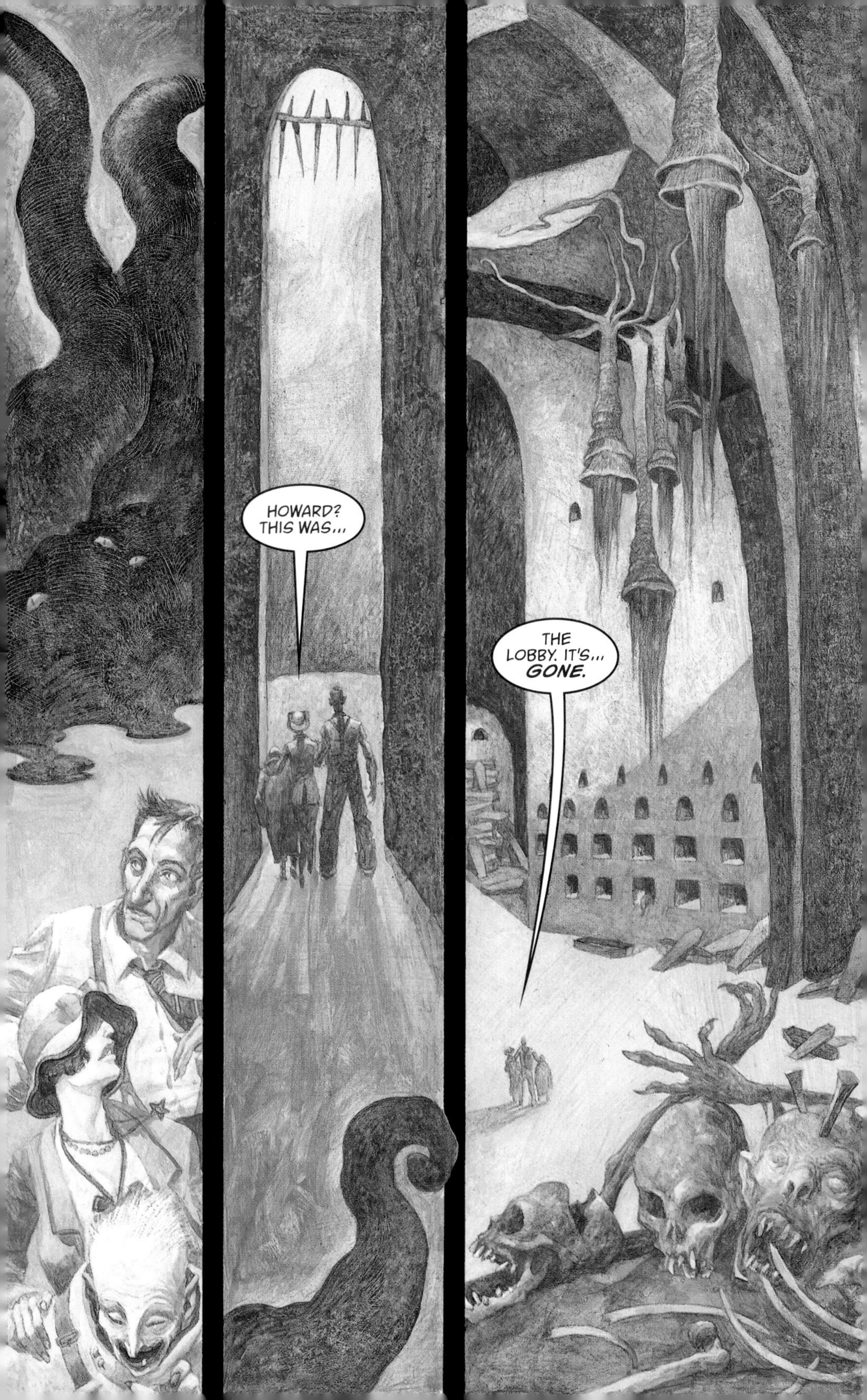
HOWARD? THIS WAS...
THE LOBBY. IT'S... GONE.

SONIA! DO YOU *HEAR* ME?

IT'S... GONE.

THAT'S THE ONLY WAY OUT.

OF COURSE... LIKE YOUR STORY...

SONIA, YOU GO FIRST, HELP MOTHER DOWN ONCE YOU GET OUTSIDE.

FORGIVE MY RUDENESS...

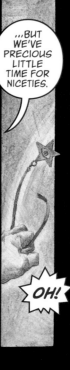

...BUT WE'VE PRECIOUS LITTLE TIME FOR NICETIES.

OH!

SONIA! *NOW!*

SSH- TTH- TA- SH- SH-TCH!

CLIMB! FOR THE LOVE OF GOD, *CLIMB!*

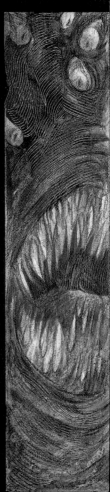

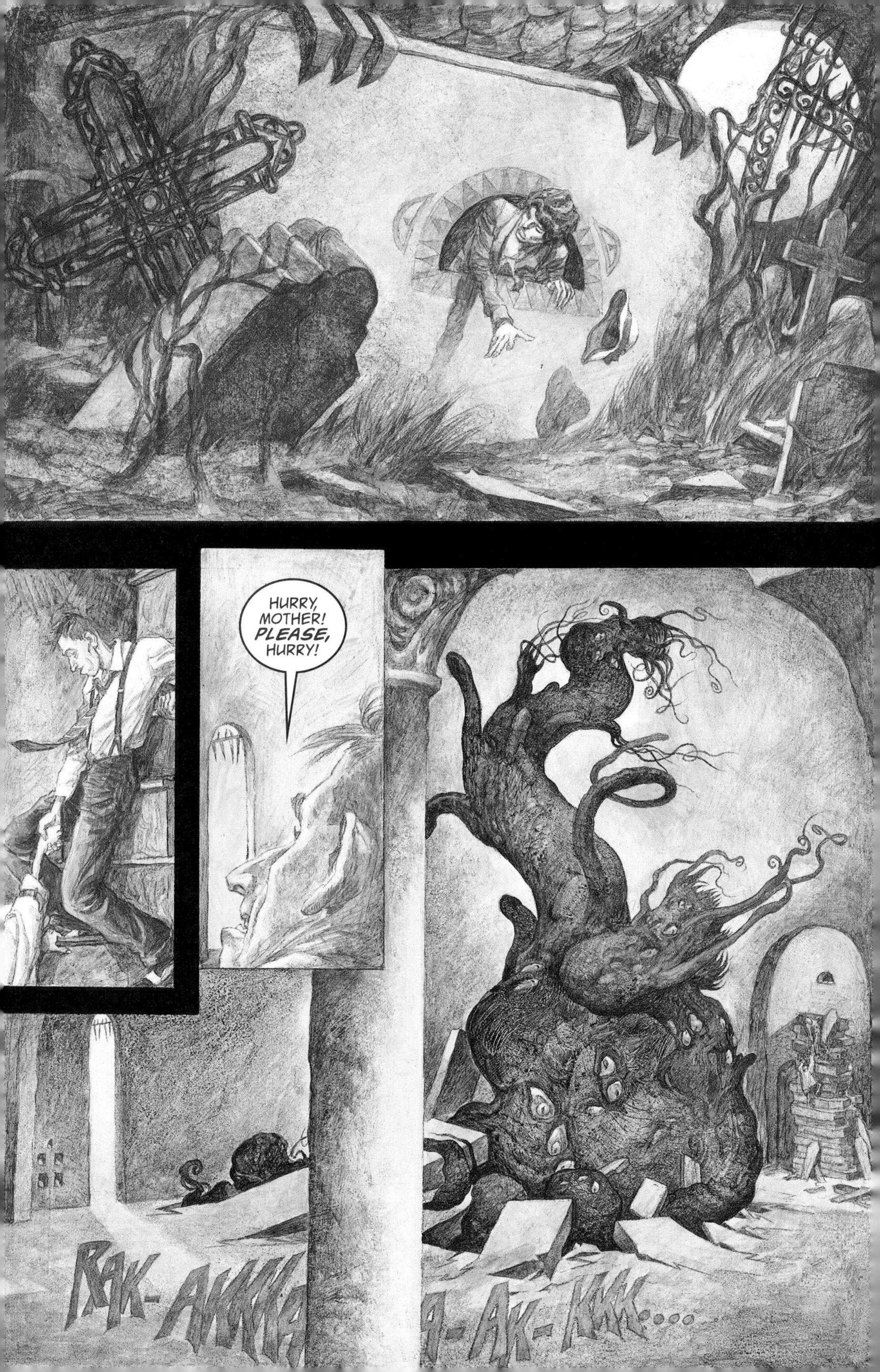
HURRY, MOTHER! PLEASE, HURRY!
RAK-AKKKA-A-AK-KKK...

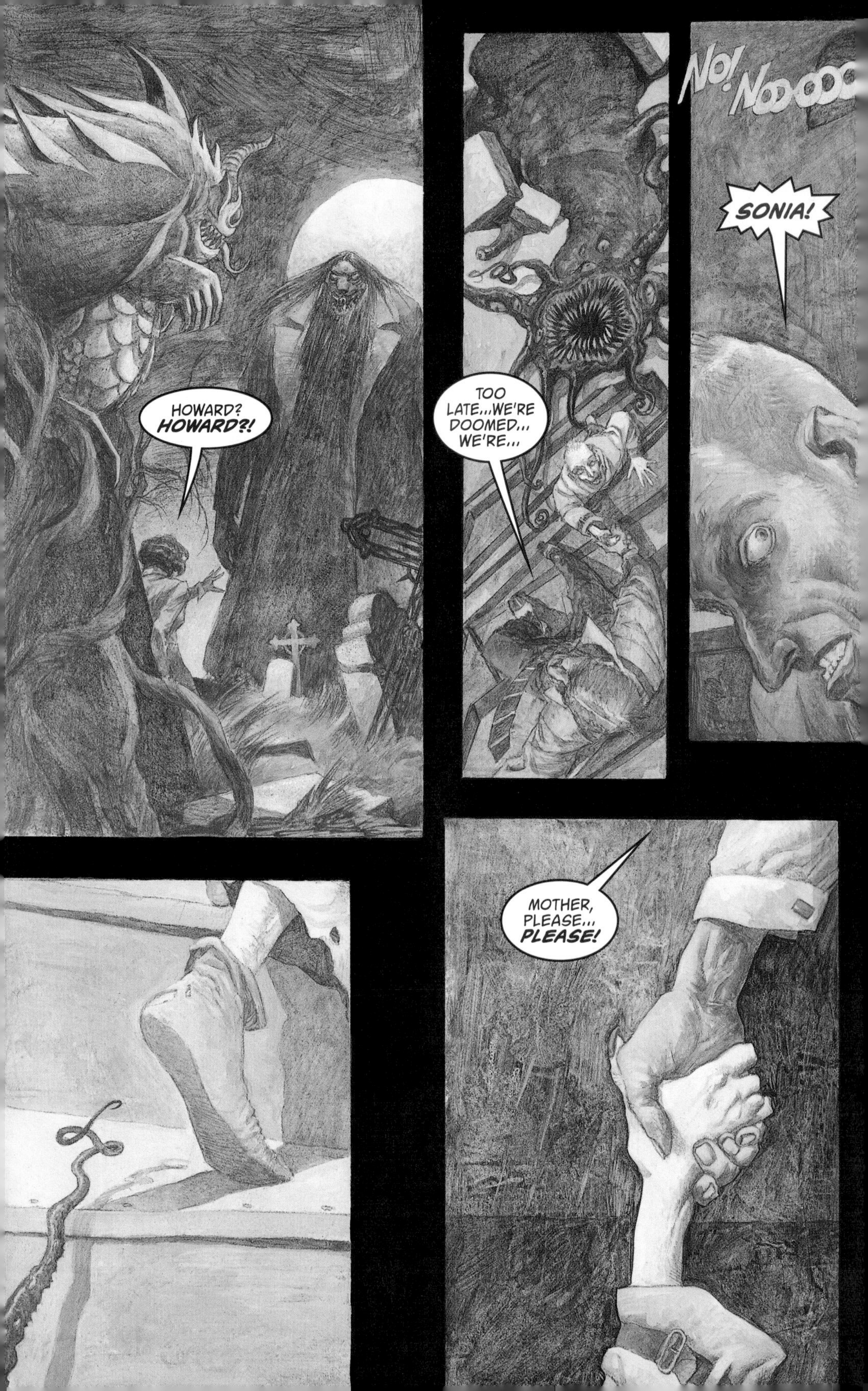
HOWARD? HOWARD?!
TOO LATE...WE'RE DOOMED... WE'RE...
NO! NOO-OOO
SONIA!
MOTHER, PLEASE... PLEASE!

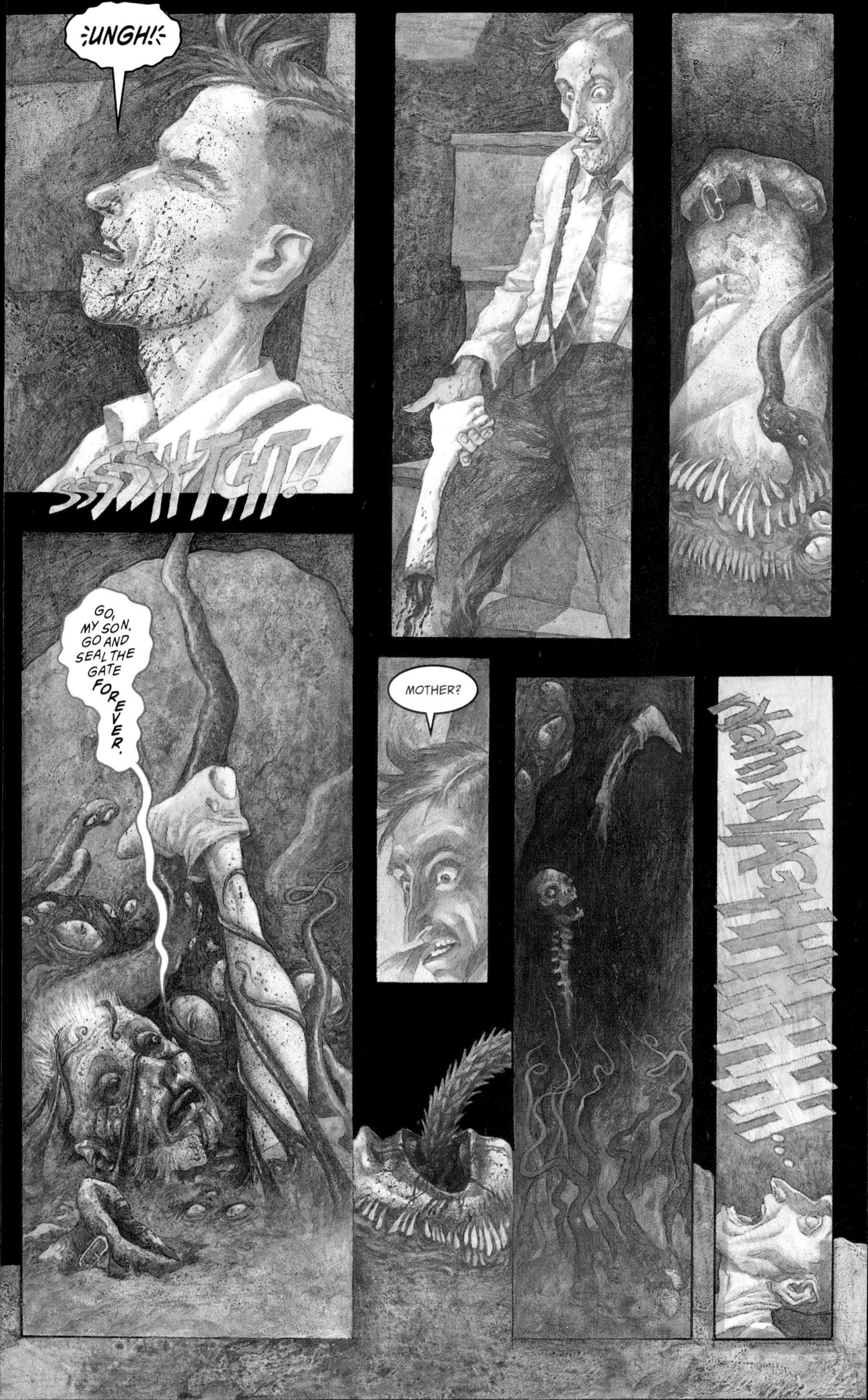
UNGH!
sssSHTCHT!!
GO, MY SON. GO AND SEAL THE GATE FOREVER.
MOTHER?
rrahhNYAGHHHHHH!

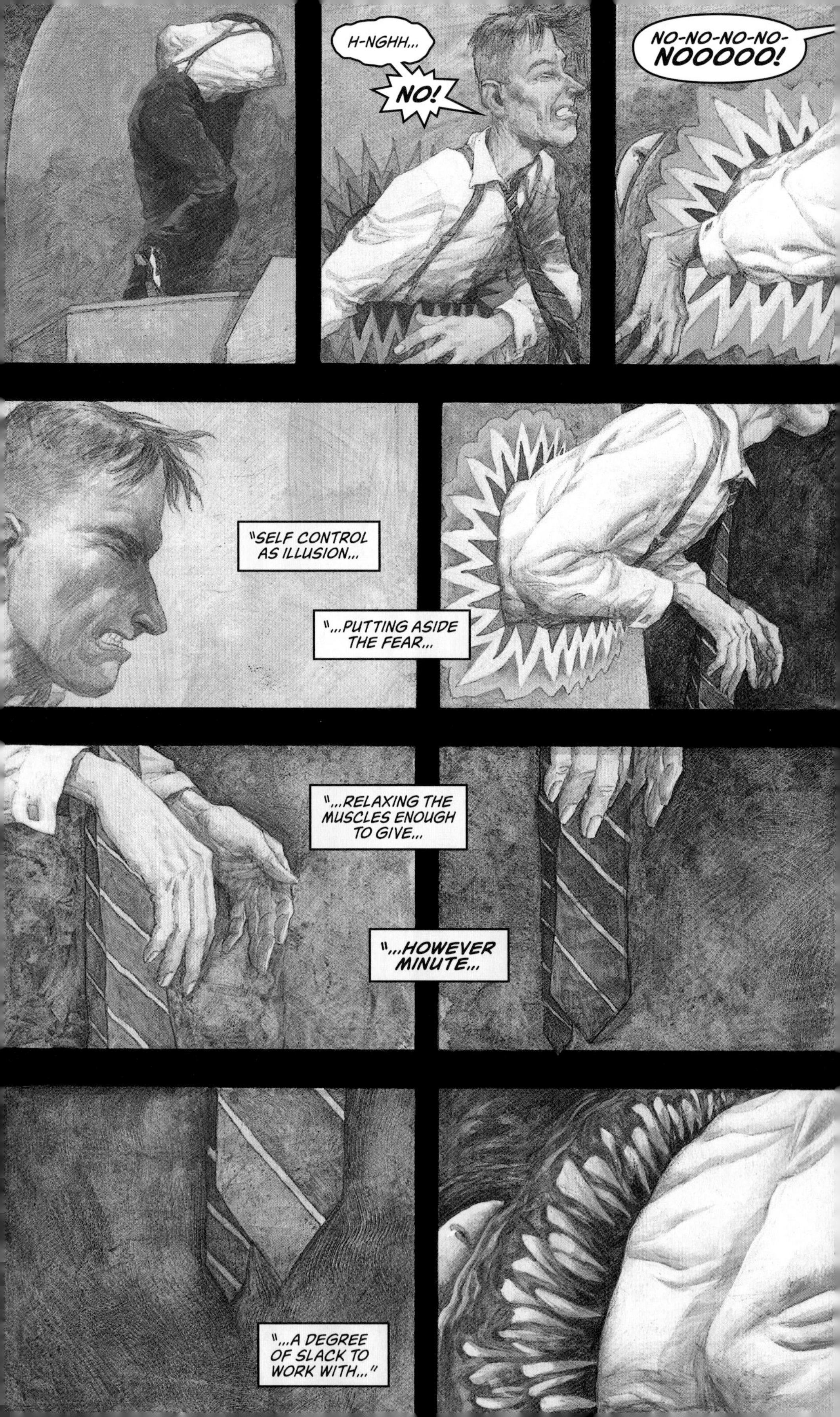
H-NGHH...
NO!
NO-NO-NO-NO-NOOOOO!
"SELF CONTROL AS ILLUSION...
"...PUTTING ASIDE THE FEAR...
"...RELAXING THE MUSCLES ENOUGH TO GIVE...
"...HOWEVER MINUTE...
"...A DEGREE OF SLACK TO WORK WITH..."

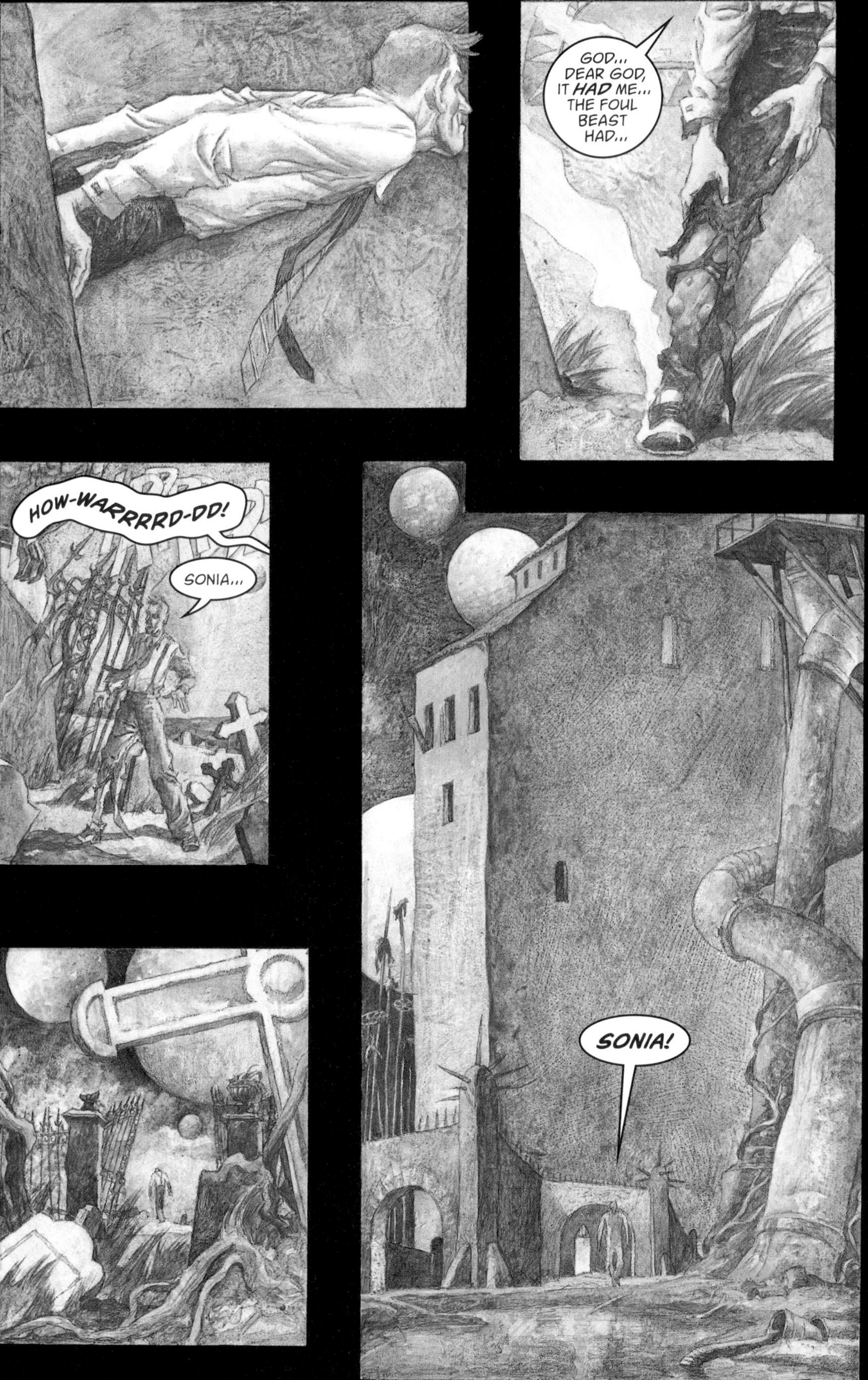
GOD... DEAR GOD, IT HAD ME... THE FOUL BEAST HAD...
HOW-WARRRRD-DD!
SONIA...
SONIA!

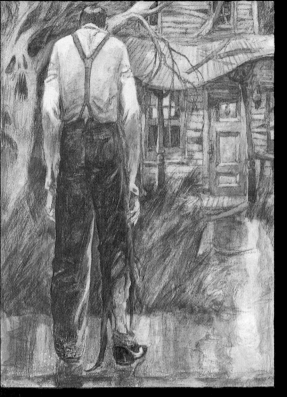

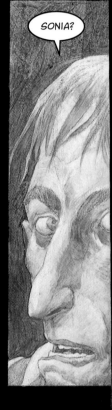

SONIA?

Welcome home, Carter. Surely you know THIS place. The shunned house. The place where all of your horrors, your unmentionable terrors reside.

SONIA!

Yes, yes...Sonia IS here. Come and find her. She's waiting for you.

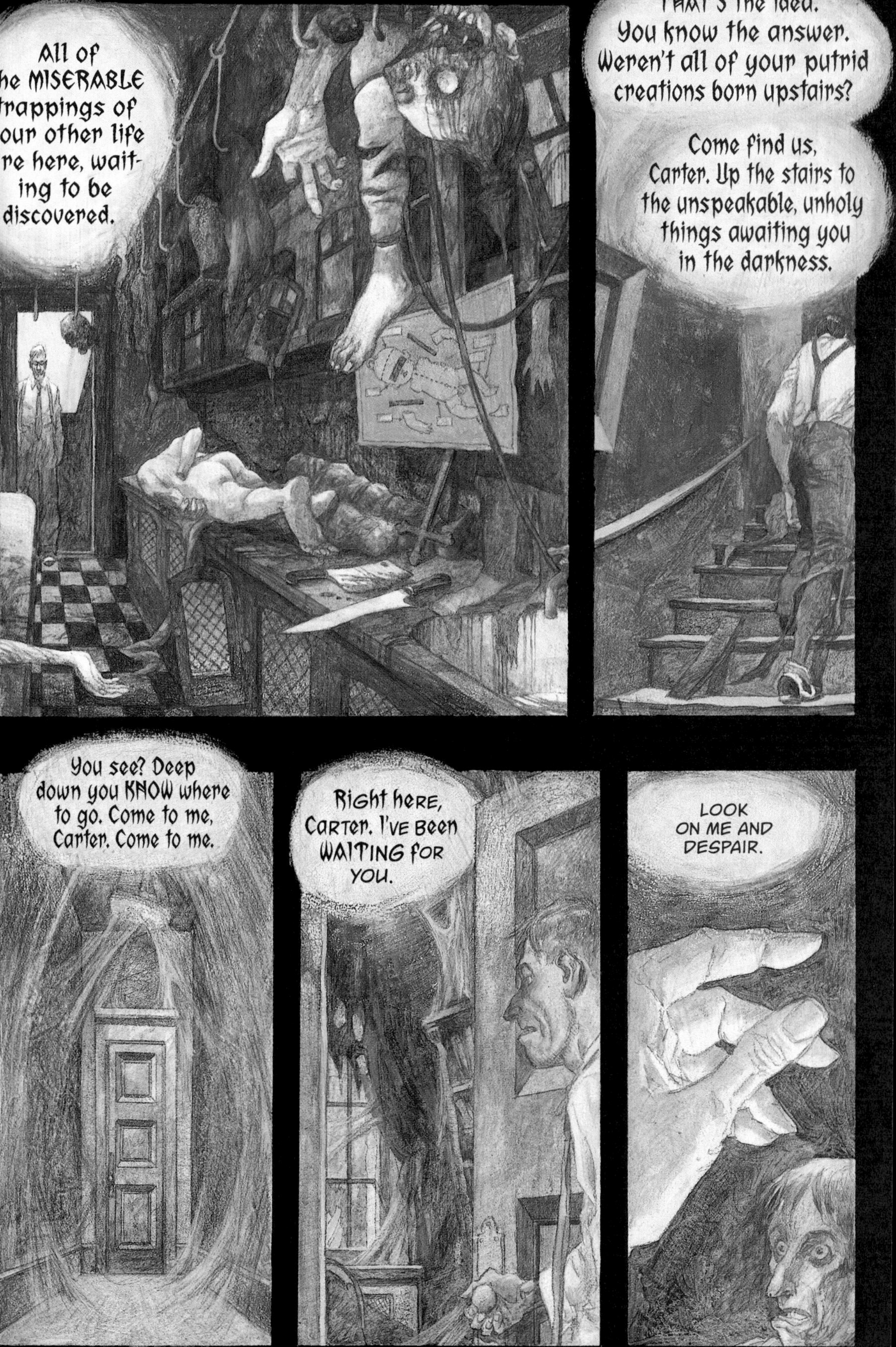
All of
he MISERABLE
rappings of
our other life
re here, wait-
ing to be
discovered.
THAT'S the idea.
You know the answer.
Weren't all of your putrid
creations born upstairs?
Come find us,
Carter. Up the stairs to
the unspeakable, unholy
things awaiting you
in the darkness.
You see? Deep
down you KNOW where
to go. Come to me,
Carter. Come to me.
Right here,
Carter. I've been
WAITING for
you.
LOOK
ON ME AND
DESPAIR.

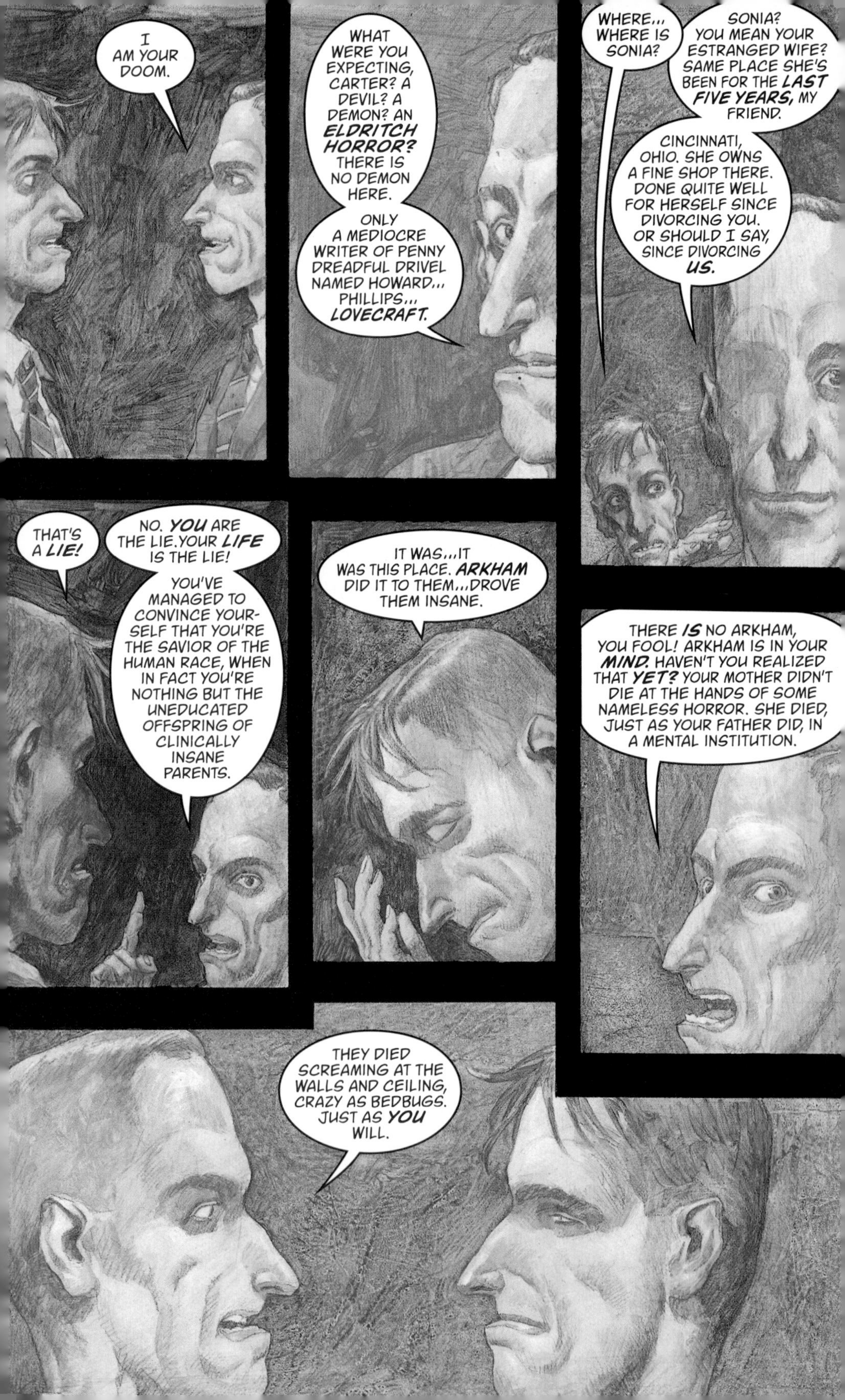
I AM YOUR DOOM.
WHAT WERE YOU EXPECTING, CARTER? A DEVIL? A DEMON? AN ELDRITCH HORROR? THERE IS NO DEMON HERE.
ONLY A MEDIOCRE WRITER OF PENNY DREADFUL DRIVEL NAMED HOWARD... PHILLIPS... LOVECRAFT.
WHERE... WHERE IS SONIA?
SONIA? YOU MEAN YOUR ESTRANGED WIFE? SAME PLACE SHE'S BEEN FOR THE LAST FIVE YEARS, MY FRIEND.
CINCINNATI, OHIO. SHE OWNS A FINE SHOP THERE. DONE QUITE WELL FOR HERSELF SINCE DIVORCING YOU. OR SHOULD I SAY, SINCE DIVORCING US.
THAT'S A LIE!
NO. YOU ARE THE LIE. YOUR LIFE IS THE LIE!
YOU'VE MANAGED TO CONVINCE YOURSELF THAT YOU'RE THE SAVIOR OF THE HUMAN RACE, WHEN IN FACT YOU'RE NOTHING BUT THE UNEDUCATED OFFSPRING OF CLINICALLY INSANE PARENTS.
IT WAS... IT WAS THIS PLACE. ARKHAM DID IT TO THEM... DROVE THEM INSANE.
THERE IS NO ARKHAM, YOU FOOL! ARKHAM IS IN YOUR MIND. HAVEN'T YOU REALIZED THAT YET? YOUR MOTHER DIDN'T DIE AT THE HANDS OF SOME NAMELESS HORROR. SHE DIED, JUST AS YOUR FATHER DID, IN A MENTAL INSTITUTION.
THEY DIED SCREAMING AT THE WALLS AND CEILING, CRAZY AS BEDBUGS. JUST AS YOU WILL.

I'M **NOT** CRAZY.

IT'S ALL RIGHT, REALLY. NO ONE COULD **POSSIBLY** BLAME YOU FOR YOUR MENTAL CONDITION.

RAISED BY A MOTHER WHO, IN HER HEART, ALWAYS WANTED A GIRL. BEING MADE TO WEAR THAT DRESS. YOUR FATHER COMMITTED TO A MENTAL INSTITUTION WHEN YOU WERE BUT FOUR YEARS OLD...

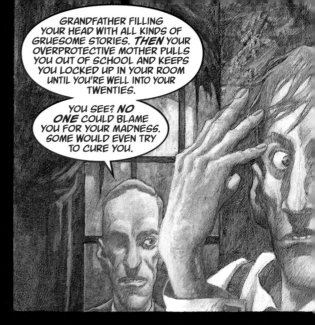

GRANDFATHER FILLING YOUR HEAD WITH ALL KINDS OF GRUESOME STORIES. **THEN** YOUR OVERPROTECTIVE MOTHER PULLS YOU OUT OF SCHOOL AND KEEPS YOU LOCKED UP IN YOUR ROOM UNTIL YOU'RE WELL INTO YOUR TWENTIES.

YOU SEE? **NO ONE** COULD BLAME YOU FOR YOUR MADNESS. SOME WOULD EVEN TRY TO CURE YOU.

SONIA.

SWEET SONIA. SHE TRIED SO HARD. BUT, IN THE END, YOUR INSANITY DROVE EVEN **HER** AWAY.

AND NOW, HERE YOU ARE, SITTING AT YOUR WRITING DESK, TRYING **DESPERATELY** TO CONVINCE YOURSELF THAT **NONE** OF THE EVENTS OF YOUR LIFE ARE **YOUR** FAULT.

YOU WANT TO BLAME ALL OF YOUR INADEQUACIES AS A SON, A HUSBAND, A **HUMAN BEING,** ON THESE HORRIFIC MONSTERS THAT LURK **JUST OUTSIDE** THE REALM OF HUMAN CONSCIOUSNESS.

THE TRUTH OF IT IS...THERE'S NO ONE TO BLAME BUT YOURSELF.

I...

I...AM THE MONSTER.

DON'T BE SO HARD ON YOURSELF. IT'S NOT YOUR FAULT. THE CARDS WERE STACKED AGAINST YOU. A PRECOCIOUS BOY WHO FOUND HIS WAY INTO HIS FATHER'S LIBRARY, AND READ A BOOK THAT GAVE HIM **ALL KINDS** OF IDEAS.

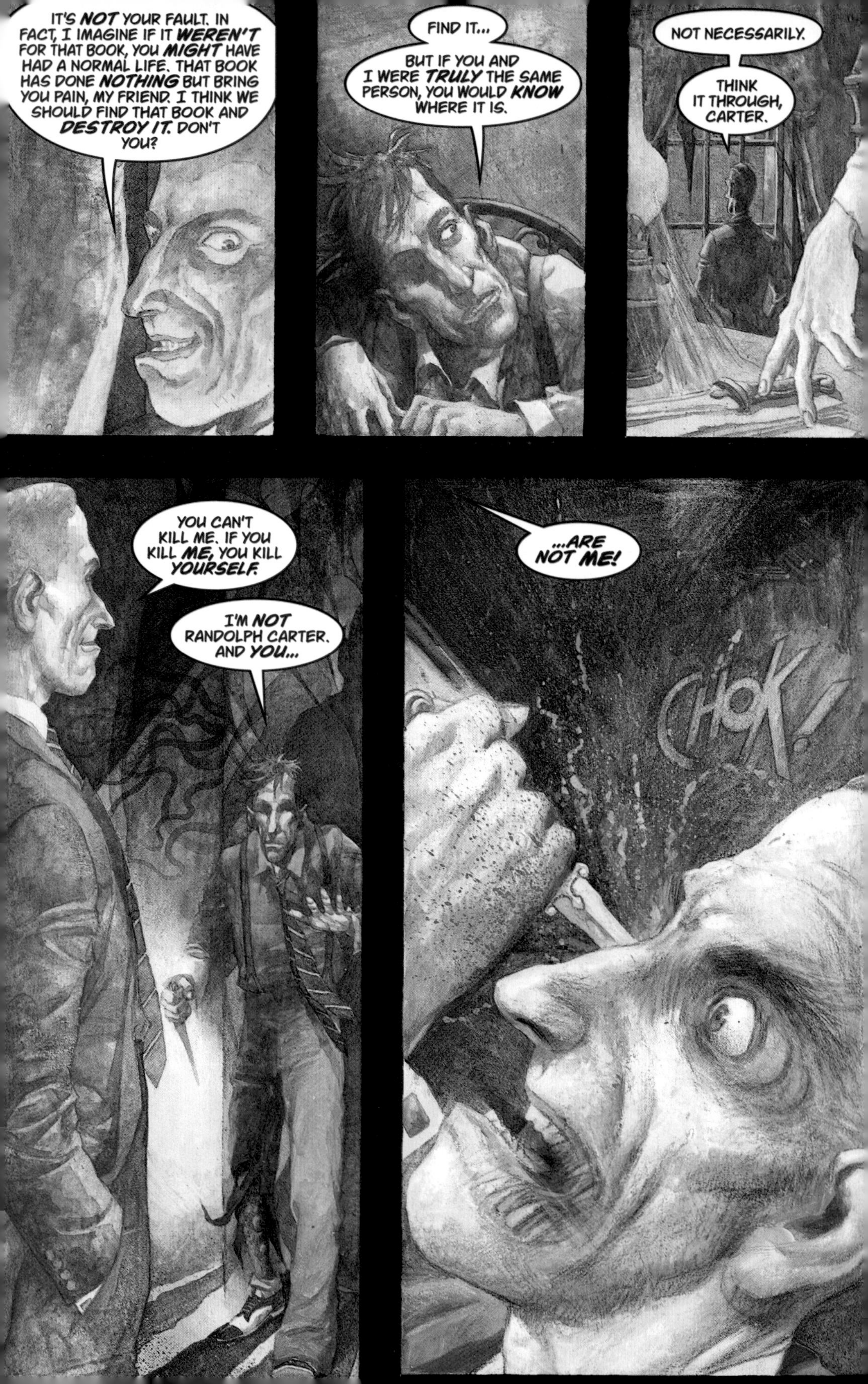
IT'S NOT YOUR FAULT. IN FACT, I IMAGINE IF IT WEREN'T FOR THAT BOOK, YOU MIGHT HAVE HAD A NORMAL LIFE. THAT BOOK HAS DONE NOTHING BUT BRING YOU PAIN, MY FRIEND. I THINK WE SHOULD FIND THAT BOOK AND DESTROY IT. DON'T YOU?
FIND IT...
BUT IF YOU AND I WERE TRULY THE SAME PERSON, YOU WOULD KNOW WHERE IT IS.
NOT NECESSARILY.
THINK IT THROUGH, CARTER.
YOU CAN'T KILL ME. IF YOU KILL ME, YOU KILL YOURSELF.
I'M NOT RANDOLPH CARTER. AND YOU...
...ARE NOT ME!
CHOK!

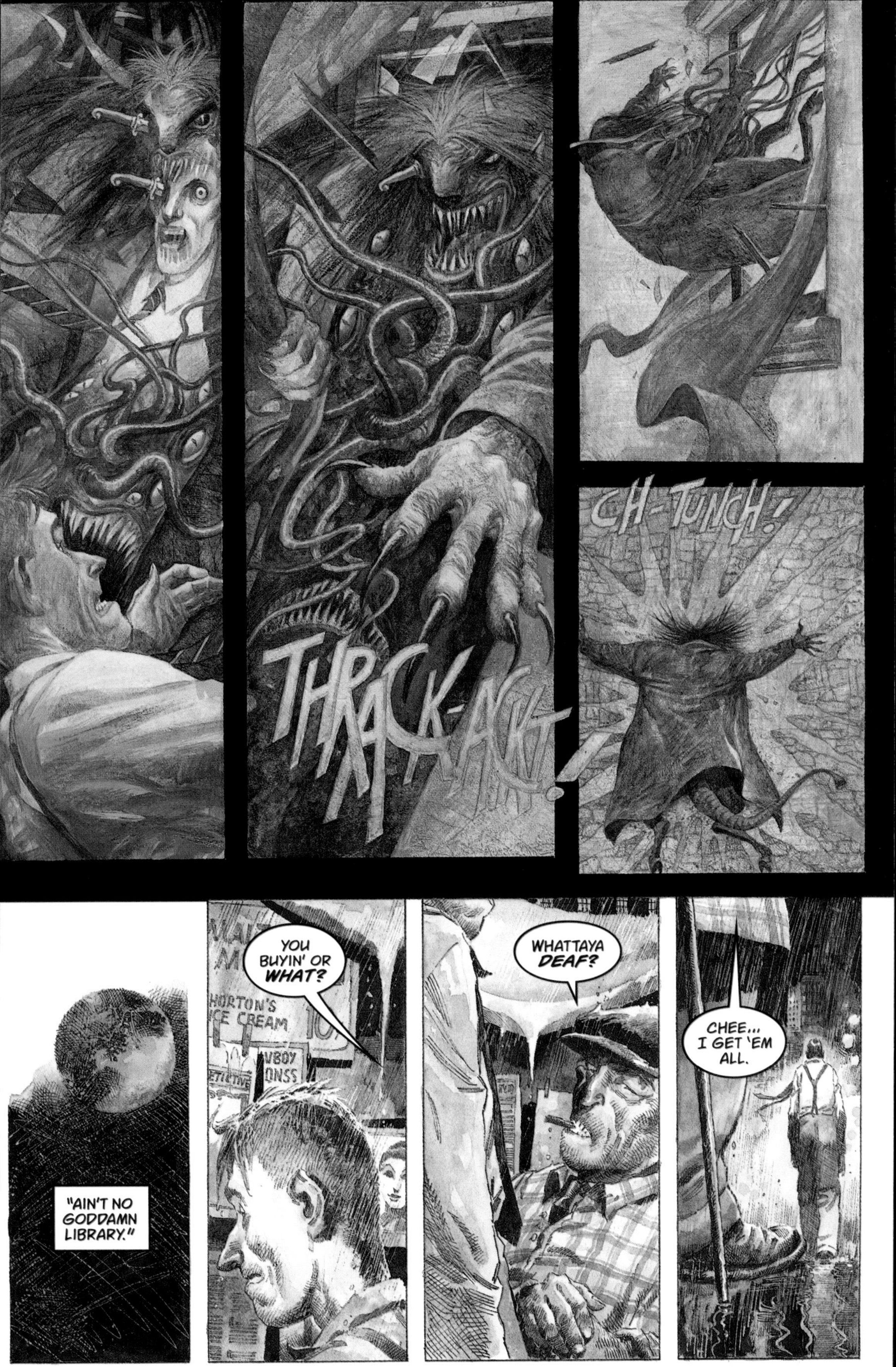
THRACK-ACK!
CH-TUNCH!
"AIN'T NO GODDAMN LIBRARY."
HORTON'S ICE CREAM
YOU BUYIN' OR WHAT?
WHATTAYA DEAF?
CHEE... I GET 'EM ALL.

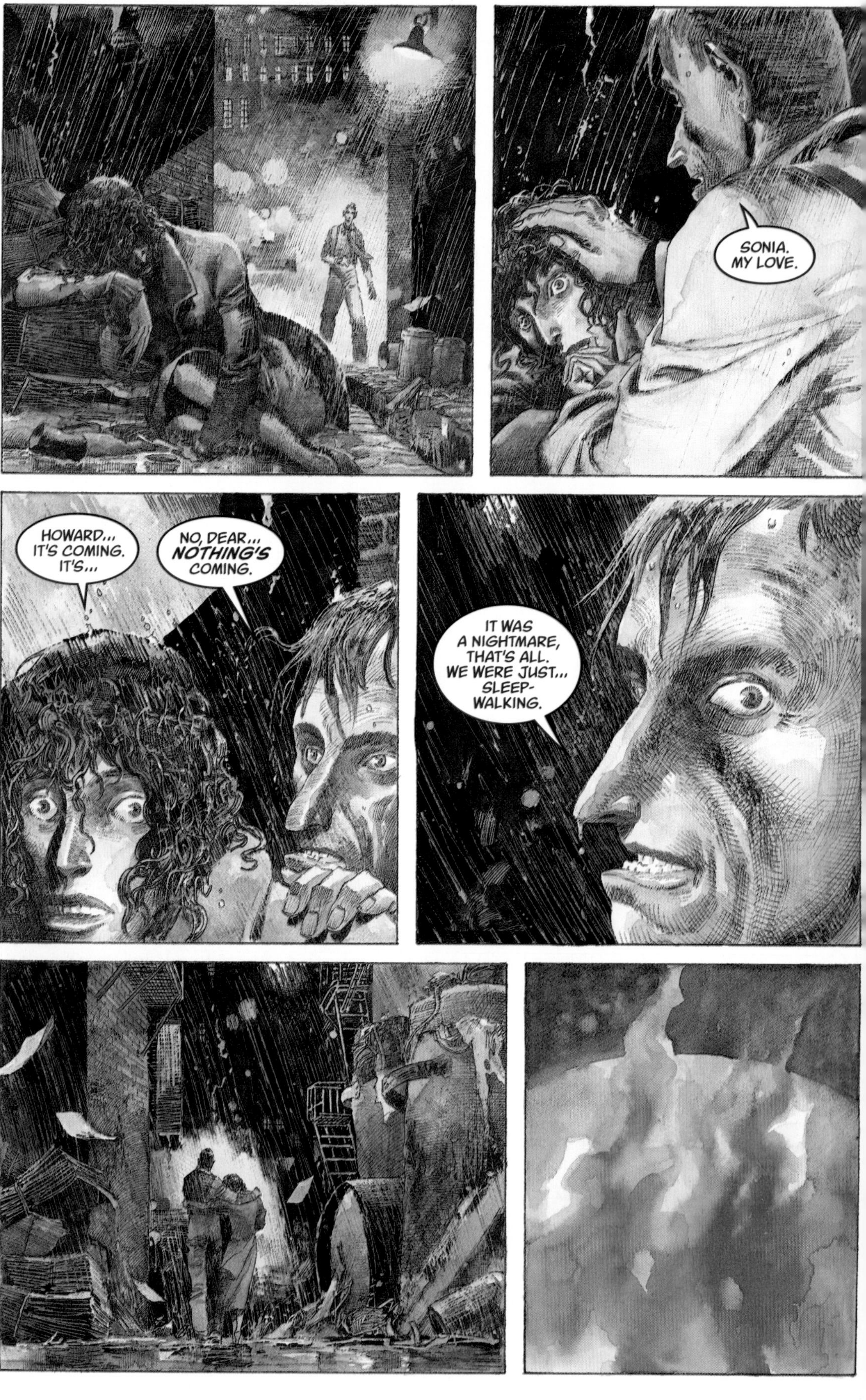
SONIA. MY LOVE.
HOWARD... IT'S COMING. IT'S...
NO, DEAR... NOTHING'S COMING.
IT WAS A NIGHTMARE, THAT'S ALL. WE WERE JUST... SLEEP-WALKING.

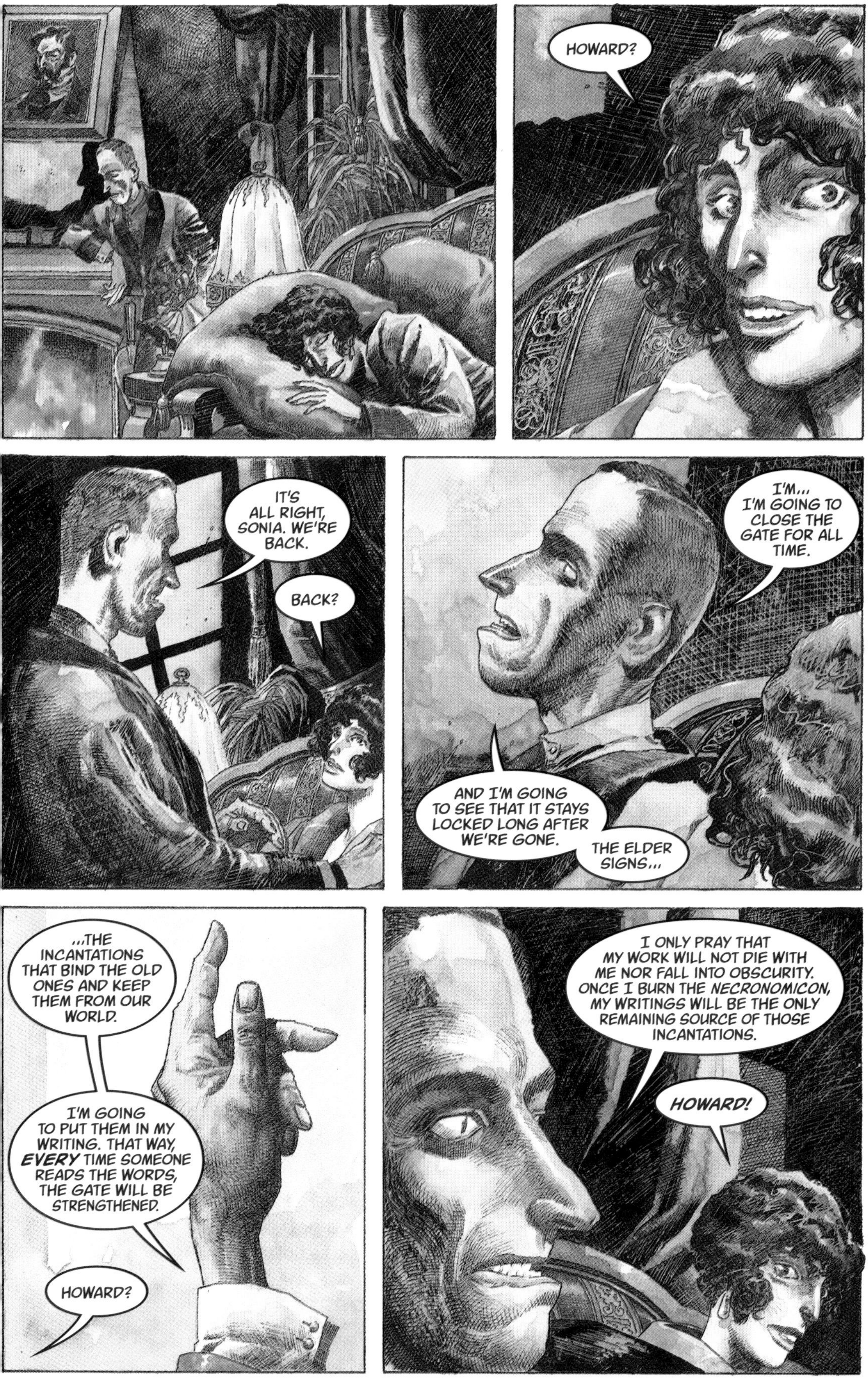
HOWARD?
IT'S ALL RIGHT, SONIA. WE'RE BACK.
BACK?
I'M... I'M GOING TO CLOSE THE GATE FOR ALL TIME.
AND I'M GOING TO SEE THAT IT STAYS LOCKED LONG AFTER WE'RE GONE.
THE ELDER SIGNS...
...THE INCANTATIONS THAT BIND THE OLD ONES AND KEEP THEM FROM OUR WORLD.
I'M GOING TO PUT THEM IN MY WRITING. THAT WAY, EVERY TIME SOMEONE READS THE WORDS, THE GATE WILL BE STRENGTHENED.
HOWARD?
I ONLY PRAY THAT MY WORK WILL NOT DIE WITH ME NOR FALL INTO OBSCURITY. ONCE I BURN THE NECRONOMICON, MY WRITINGS WILL BE THE ONLY REMAINING SOURCE OF THOSE INCANTATIONS.
HOWARD!

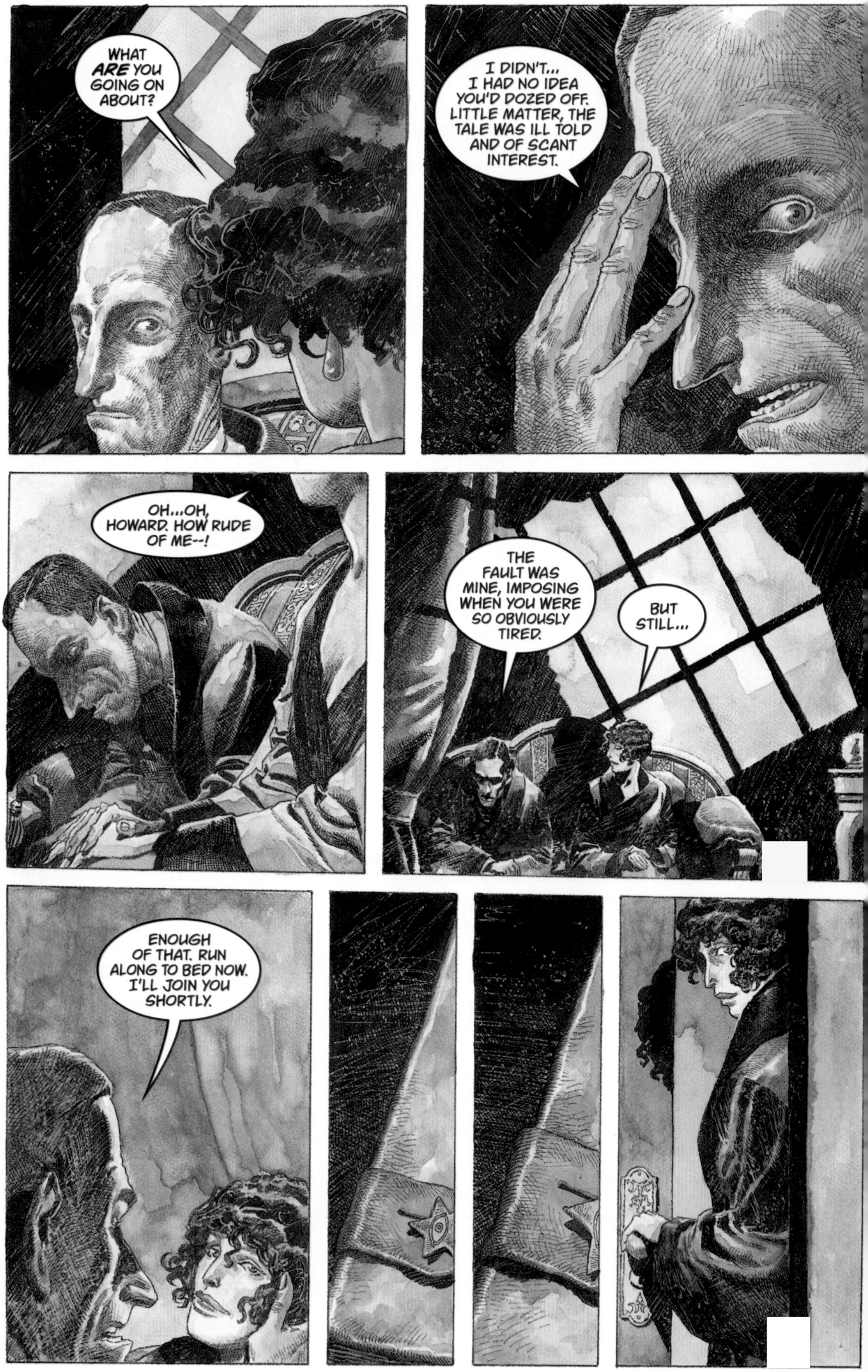
WHAT *ARE* YOU GOING ON ABOUT?
I DIDN'T... I HAD NO IDEA YOU'D DOZED OFF. LITTLE MATTER, THE TALE WAS ILL TOLD AND OF SCANT INTEREST.
OH...OH, HOWARD. HOW RUDE OF ME--!
THE FAULT WAS MINE, IMPOSING WHEN YOU WERE SO OBVIOUSLY TIRED.
BUT STILL...
ENOUGH OF THAT. RUN ALONG TO BED NOW. I'LL JOIN YOU SHORTLY.

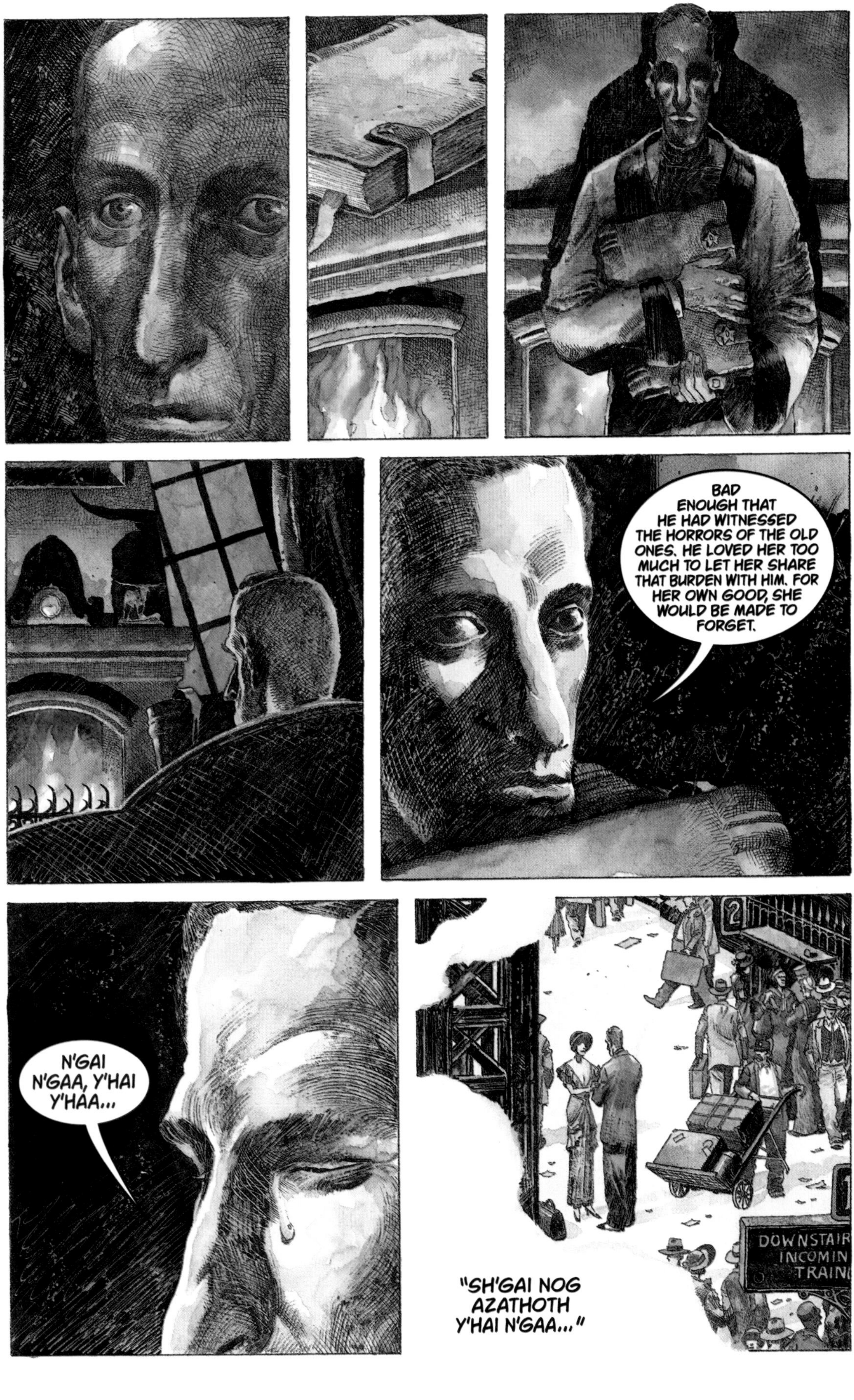

BAD ENOUGH THAT HE HAD WITNESSED THE HORRORS OF THE OLD ONES. HE LOVED HER TOO MUCH TO LET HER SHARE THAT BURDEN WITH HIM. FOR HER OWN GOOD, SHE WOULD BE MADE TO FORGET.
N'GAI N'GAA, Y'HAI Y'HAA...
2
DOWNSTAIR INCOMIN TRAIN
"SH'GAI NOG AZATHOTH Y'HAI N'GAA..."

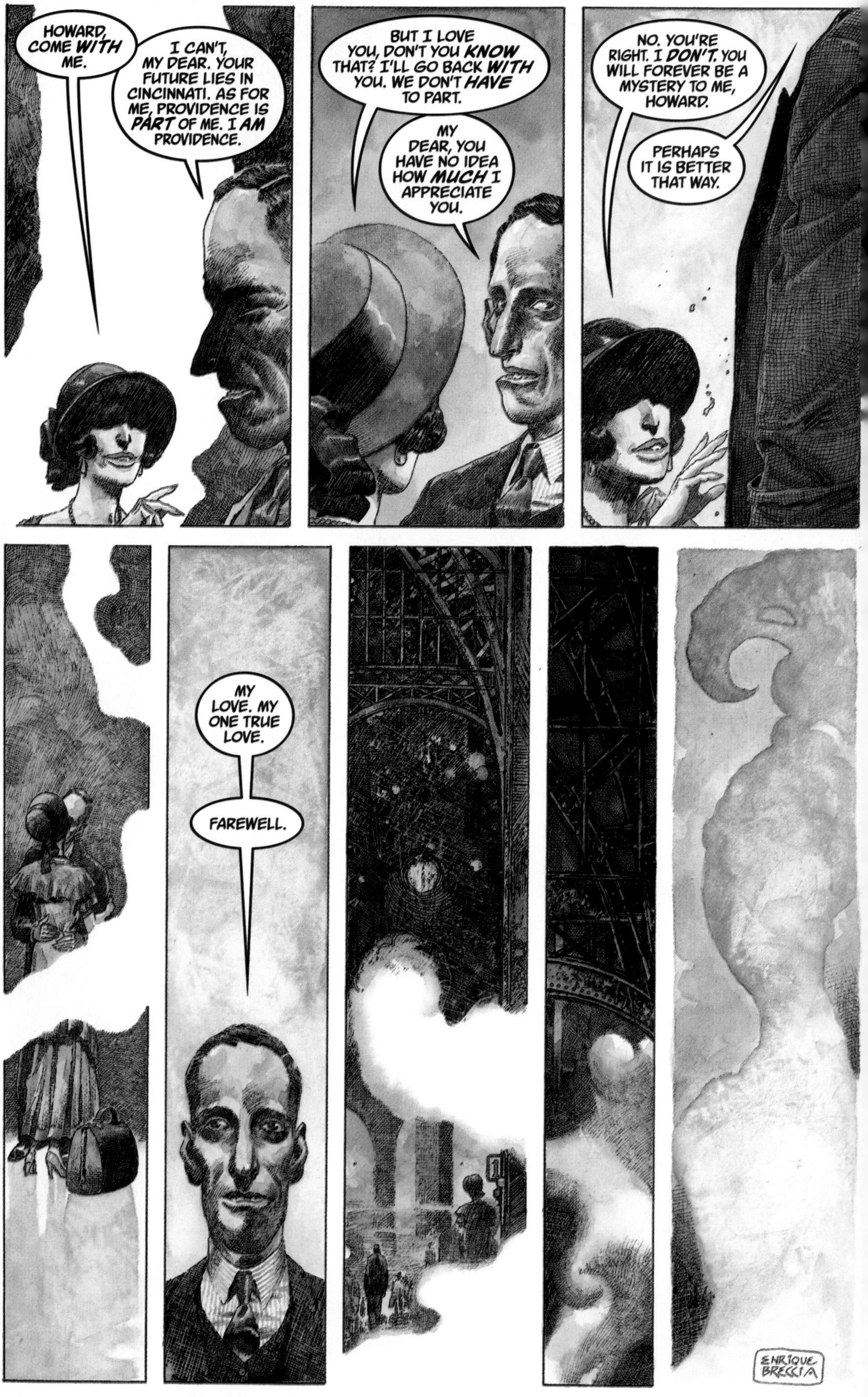
HOWARD, COME WITH ME.
I CAN'T, MY DEAR. YOUR FUTURE LIES IN CINCINNATI. AS FOR ME, PROVIDENCE IS PART OF ME. I AM PROVIDENCE.
BUT I LOVE YOU, DON'T YOU KNOW THAT? I'LL GO BACK WITH YOU. WE DON'T HAVE TO PART.
MY DEAR, YOU HAVE NO IDEA HOW MUCH I APPRECIATE YOU.
NO. YOU'RE RIGHT. I DON'T. YOU WILL FOREVER BE A MYSTERY TO ME, HOWARD.
PERHAPS IT IS BETTER THAT WAY.
MY LOVE. MY ONE TRUE LOVE.
FAREWELL.
ENRIQUE BRECCIA

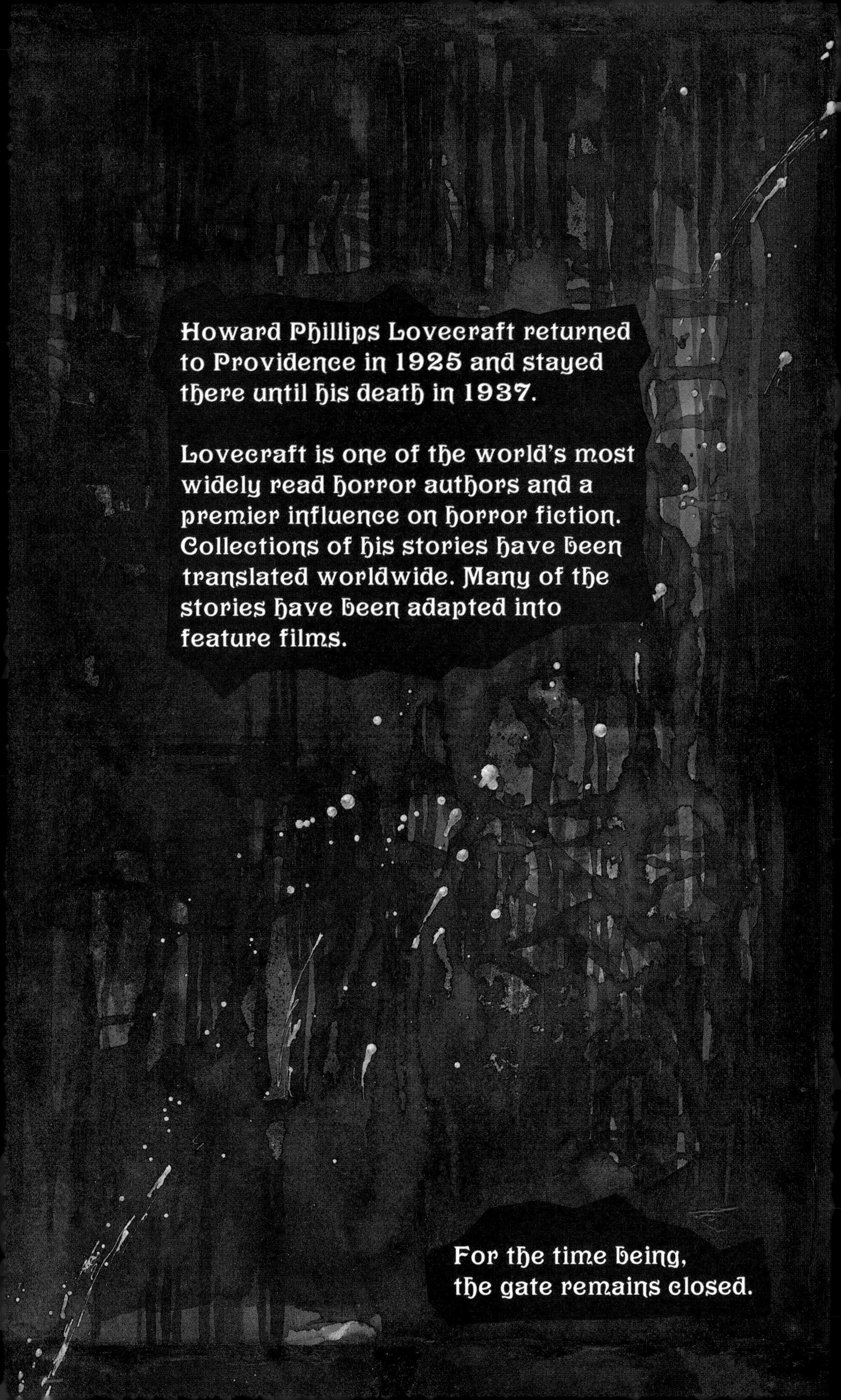
Howard Phillips Lovecraft returned to Providence in 1925 and stayed there until his death in 1937.
Lovecraft is one of the world's most widely read horror authors and a premier influence on horror fiction. Collections of his stories have been translated worldwide. Many of the stories have been adapted into feature films.
For the time being, the gate remains closed.

Biographies

Hans Rodionoff

Hans Rodionoff found a copy of the Necronomicon in his early childhood and was never the same. Growing up in Innsmouth, he spent his days lifeguarding and surfing his local break of Dagon Point. But secretly, in the darkest recesses of his heart, he wanted to be a comic book artist. While studying illustration at Miskatonic University, he took an introductory film class and fell in love with celluloid. Since that time he has devoted himself to screenwriting, collaborating with horror maestros such as John Carpenter and Clive Barker.

Enrique Breccia

A self-taught artist, Enrique Breccia has been drawing comics for over 20 years, his work having been published in Europe, America, and his homeland, Argentina. Stateside, his work for DC Comics includes **Batman Black and White** and **Legion Worlds**. Today, he lives with his second wife and youngest son in Mar del Sur, 600 km from the Capital City of Argentina, in a house only a few steps from the Atlantic Ocean and with an open field behind him. There, he has devoted himself to his three greatest passions: drawing, painting and woodcarving.

Keith Giffen

Keith Giffen kicked off his two-and-a-half decade career in the comic book field by working alongside writer Paul Levitz to energize DC Comics' **Legion of Super-Heroes** into a franchise property. Later in the '80s, he and writer J. M. DeMatteis revitalized **Justice League of America**, turning it into DC's top-selling book. In the '90s, he co-created **Lobo** with writer Roger Slifer, generating one of the most successful original comic book characters in the past thirty years. Giffen, who is currently writing **Reign of the Zodiac** and **Lobo Unbound** for DC Comics, presently resides in New Jersey.

Look for these other Vertigo books:

All Vertigo titles are Suggested for Mature Readers